MAKING BUSINESS FRENCH WORK:

MODELS, MATERIALS, METHODOLOGIES

Second of a two-volume series of the AATF Commission on
French for Business and Economic Purposes

MAKING BUSINESS FRENCH WORK:

MODELS, MATERIALS, METHODOLOGIES

Edited by :
Steven J. Loughrin-Sacco
San Diego State University

Jayne Abrate
American Association of Teachers of French

A Publication of the
American Association of Teachers of French (AATF)

SDSU CIBER Press
San Diego State University
5500 Campanile Drive, BAM 428
San Diego, CA 92182-7732
Phone: (619) 594-6023
Fax: (619) 594-7738
ciber@mail.sdsu.edu

A Tribute to Alvord G. Branan

This second volume of the AATF Series on French for Business and the Professions is dedicated with humble appreciation to Alvord G. Branan, who retired as Professor of French and Co-Director of the SDSU Center for International Business Education and Research (CIBER) at the end of summer 1997. He and his dear wife Elisabeth have now joined the ranks of the retired in the south of France. For those readers not familiar with Professor Branan's accomplishments, we cannot do them justice here. What we can do is attempt to illuminate to some extent the quiet and yet dramatic role he played in bringing to prominence the many extraordinary benefits of linking business faculty with colleagues in languages and area studies. Through his role as a CIBER Co-Director, the only language teacher among business faculty, Professor Branan led the charge for interdisciplinary education and the integrative role played by language in the business curriculum. He also co-chaired the annual CIBER Business Language meeting, held in alternating years at SDSU and UCLA, with Dr. Russell Campbell of UCLA, and served as the founding Chair of the Business Language Committee of the Association for International Business Education and Research.

Dr. Branan's activities on behalf of French and French for Business were sufficiently known to colleagues in France such that in 1995 he was made *Chevalier dans l'Ordre des Palmes Académiques*, the highest award that the French government bestows on members of the academic community. His provocative and insightful representation of the language of business being an important part of the business of language was to play a critical role in ensuring that many of the CIBERs would pay particular attention to faculty development initiatives for language professionals seeking additional qualifications in languages for professional purposes.

Professor Branan's credentials include a B.S. in Business Administration from the University of Florida, an advanced degree from Thunderbird, and a Ph.D. in French from Tulane University. This breadth of preparation allowed him to span multiple disciplines and forge unifying, creative partnerships which then served as catalysts for change and the development of more reasoned and prudent perspectives by colleagues in business and the liberal arts. His outreach efforts led to partnerships with International Business programs, K-12 schools, language magnet programs, and the more traditional strongholds of language education, universities and community colleges.

Professor Branan leaves a portfolio of business language activities and models unmatched among language educators. For those of us fortunate to serve as colleagues, his absence from the profession represents a gap which is recognized by many and felt by even more.

This volume typifies the melding of scholarly and pragmatic pursuits which Alvord Branan championed during his career at San Diego State University. We trust that the contents of this volume pay appropriate tribute to his years of service to our discipline and in some way acknowledge our debt and thanks to him.

David P. Earwicker
Managing Director, CIBER
Senior Editor, San Diego State University
CIBER Press

Steven J. Loughrin Sacco, Ph.D.
Chair, International Business Program
Co-Director, CIBER
Professor of French
San Diego State University

TABLE OF CONTENTS

Acknowledgements

Publishing an edited volume is always a major undertaking. Fortunately, several individuals greatly facilitated the successful publication of volume 2. We would like to begin first by thanking Patricia W. Cummins, Editor of volume 1, for her helpful suggestions in the design and production of volume 2 and for reviewing several articles. At San Diego State University, we would like to thank David P. Earwicker, Managing Director of the Center for International Business Education and Research (CIBER), for his behind-the-scenes choreography of all aspects of design and publication. Thanks to Erwin Wilson, a French businessman and Business French instructor, who reviewed several articles. Carla Clements, CIBER program assistant, was especially helpful in document design and contacts with the printer. Wayne Stromberg and Rich Mosler from the National Language Acquisition Resource Center provided excellent computer support. Claudia Allen was a lifesaver because of the last-minute changes she made to the manuscript. Our thanks to Kirk Albrektsen of Pacific Printing for his assistance in the publication of the volume. We are most indebted to Florence Miquel-Bonhomme, a graduate student in French, who directed the physical publication of volume 2. She designed the volume cover, the overall layout, and critiqued all manuscripts for clarity of expression as well as grammatical and orthographic accuracy. Finally, we are deeply indebted to all who submitted manuscripts for volume 2 and to the 15 authors whose articles were accepted for publication.

Introduction

Following volume 1, *Issues and Methods in French for Business and Economic Purposes*, is indeed a tough act! Patricia W. Cummins compiled and edited an excellent collection of articles and resources from veteran Business French educators. The Commission on French for Business and Economic Purposes is pleased to present volume 2, *Making Business French Work: Models, Materials, Methodologies*, as the second of a two-volume series. Like volume 1, *Making Business French Work* is a collection of articles from veteran Business French educators. Volume 2 contains 13 articles (9 written in English and 4 in French) and includes 12 new contributors. *Making Business French Work* is divided into four sections, focusing on the future of our discipline, the importance of *l'interculturel* in Business French programs, the exciting potential of case studies, and new and innovative methods and materials. Preparations for volume 2 began in April 1997 and were completed in time for display at the 1997 AATF/ACTFL annual conference in Nashville and subsequent distribution in January 1998.

Irène Finel-Honigman sets the tone for the volume with her article "The Internationalization of Business French: Strategies for the Next Century." She astutely reminds us that France plays a strategic economic and political role in global affairs and will continue to do so as we enter the next century. Finel-Honigman outlines how French will not fall by the wayside, as many predict, but will become the second global language of business and economics. Despite France's positive future in global affairs, she warns that continued elitism and insularity in traditional French literature programs may lead to their demise. She urges all French departments to revitalize their curricula by adding economic and geopolitical contexts to traditional literature programs.

The second of three articles focusing on the future of Business French is **Hervé de Fontenay**'s "Le Français des Affaires et des Professions: Langue 'Hexagonale' ou 'Internationale?'" De Fontenay exposes a major weakness in Business French programs: the exclusion of Quebec in Business French programs. De Fontenay argues that the exclusion of Quebec and the rest of the Francophone world will relegate French to a position of "hexagonal" language. As a preliminary step toward keeping French an "international" language, he describes the newly established alliance between the Quebec and Paris Chambers of Commerce and Industry.

Eileen Angelini completes the section on the future of Business French with her article "Meeting the Needs of the Non-Traditional Language Program." Angelini points out that traditional graduate literature programs are not producing educators prepared to teach in the majority of undergraduate French programs. Junior French faculty who find themselves in this situation will profit from information she provides on professional development.

Fernande Wagman, a contributor in volume 1, begins the section on the importance of *l'interculturel* in Business French programs. In her article, "Faire des Affaires ou le Commerce des Hommes," Wagman uses the image of the iceberg for illustrating the complexity of French culture. She highlights the gamut of intercultural behavior that comprises the unseen portion of the cultural iceberg. It is in probing below the surface that our students will be better able to understand the French mentality.

Along these same lines, **Raymond Eichmann** presents what he considers as the 10 "comportements culturels" that US students must study in the Business French class. Eichmann categorizes and describes these "comportements," which include "l'harmonie de l'ensemble," "l'horreur de l'imprécis," "la peur de risque," "le Manichéisme français," and "l'esprit de clan." He suggests that ignorance of these "comportements" may be at the heart of many US-French business misunderstandings.

Completing the intercultural section, **Michel Gueldry** presents an intriguing article which describes his graduate-level Business French course at the Monterey Institute for International Studies. He argues that most curriculum development in Business French has focused on the undergraduate level. His article describes the intercultural content of his course, and argues for the merger of Business French and the social sciences into one course. Without overtly doing so, Gueldry's article challenges those of us who teach undergraduate Business French courses to re-examine our course content and focus.

Beginning the two-article section on the use of case studies in the Business French classroom is **Salvatore Federico** and **Catherine Moore's** article "L'Utilisation des Cas Pratiques dans la Classe de Français des Affaires." Federico and Moore are pioneers in the use of case studies in Business French as evidenced by their textbook *Cas Pratique pour le Français des Affaires*. In their article, they trace the history of the case-study approach and describe how case studies can best be used in the Business French classroom.

Steven Loughrin-Sacco and **Michael Fronmueller** introduce case studies of a different type: case studies targeting key Quebec companies and industries. Loughrin-Sacco and Fronmueller echo Federico and Moore's call for the use of case studies in the Business French classroom and de Fontenay's call for the inclusion of Quebec in Business French programs.

Critics of Business French often point to the vocational nature of our courses, citing the absence of literature as one example. **Allen Wood's** article "Negotiating Literature in the Business French Class" dismisses this criticism by illustrating how the Business French course can include both *la Bourse* and Balzac. In his article, Wood describes how he weaves four works of literature into the study of French business practices. Wood provides the reader with an extensive bibliography of literary sources useful in designing similar courses.

Annette Sampon-Nicolas espouses a reality-based approach to the teaching of Business French in her article "Bringing it Back Home: French for Business Explores the USA." She describes four research projects that her students conduct using the Internet. In project 1, students search for jobs in France and prepare their applications for potential jobs in the future. In project 2, students explore the role and function of the French Trade Commissions. In projects 3 and 4, students research French companies or products that have a high profile in the US. Sampon-Nicolas' goal is to make the Business French curriculum more relevant to her students and make them more marketable to both US and French companies.

Juanita Casagrande is another proponent of a reality-based Business French program, as evidenced by her article "The Product is the Thing." Her approach is to have students select an existing US product that is not sold in France and prepare a campaign to market and sell the product in France. In order to accomplish this task, students must conduct extensive research into French consumer behavior, advertising and sales techniques.

Teaching Business French for the first time is a daunting experience. Educators are often overwhelmed with decisions concerning goals and objectives, the selection of a textbook, professional development opportunities, etc. **Nicole Meyer**'s article, "Ten Tips for the First-Time Business French Teacher," will equip the novice Business French educator with practical suggestions on these and other issues.

At a time when few language departments and business schools have forged strategic alliances, **Jo Ann Hinshaw,** author of "Radishes & Butter," introduces a unique program at the University of Maryland called "Business, Culture & Languages." In this program, students complete a double major in International Business and Foreign Languages. The program distinguishes itself by offering students "flexible options, an interdisciplinary curriculum, and a menu of 'non-traditional' courses using interactive methodologies and technology." Hinshaw's program will spark ideas for the development of similar programs elsewhere.

We hope that you find *Making Business French Work* a valuable addition to your professional library, and we look forward to your comments on this volume.

Steven J. Loughrin-Sacco   *loughrin@mail.sdsu.edu*

Jayne Abrate   *abrate@siu.edu*

PART 1

THE FUTURE OF
BUSINESS FRENCH

INTERNATIONALIZATION OF BUSINESS FRENCH: STRATEGIES FOR THE NEXT CENTURY

Irène Finel-Honigman

Economic Contexts

For the next decade, French as a commercial and economic language needs to be placed in the context of France's position in global financial and economic institutions: the site of the European Union Parliament, EU Commission, the Organization of Economic Cooperation and Development and the new World Trade Organization in Francophone cities; the implications of French Canada's linguistic policies on enforcement and expansion of NAFTA, and the growing role of Francophone countries in US-EU emerging markets strategies. As the French-US relationship evolves from a historical-political alliance to a far more dynamic, albeit at times tense, economic and strategic alliance, France will be a lead competitor in the Chinese Economic Area, the projected Middle East economic development zones, in West Africa and in parts of the CARICOM alliance of Caribbean and Central American countries.

In the 1980s business and economic French evolved in the US classroom from the study of a specialized semantic field to a broader analysis of France's growing role in international finance, technological innovation and the European Community. Le français des affaires, sponsored by the French government and the chambers of commerce, especially the Chambre de Commerce et d'Industrie de Paris (CCIP) under Jacques Cartier, and the French American Chamber of Commerce under the leadership of Serge Bellanger, was instrumental in increasing the visibility and knowledge of France as a dynamic business presence in the United States.

At the end of the 1990s, French language educators have to reevaluate and enhance the subject to meet the demands of language, business and international relations students who will interact with France as the spokespeople for the European Union. They will be involved with France as competitor, partner or analog in most international commercial, military, high technology, negotiating or policy fields. In EU crossborder initiatives, France is strategically placed at the hub of European regional development with Lyon-Geneva-Turin, Strasbourg-Basel-Frankfurt, and the "Chunnel." As the world's fourth-largest export power and second-largest services exporter, France is in 1996 the US's third-largest trade partner in the EU after the UK and Germany. In US trade publications and in the US press preceding the G7 Economic Summit in Lyon in 1996, France was viewed as an "aggressive" competitor "expert in economic espionage," and the EU gateway for US investments and exports. In the areas of information technology, aeronautics, agriculture, optics, medical technology, France is the US's most important competitor. As France, like Japan, Germany and the UK, continues to allocate a comparatively greater amount of resources, manpower and subsidies to export promotion than the United States, this competitive status will continue unabated into the next decade. In new trade debates on standards compliance, ecolabeling, information technology agreements and intellectual property, France and the US will be key players as partners or adversaries. American students should learn, through both the traditional and nontraditional French curriculum, how to effectively communicate and deal with this complex, and at times, difficult ally.

Cultural Contexts

Although English is globally accepted as the language of trade and technology, since 1993 multilateral, bilateral and regional agreements have proven that a single language for all negotiating and transactional needs is not always sufficient in a global economy. A discussion of the General Agreement on Trade and Tariffs (GATT) debate, multilateral institutions and agreements demonstrates how Americans negotiate in the indicative, while the French negotiate in the conditional. Americans seek end-results and profit-based decisions while the French maneuver for position and often seek long-term, non-tangible results.

In the 1993 GATT negotiations, the Uruguay Round almost failed to come to completion in the last week of December 1993 because of French-US differences on agricultural, services and audiovisual issues. As the late President Mitterrand said in a television interview in October 1993: "Nos cultures ne sont pas à négocier." By demanding and winning the cultural exemption clause on audiovisual access, France not only transposed economics into culture and ideology but put to the test the European system of values, language and cultural identity. The 47 countries which stood by the French position, including all members of the EU which backed France, reaffirmed their right to maintain national and linguistic integrity. In long-term economic strategy, very little was gained; in cultural terms, a very important statement was made. These issues are not mere trade problems limited to a few industrial sectors, but they affect global trade policies and subsequently the policies of companies and nations as negotiations have to resume through July 1998. GATT negotiations prove that in the arena of international trade and transactional diplomacy, the US cannot act as a hegemonic force but needs to forge consensual alliances with its strongest partners, the EU and Japan.

Teaching contemporary Business French should not be perceived as a violation of the literary canon but an integration of historiography and essay genres. Reading Malraux, de Tocqueville, Laclos, Michelet, Taine, de Gaulle, Voltaire or Montesquieu helps the student understand the basis for French financial, monetary and diplomatic decisions. French politicians and media assume that the public understands the linkages between history and business. Where the United States separates culture from economics, the French integrate it as part of the identity of France.

When the US stock market crashed in 1987, the French economic press did not hesitate to refer to John Law's financial fiasco in 1720. In July 1996, the French media seriously debated the issue of Clovis, a 5th century potential creator of the French state. French leaders de Gaulle, Mitterrand, and Balladur were historians and thus deeply influenced by the role of history in political and economic decision making. During the GATT debate, Balladur's admiration for de Tocqueville and Mauriac was noted in the French press. The history of the *franc fort*, France's powerful monetary policy, cannot be understood in context without referring back to the position of French financial markets described in Balzac, Valles and Zola. As Eugen Weber wrote: "*Nos ancêtres* may be fading away but in France, the dead live longer than in other places."

For the American student and business person, French business letters appear heavy and quaint in their elaborate endings and formulaic exigencies. It is important to emphasize the correlation between the modern French business letter and its antecedents in the 18th century epistolary novel when stylistic formality and courtesy were tools of deception and manipulation. Expertise at negotiating comes from centuries of practice as French was the only acceptable language for negotiations, treaties and official speeches in international fora throughout the 18th and 19th century. For all of Europe, including Poland, Romania, and Russia, as well as the UK, (until Prime Minister Benjamin Disraeli was granted permission to negotiate in English because of his atrocious accent) French was the written and spoken language of diplomacy.

Pluralingualistic Policies

In a global business environment, dominated by multinational corporations, crossborder alliances, and mergers, American English, although the first language, is not the unequivocal choice of all nations for cultural, political or transactional communication. It is not, as perceived by the US press in the aftermath of the GATT negotiations, that France seeks linguistic totalitarianism, but rather that it encourages *pluralinguisme* with French as "spokes language" (porte parole) for the EU. French polls in 1995 showed that 78% of French persons favored a policy of *pluralinguisme* and increased foreign language acquisition. Europeans, by necessity and economic reality already bi- and often trilingual, understand the need to interact inside and outside the boardroom in their counterpart's language. The late Ambassador Pamela Harriman, the well-received and Francophone American Ambassador to France made the following point: "It makes it easier that many important Frenchmen by now are virtually bilingual. Americans are lazy about languages and they really loathe being put in a position where they feel at a disadvantage" (Interview in *Elle*).

As American English achieved a status of linguistic and cultural dominance after 1945 based on economic rather than intellectual criteria, the United States was in the unusual position until the late 1970s of being able to export and import, to transact and negotiate in English. While the European Union understood the need to incorporate crossborder language training as a part of international technical assistance initiatives, to formalize the status of such training in international treaties, and to provide public funding, the United States has left the teaching of languages, both traditional and specialized, within the bounds of school systems and universities.

The initiatives created under the Omnibus Trade and Competitiveness Act of 1989, which established the CIBERs (Centers for International Business Education and Research) with their language and culture modules, and the limited initiatives instigated by the US Department of Commerce and the US Department of Education under the late Secretary Brown in 1995, have created a framework for greater cooperation within universities and with the private sector. However, funding has been reduced or has remained static in most of these programs.

Relegated on the federal level to the Department of Education and dependent solely on ad-hoc state or private university and corporate initiatives for development of language and international trade programs, the relationship between education and export promotion never became part of public policy. The NAFTA agreement, which establishes commercial, regulatory and economic market integration between Canada, Mexico and the US, does not contain a single reference nor a single clause related to language issues. Never discussed are issues related to transacting, negotiating, accessing and opening markets anchored in Spanish, nor are French cultural, historical, and socioeconomic contexts ever discussed. Linguistic policies are still seen as separate ethnic issues, without any direct correlation to geoeconomic integration.

The Maastricht Agreement built in directives and articles (Articles 3, 3B, 128) which specifically guarantee funding for crossborder educational initiatives. From ERASMUS in 1987 and LINGUA in 1989 for foreign language competence, EURYDICE, for information and cooperation, and COMETT for technology and education, French adult education centers and business schools are highly sensitized to maintaining foreign language requirements in university and MBA programs. Consolidation in SOCRATES (1995), which includes open and distance learning and adult education, reinforces education, communication skills and crossborder trade interdependency.

Geopolitical Contexts

In the political realm it is important to establish a correlation between Francophone studies and Business and Economic French. French-speaking countries in Africa, Asia, the Caribbean, as well as former French colonies, are also important economic markets for France, the EU and the United States. As the United States has learned in its Big Emerging Markets initiative in non-OECD countries, country access and breakdown of regulatory, political and corporate barriers can depend on cultural, linguistic, and historical affinities. The European and French models can serve as a point of reference.

In Southeast Asia, West Africa, the Caribbean and Latin America, areas of emerging and developing markets, French has been the official or second leading language for over a century. There are profound historical and cultural affinities in countries such as Vietnam, Turkey, Romania and former French West Africa. Older leaders, ministers and senior-level bureaucrats, who are the rule rather than the exception, have been educated in France and are indebted to France for pedagogical materials, teacher training, scholarships and French government-subsidized schools. In many of these countries, despite changing and often closed political regimes, France has maintained educational funding and has been directly responsible for a rise in literacy and accessibility to Western education:

> Guan Jinsheng already runs China's biggest securities house. But he is ambitious. "I am building the Merrill Lynch of China," he says. "Make that the Merrill Lynch and the Nomura Securities of China." He tells how he was prevented from learning French at university at the onset of the Cultural Revolution. But he continued his studies, first in private and then in Belgium, where he took a Master's in French Literature. More comfortable in French than in English, he quotes liberally from such authors as Voltaire and Victor Hugo" (*Euromoney*, February 1995, p. 63).

Although American enterprises, multinationals and financial institutions enter these markets with a highly publicized presence and vast outlays of capital and resources, they often lack institutional relationships with leaders and companies and they are rarely seen as long-term investors. The French, like the British and Germans, are often far more low-profile in their initial approach, but they are viewed as making long-term commitments to the local economy. Specialized language training, in the technical, financial and scientific sectors, is an important segment of the European Union and especially France's technical assistance and training initiatives for both mature and emerging markets. Developing, updating and enhancing specialized terminology to meet communication and conveyance of information needs in new market economies in Eastern and Central Europe, Russia, the NIS and Africa is pertinent to increasing market access, facilitating negotiations and fostering future export markets. Therefore, the teaching and learning of specialized language, especially "le français des affaires," has a new dimension, not only as an essential communication tool for international business but also as an integral component of public-private sector initiatives in economies which have to rapidly adapt to Western business culture.

One of the French-US debates on the renewal of United Nations Secretary General Boutros-Boutros Ghali's mandate for a second term underscores profound French-US differences concerning linguistic as well as diplomatic policies. The original UN charter of June 26, 1945 had five official languages: English, Russian, Chinese, Spanish and (due to de Gaulle's insistence) French. Since 1946, French has become the second UN working language, its position strongly reinforced in 1960 by the entry of liberated West African nations and by the 1975 addition of Moldavia, Armenia, Vietnam and Monaco. In the intervening two decades, as described in Jean Gazarian's article "Le Français au sein des institutions multinationales" (*France-Amérique*), French has been reduced to a lesser status with the advent of all but four language databanks in English. However, in November 1995, when the charter on pluralingualism had to be renewed, 100 members voted to maintain French and English as working languages, 35 voted against and 29 abstained. The United States was the only major power to oppose pluralingualism. Under Secretary Boutros-Boutros Ghali, a French-educated Egyptian, French had been strongly supported and often used in his official speeches. Despite the clear US warning that they would refuse to renew his mandate, President Chirac invited him to France during the G7 meeting in Lyon, and the Minister of Cooperation, Jacques Godfrain, endorsed his leadership by also praising his great efforts on behalf of Francophone endeavors.

Business French: Inclusionary Evolutions

"Un Gaulois chic était un Gaulois qui parlait latin": (Professor Alain Rey, AATF keynote address, July 15, 1996). This charming aphorism actually expresses an important call for linguistic tolerance and is a reminder that present day French derives from a complex pluralinguistic evolutionary process. As the US denigrates or ignores the importance of other languages, and as France sporadically tends to revert to linguistic autocracy, it is important that French language educators, administrators and students understand that linguistic policies which help preserve and disseminate the language must be supported but must not become linguistic policing. The development of languages other than English, as tools of technical and economic communication, is a two-edged sword. In industrial technology, computer science and finance, new products and instruments continue to originate in the United States and, therefore, can and often should be inserted "as is" in other languages.

Among recent financial and commercial operations, derivatives, a set of complex financial vehicles, and countertrade, a trade financing mechanism with increased use in emerging economies, have technical terminology which becomes awkward and even misleading when translated into French or German. BOT (build-operate-transfer), clearing, offsets, and switch, part of the English terminology of countertrade, are accepted usage in French trade finance publications and should not require translation. Political agreements which are designated by English acronyms become incomprehensible when translated into French and new acronyms are created: i.e., GATT (AGETAC), NAFTA (ALENA). Therefore, the premise in 1994 to institute a French language law, the *Loi Toubon* (a reincarnation of the *Bas-Lauriol* law of 1975) was correct in intent but flawed in strategy and potential objectives. Although the law is necessary to preserve each language and to enrich and adapt languages to meet new socioeconomic, scientific and technological concepts, it is illogical in a global environment to require separate terms from separate etymological and historical roots which isolate rather than integrate usage and accessibility.

Business and Economic French, like the study of scientific or any other form of French, has to find a compromise between incorporating new terminology, and maintaining its stylistic and historical integrity. The semantic field needs to be enlarged, not reduced or displaced. Teaching students the basic issues of the European Monetary System and the creation of the names of the single currency from ECU to EURO is also a lesson in etymology and cultural history. The ECU (acronym for European Currency Unit suggested by Valéry Giscard d'Estaing in 1975) was in fact a very old French coin introduced as account money (*écu de marc* and *écu de soleil* in the 1570s) for settlement of foreign transactions.

Transformed, distorted and recreated from the 15th to the 18th century as Europe experienced the unification and dislocation of empires and alliances, languages flourished along trade routes as merchants became crossborder emissaries of goods, currencies and words. In financial English and French terminology, words flowed between their street origins in 17th century England and their formal reappearance into French a century later: *balancer/balance/bilan*; *Grand Livre* (because of its vast weight and size) from the German *legen* to the English *ledger*; *changeur (d'argent)* to *cambio* to *cambiste*; *dette* (from Latin *debitus*) *debt*, *debenture*; *asset* (*asseoir*) to *actif*. Beginning Business French students are often amazed that, with a few guesses at etymology and knowledge of the context, they can read a financial statement or short company report. It is essential to focus on the usage, and cultural content of French rather than on specifying terminological country of origin.

Conclusion

But the issue still remains "on peut mal parler l'anglais, culturellement il n'est pas acceptable de mal parler le français" (Jean Gazarian, *France-Amérique*). The goal is a noble and valuable one. When President Chirac came to the US on his first official visit in February 1996, despite being fluent in English, he gave his speech to Congress and at a State Department luncheon in French. It was not for fear of being misunderstood in English but rather in order to impress upon France's strategic ally and friend the importance, perfection and precision of the message in French.

President Chirac came not only as President of France, but as spokesperson for what he predicted could be a 26 to 30-nation Eurobloc in the next decade. This is the market in which future US business, language, science and history students will have to compete. The next generation of American business managers and exporters of US products to new markets need to understand the economic significance of languages and culture as they learn the role of cultural variables in economics. The historical and cultural influence of French and English is evenly divided among former third-world countries, now designated as emerging and developing markets.

Educators in foreign language departments and business schools and policymakers in commercial, trade and export strategy will have to coordinate their goals in order to guarantee US students the ability to access the international job market. US educators need to adopt the UK MBA model:

> English may be the international language of business, but the internationalization of the economy means it is no longer enough for English speakers to have a smattering of schoolboy French. At London Business School all students on the MBA programme are required to have sufficient fluency in another language to be able to negotiate in business, in writing and in person before they can graduate (*Financial Times*, October 3, 1996).

Isolated, the French language will slowly become just another language; integrated, French can become the second global language and a true cultural facilitator.

LE FRANÇAIS DES AFFAIRES ET DES PROFESSIONS: LANGUE «HEXAGONALE» OU «INTERNATIONALE»?

Hervé de Fontenay

Introduction

Les étudiants qui décident d'apprendre le français aux États-Unis sont, dans l'immense majorité des cas, exposés à un matériel pédagogique français qui présente la langue dans le contexte socio-culturel de la France. Une étude de douze méthodes de français langue étrangère largement utilisées aujourd'hui aux États-Unis montre en effet que ces méthodes ne consacrent, en moyenne, pas plus de 5% de leur contenu à d'autres pays ou régions du monde où le français a une place prédominante. Joseph A. Wieczorek, l'auteur de cette étude, écrit à ce sujet ceci :

> Such texts ignore to a large extent the cultural diversity and sociolinguistic contributions of the 42 countries and regions that boast French as a primary, secondary, or tertiary language (cf. *Atlas de la francophonie* 1989). From a sociolinguistic standpoint, it is untenable to concentrate on one particular geographic area while functionally ignoring much of the Francophone world.[1]

Qui plus est, il arrive bien souvent que les textes ou descriptions se rapportant à ces pays/régions soient biaisés ou présentent des faits erronés, reflétant ainsi une image singulièrement fausse de ces pays/régions, de

25

leur réalité socio-économique, de leur culture. Wieczorek cite plusieurs exemples dont un court texte tiré de *The Advanced Placement Guidelines* dans lequel le joual est présenté comme étant <u>le</u> dialecte québécois, laissant ainsi entendre que ce dialecte – particulièrement difficile à comprendre pour les Parisiens (mis en scène dans ce texte) – est <u>la</u> norme dialectale du Québec. Ce qui est vrai pour le français «général» l'est encore davantage pour le français de spécialité. Le cas du Québec est probant. La province, qui entretient, avec les États-Unis, des échanges économiques plus importants que la France, est à toutes fins utiles absente des contenus de cours de français de spécialité. Situation regrettable pour le Québec bien entendu, mais aussi – et surtout – pour le français. Certaines conditions sont nécessaires pour qu'une langue maintienne son statut de langue internationale. Le français dispose d'un puissant moyen, la francophonie, que malheureusement de nombreux francophones sous-estiment ou négligent. Au recul du français sur la scène internationale depuis quelques années devrait correspondre non pas un repli sur soi, mais bien une ouverture, une volonté d'agir et d'élargir sensiblement le champ d'action dans l'enseignement du français. Le projet d'un examen de français des affaires et des professions conjoint entre la France et le Québec répond à cette logique et illustre la voie à suivre pour s'assurer que le français conserve son statut de langue internationale.

Le français de spécialité

Aux États-Unis, plusieurs cours de français des affaires mènent aux examens de la Chambre de commerce et d'industrie de Paris (CCIP), le *Certificat pratique* et le *Diplôme supérieur*. Ces certifications mesurent bien entendu une connaissance de la langue, des pratiques des affaires et des réalités sociales, économiques et politiques telles qu'on les retrouve en France et en Europe. Comme la finalité conditionne les contenus, il est logique que le matériel pédagogique du français de spécialité utilisé aux États-Unis transmette cette vision que le français, langue du commerce et du travail, se vit et se définit essentiellement en France[2]. Dans le livre

26

L'Hôtellerie en français[3] par exemple, le Canada est mentionné une fois dans un exercice portant sur la chaîne hôtelière Arcade. On n'y fait aucune référence au Québec, pas plus d'ailleurs qu'a d'autres destinations francophones. Le Québec est pourtant une destination touristique de première importance, et les Québécois sont de grands voyageurs. Quant au matériel périphérique ou d'appoint destiné aux activités communicatives, les professeurs ont recours à des magazines comme *L'Expansion*, *Le Point*, *Le Nouvel Économiste*, *L'Express*, etc. Là encore, on constate une absence de références autres qu'«hexagonales». On relève parfois, dans les documents de présentation, l'intention d'inclure des textes/références venant d'autres pays de la francophonie, mais cela s'arrête trop souvent à l'intention. Quant aux cours plus spécialisés, portant par exemple exclusivement sur le Québec, il va sans dire qu'ils sont l'exception[3]. La plupart des professeurs reconnaissent cette lacune tout en faisant valoir du même souffle que les programmes étant déjà fort chargés, il serait peu réaliste, et dans certains cas impensable, d'y ajouter un contenu supplémentaire. Nombreux sont ceux qui invoquent également leur manque de connaissances de la réalité socio-économique de pays/régions francophones autres que la France. Ces objections, si pertinentes soient-elles, ne sont que des objections, et non des arguments contre une révision ou une réorientation des programmes. Plutôt que de les brandir comme des fins de non-recevoir déguisées, on devrait s'en servir pour alimenter la réflexion sur les moyens à mettre en œuvre pour repenser les programmes. D'ailleurs, à bien des égards, il s'agit plus de changer d'attitude que d'alourdir les programmes. Il ne faut pas non plus surestimer les connaissances qu'un professeur doit acquérir pour être capable de «présenter» certains aspects linguistiques, socio-économiques et culturels d'un autre pays francophone. Quant à la documentation, rappelons que l'augmentation fulgurante des sites Internet en français offre des sources d'information encore inconnues jusqu'à récemment et ouvre de multiples perspectives pédagogiques. Certains professeurs, conscients des enjeux et motivés par une curiosité louable, ont déjà apporté des changements à leur programme et à leur matériel. Ces changements sont toutefois trop rares, trop timides et ne reflètent que très partiellement les réalités francophones et la réalité du fait français dans le monde.

La situation du français

Il n'est pas besoin de consulter de grandes études statistiques pour constater la nette régression du français sur la scène internationale. Élimination du français comme seconde ou troisième langue étrangère obligatoire dans les programmes scolaires de nombreux pays, disparition du français dans les écoles de formation de diplomates, baisse marquée des inscriptions dans plusieurs écoles de français langue étrangère, etc.[4] On se laisse parfois aller à croire qu'un tel recul n'affecte sérieusement que les «experts» de la langue, les intellectuels, les politiciens, les professeurs de langue, globalement tous ceux qui travaillent dans les «industries de la langue». Il n'en est rien. Les francophones sont *tous* touchés, et à des niveaux qu'ils ignorent le plus souvent. André Gélinas, dans sa préface à un ouvrage qui a reçu le *Prix de la Francophonie Jean-Humblet 1997*, écrit à ce sujet :

> Qu'ils soient consciemment perçus comme tels ou non, les facteurs intangibles ou matériels du déclin linguistique francophone se traduisent, chez les individus, par une perte de confiance en eux, un manque de créativité, une peur exacerbée des risques, un sentiment de vulnérabilité, et une grande crédulité. Vis-à-vis du monde extérieur, les groupes francophones souffrent d'une perte de crédibilité et sont témoins de la paupérisation de leurs industries culturelles et collectives [5].

La régression du français s'est particulièrement fait sentir aux États-Unis. Entre 1990 et 1995, les inscriptions en français dans les établissements collégiaux et universitaires américains ont baissé de 24,6%, alors qu'elles augmentaient de 35,8% en chinois, et de 13,5% en espagnol. En fait, parmi les douze langues les plus communément enseignées, le français et l'allemand sont les seules avec le latin, à avoir connu une baisse d'inscriptions entre 1968 et 1990[6]. Il semble bien que la situation ne se soit pas redressée depuis. Pour certains, le français de spécialité a été une tentative de réponse : en multipliant les cours de français des affaires, on offrait un enseignement plus fonctionnel et on se rapprochait des besoins légitimes d'étudiants qui considèrent que la connaissance d'une langue étrangère a une valeur monnayable et permet d'offrir une plus-value non négligeable sur un marché du travail très compétitif. Augmentation donc des cours de français de spécialité. Pourtant, là aussi certains indicateurs ne trompent pas. Dans une enquête récente sur les cours de langues offerts dans les programmes MBA aux États-Unis, le français se situe en dernière place parmi les cinq premières langues réclamées par les employeurs, derrière le japonais, l'espagnol, l'allemand et le chinois. Toutefois, il se situe en deuxième place, derrière l'espagnol et à égalité avec le japonais et l'allemand, parmi les langues les plus réclamées par les étudiants[7]. Cette situation reflète-elle notre réalité économique à l'heure de la globalisation des marchés ou vient-elle du fait que le français est encore – trop souvent, malheureusement – victime de «cette vision simpliste et manichéenne qui ferait de l'anglais la langue des affaires et du français celle des arts et des belles-lettres»[8] ? Les stéréotypes ont la vie dure et n'aident en rien le français des affaires : d'une part le français est toujours perçu comme «the language of the elite, reserved to good students and good schools, locked into its image of perfectionism», d'autre part le monde du commerce et des affaires en France est souvent perçu par les Américains comme «inefficiency, noncompetitiveness and lack of marketing skills»[9]. Ces stéréotypes, qui visent d'abord la France et les Français, auraient sans doute moins de prise sur l'image de la langue française si celle-ci était davantage associée à la francophonie.

Français hexagonal ou français international?

La vitalité du français comme langue internationale et la perception que l'on peut en avoir dépendent plus que jamais d'une prise de conscience. Les francophones doivent en effet reconnaître eux-mêmes la valeur et le dynamisme potentiels de la francophonie. Or celle-ci est mal connue et son poids politique et économique, par conséquent, mal évalué, un poids pourtant loin d'être négligeable comme le souligne Charles Durand :

> La Francophonie officielle actuelle rassemble environ un demi-milliard d'individus répartis sur cinq continents. 120 millions sont alphabétisés dans cette langue et 300 millions de personnes ont une connaissance du français oral à des degrés divers, dans les pays membres. On estime à environ 200 millions le nombre de gens ayant étudié le français à des niveaux variables dans les pays non francophones. Le poids économique de la Francophonie, compte tenu du grand nombre de pays pauvres qui la composent, représentent malgré tout 10,9% du PNB mondial et 13% des exportations. Le potentiel de développement des pays pauvres de la Francophonie pourrait facilement porter ces chiffres au quart du commerce mondial, créant ainsi un ensemble planétaire qu'il serait difficile d'ignorer[10].

On peut chercher les raisons de cet état de fait dans la dispersion géographique et le morcellement des communautés francophones, ou dans l'absence de pays – en dehors de la France – dont le français est la seule langue nationale, ou encore dans la difficulté que les Français eux-mêmes éprouvent à accueillir, sur le plan linguistique, culturel et socio-économique, cette nouvelle réalité qu'est la francophonie[11]. Quoi qu'il en soit, les professeurs de français de spécialité jouent un rôle crucial dans le maintien du français comme langue de travail, de commerce, de référence à l'échelle internationale. Ils ont en effet une position privilégiée pour changer certaines perceptions et offrir à leurs étudiants un portrait plus juste des réalités socio-économiques reliées à l'usage du français. Les Américains qui apprennent le français ne devraient-ils pas savoir, par exemple, que le Québec à lui seul entretient avec les États-Unis des échanges économiques plus importants que la France ?

La situation actuelle n'est pas seulement regrettable pour les pays/régions concernés, elle l'est aussi, malheureusement, pour la langue française. Ne pas refléter suffisamment la réalité socio-économique de la francophonie (ses réalisations comme ses difficultés), la traiter négligemment ou encore de manière «folklorique», c'est laisser les étudiants américains, souvent peu sensibilisés aux réalités internationales, conclure que la présence et le poids du français dans le monde est une «réalité historique» plutôt qu'une réalité contemporaine. C'est piéger le français dans un référent culturel unique (l'Hexagone) dont les Américains ont en plus, malheureusement, une vision souvent stéréotypée. Faire des affaires en français serait donc faire des affaires en France, avec des Français et comme les Français. Cette tendance à l'ethnocentrisme – même inconsciente, même causée par une méconnaissance – renforce encore davantage la perception selon laquelle le français est une langue difficile, élitiste, normative, vivant mal son évolution parce qu'uniquement ancrée dans le contexte culturel du seul pays dont la seule langue nationale est le français. L'anglais, l'espagnol ou même l'allemand sont perçus comme des langues moins dépendantes de leur contexte[12]. Ces langues semblent davantage capables de s'enrichir à même les apports des différents pays/régions qui les parlent. Le français ne semble pas avoir cette souplesse, ce qui fait dire au président de l'Observatoire de la langue française[13], Yves Berger :

> Quelque chose m'inquiète dans la langue française, aussi fort que je l'aime. Elle est faite de telle façon qu'elle repousse, sans le vouloir il va sans dire, les richesses qui pourraient lui venir des langues francophones. Je relisais un petit livre important qui s'appelle *Les mots de la francophonie*[14], un dictionnaire, où des mots du Togo, du Québec, de pleins

31

d'autres pays de la francophonie sont rassemblés. Je n'ai pas trouvé un mot sur dix qui ait pénétré le vocabulaire français. Ça, c'est grave. La langue française manque de souplesse et ça, c'est alarmant[15].

Trop de professeurs, d'auteurs, d'éditeurs, de conseillers pédagogiques sous-estiment l'importance de la francophonie et en traitent, pourrait-on dire, «par la bande», comme un supplément «couleur locale» en quelque sorte. Non seulement cela reflète bien mal la réalité du français, mais c'est en plus une erreur stratégique grave. La question n'est pas de savoir si la francophonie existe, mais de décider si on veut qu'elle survive et qu'elle occupe la place qui lui revient. À la question de savoir si l'on peut encore compter sur la francophonie, Yves Berger répond ceci: «Si la francophonie n'existait pas, ça serait terminé». On ne peut être plus clair.

Liens entre langue et culture dans le commerce international

L'importance de l'interculturel dans le monde des affaires est une évidence. Une littérature imposante existe sur ce sujet. Comme il en existe d'ailleurs sur le poids que peut avoir la connaissance d'une langue étrangère dans le commerce international. Les liens entre la langue et la culture dans le commerce international ont par contre été moins étudiés. Des liens pourtant solidement tissés qui établissent une interdépendance entre ces deux pôles : l'interculturel dans le commerce international ne peut être efficace sans une bonne connaissance de la langue ; une compétence linguistique ne peut être véritablement efficace dans le commerce international sans une connaissance suffisante de la culture[16]. Ces liens nous intéressent particulièrement dans le cadre de cet article. Si la France et le Québec partagent le français, cela ne veut pas dire qu'ils partagent la *même* langue ni la *même* culture. En Europe, une étude d'IBM[17] a montré que les Flamands s'identifiaient culturellement plus à la

France qu'aux Pays-Bas, même si leur langue est très proche du néerlandais. Il semble que la situation soit du même ordre pour les Québécois qui partagent culturellement autant, sinon plus, avec les États-Unis qu'avec la France. Cela signifie que la façon de faire des affaires au Québec est fort différente de celle qui prévaut outre-atlantique[18]. La différence culturelle est bien évidemment liée à des différences linguistiques, tant au niveau de la forme que du fond. Autre culture francophone donc qui devrait être perçue comme un signe de richesse, comme la preuve du dynamisme et de la capacité d'adaptation du français: cela devrait d'ailleurs être la cas pour l'ensemble des cultures francophones dans le monde. N'est-ce pas en effet ces différences qui disent le mieux que le français est une langue globale, comme l'anglais ou l'espagnol. Malheureusement, les francophones eux-mêmes, et au premier chef les élites françaises, ont énormément de mal à reconnaître leur appartenance à une culture francophone globale[19]. Les écarts linguistiques, par exemple, que ce soit au niveau de l'accent, de l'intonation, du lexique et de la syntaxe, passent mal en France. Dans la majorité des milieux de travail, ils sont plus ou moins consciemment rejetés. Il arrive même qu'à l'étranger, lors de rencontres d'affaires, des Français s'adressent à des francophones originaires d'autres pays/régions en anglais à cause entre autres de ces écarts linguistiques. Le français est une langue partagée par plusieurs cultures distinctes. Toutefois, la culture dominante, qui se sent dépositaire de la langue, accepte difficilement de la partager et tolère mal les écarts.

Le Cas du Québec

En général, les étudiants de français aux États-Unis connaissent peu, mal ou pas du tout le Québec. La situation est encore plus sérieuse pour les étudiants de français de spécialité qui, s'ils connaissent certains faits sur l'économie française et la culture des affaires en France, ignorent presque tout de la réalité socio-économique du Québec. Rien d'étonnant à cela puisqu'il n'existe pratiquement pas de cours spécialisés traitant du français des affaires au Québec ni de matériel pédagogique qui pourrait s'insérer aisément au curriculum général du français des affaires. Le Québec produit pourtant bon an mal an un nombre impressionnant de livres ou de méthodes de français, langue étrangère, et d'outils pédagogiques de référence. La recherche dans ce domaine y est fort active. Les livres traitant du français de spécialité sont bien entendu en nombre plus restreint, leur apport est toutefois loin d'être négligeable. Par ailleurs, le Québec n'offre pour l'instant pratiquement aucun incitatif qui encouragerait les étudiants américains à poursuivre leur spécialisation dans la province : bourses d'études, stages en entreprise, etc. La France, elle, est très active sur ce terrain. Par le biais de certains organismes ou établissements (consulats, Chambre de commerce et d'industrie de Paris, etc.), elle offre plusieurs programmes. En fait, la France est le pays occidental qui, toutes proportions gardées, offre le plus de possibilités aux étudiants étrangers. Les professeurs de français peuvent par exemple redevenir étudiants et faire un stage de perfectionnement en français de spécialité à l'université d'été de la CCIP. Le Québec n'offre pour l'instant rien de comparable. Comment s'étonner, donc, de la place congrue que la province occupe dans l'enseignement des affaires et des professions à l'étranger[20] ? Cette situation est regrettable et tout à fait inacceptable pour l'enseignement du français des affaires et des professions aux États-Unis. Ne serait-il pas important, et intéressant, que les étudiants américains sachent par exemple qu'il existe 43 ordres professionnels au Québec et qu'ils peuvent exercer dans cette province à condition de détenir une attestation de français délivrée par l'Office de la langue française. Qu'ils apprennent qu'il existe une réglementation concernant l'étiquetage et qu'en 1996, le géant Wal-Mart a convoqué ses fournisseurs et acheteurs américains et canadiens pour les sensibiliser aux normes de francisation de l'emballage et de l'étiquetage des produits vendus au Québec ? Qu'ils découvrent par exemple qu'une entreprise québécoise, Aventure Électronique, a réussi en 1996 à convaincre le géant NEC d'adapter ses produits (claviers français, panoplie de logiciels préinstallés en français, documentation, etc.) au marché francophone québécois[21] ? Ne devrait-on pas leur montrer les différences entre le protocole épistolaire en vigueur au Québec et celui utilisé en France ?

Le Projet d'examen nord-américain

En 1995, la Commission on French for Business and Economic Purposes de l'American Association of Teachers of French (AATF) proposait à la Chambre de commerce et d'industrie de Paris (CCIP) et à deux universitaires du Québec[22] d'examiner la possibilité d'inclure dans les examens du *Certificat pratique* et du *Diplôme supérieur* de la CCIP une composante québécoise et nord-américaine. Dans leur forme actuelle, ces certifications ignorent la réalité économique de la francophonie nord-américaine, et en premier lieu celle du Québec[23], ce qui n'encourage évidemment pas les professeurs à traiter de cette réalité dans leur cours. La CCIP s'est déclarée prête à répondre à cette demande à condition toutefois de trouver, du côté du monde des affaires, un partenaire québécois qui accepte de participer au projet et de «labéliser» l'examen avec la CCIP[24]. Les représentants de l'université McGill et de l'université du Québec à Chicoutimi ont donc sollicité, par l'entremise de la Chambre de commerce du Saguenay-Lac-Saint-Jean et de la Chambre de commerce du Montréal métropolitain, la Chambre de commerce du Québec (CCQ).

Un *Comité-directeur*[25] a été créé en juin 1996, à l'occasion d'un Colloque sur le français des professions organisé par le Département de langues et de traduction de l'université McGill[26]. Ce comité s'est fixé les objectifs suivants :

1. Développer, en collaboration avec la CCIP, une composante québécoise et nord-américaine aux examens internationaux de français des affaires et des professions offerts par la CCIP en Amérique du Nord et dans le monde.

2. Créer, puis diffuser, par le biais d'un site Internet, un matériel pédagogique spécialisé sur la langue des affaires et

des professions et sur la réalité socio-économique du Québec et de la francophonie nord-américaine. Le contenu de ce site sera avant tout destiné aux professeurs de français – de français de spécialité tout particulièrement – aux États-Unis et dans le monde.

3. Encourager les entreprises et différents organismes québécois à offrir des stages en entreprise aux étudiants américains et étrangers qui étudient le commerce international.

4. Développer une collaboration entre différents partenaires (AATF, CCQ, Universités, etc.) désireux de promouvoir le français des affaires et de faire connaître la réalité socio-économique du Québec à l'étranger.

La Chambre de commerce du Québec a accepté, à la demande du *Comité-directeur*, de devenir le partenaire-hôte de ce projet, ce qui répondait à la principale demande de la CCIP[27]. En d'autres termes, la CCQ est devenue un des membres du *Comité-directeur* et «héberge» officiellement ce comité. En plus de souscrire aux objectifs du *Comité-directeur*, la CCQ a accepté d'héberger, sur son site Internet, un site secondaire qui offrira aux professeurs de français un matériel pédagogique sur le français des affaires et des professions au Québec et sur la réalité socio-économique de la province et de la francophonie nord-américaine. Enfin, elle étudiera la question des stages en entreprise pouvant être offerts aux étudiants en commerce international qui se spécialisent en français. Le 30 septembre 1997, la CCQ et la CCIP ont signé à Paris, à l'occasion de la visite du premier ministre Lucien Bouchard en France, une lettre d'entente dont les grandes lignes sont les suivantes :

a. La CCIP et la CCQ apposeront conjointement leur «label» au nouvel examen nord-américain ;

b. Le nouvel examen sera préparé par la CCIP et, dans sa partie québécoise, par les universités membres du comité-directeur ;

c. Le nouvel examen sera offert dans les centres d'examen de la CCIP, et cette dernière continuera à gérer la correction et la délivrance des examens.

La structure est donc en place et le partenariat bien amorcé ; il reste maintenant, pour le *Comité-directeur,* à assurer le financement pour la recherche et la conception du matériel pédagogique, pour l'entretien du site et enfin pour la conception et la promotion des examens eux-mêmes.

Une Mission auprès de la CCIP

Une mission menée auprès de la CCIP en mai 1997 a permis de cerner les enjeux pédagogiques du projet, d'entamer une réflexion autour d'une réforme à venir des examens de la CCIP et d'établir les bases d'une collaboration entre les partenaires québécois et l'équipe des relations internationales de la CCIP[28]. Le principal objectif de cette mission était d'étudier le format et l'organisation d'un examen nord-américain. Devait-on simplement substituer une composante à une autre ? Si oui, laquelle ? Quels étaient les principes pédagogiques à la base des choix que nous devions faire ? Lors de mes discussions avec les concepteurs du *Certificat pratique,* il est clairement apparu que d'autres enjeux étaient aussi sur la table. Plusieurs questions, pour lesquelles il faudra trouver les bonnes réponses, ont été soulevées : États-Unis, le taux d'échec élevé au *Certificat pratique* et au *Diplôme supérieur* a-t-il contribué à la baisse des inscriptions dans les centres d'examens américains ? Ce taux d'échec est-il relié au format même des certifications de la CCIP qui, par leur modèle européen (version et thème entre autres), ne correspondent guère aux pratiques d'évaluation nord-américaines ? Les certifications de la CCIP sont-elles touchées par la présence du *Diplôme d'Études en Langue française (DELF)* et du *Diplôme Approfondi de Langue française (DALF) ?* Devrait-il y avoir des passerelles entre ces deux certifications ?

Il ne s'agissait pas dans un premier temps de répondre à toutes ces questions. Toutefois, nous avons exploré des pistes prometteuses pour la réforme à venir des examens. Pourquoi, par exemple, ne pas concevoir un examen «à paliers», couvrant plusieurs niveaux de compétence. Cela permettrait de diminuer le taux d'échec et attirerait des étudiants en phase intermédiaire d'apprentissage qui perçoivent les examens actuels comme hors de leur portée. Une réussite à un premier degré encouragerait certains à poursuivre leurs études et à viser le ou les niveaux supérieurs. Le *Diplôme national de compétence en langue (DNCL)*, un examen translangues sur lequel a travaillé une équipe de l'université Stendhal, à Grenoble, offre trois niveaux de compétence. Le *Diplôme d'études en langue française (DELF)* vise un seul niveau de compétence, mais il est divisé en quatre unités autonomes ; cela permet aux étudiants de passer les unités indépendamment les unes des autres, et quand ils le désirent. Il a été également question de revaloriser l'oral et de mettre l'accent sur la compétence fonctionnelle. La traduction à l'oral pourrait être supprimée, ainsi d'ailleurs que la version dans la partie écrite. La réflexion autour de cette réforme est bien entamée, on en connaît les objectifs : 1. mieux répondre aux attentes des étudiants, comme à celles des employeurs ; 2. attirer de nouveaux étudiants ; 3. diminuer le taux d'échec ; 4. sensibiliser les apprenants de français aux réalités socio-économiques de la France et du Québec. Il s'agit maintenant que cette réflexion débouche sur des actions concrètes.

Le principal obstacle à la réalisation de ce projet est actuellement l'absence presque totale, aux États-Unis, de matériel pédagogique sur le français des affaires et des professions au Québec. C'est pourquoi la création et la diffusion de ce matériel sont au cœur du projet. Cela demande évidemment des ressources financières dont nous ne disposons pas pour l'instant. Toutefois, avec la signature de l'entente, le gouvernement québécois s'est commis et devrait être plus réceptif à nos demandes. Quant à la diffusion, nous la voulions efficace, simple et peu coûteuse ; nous avons donc opté pour un site internet d'où professeurs et étudiants pourront tirer ce qu'ils estiment le plus pertinents d'inclure dans leur programme.

Conclusion

Le déclin relatif du rayonnement de la langue française dans le monde nous oblige, pour la première fois sans doute, à cesser de prendre pour acquis son statut de langue internationale, sa force d'attraction, sa diffusion et sa pérennité. Loin de nous décourager, ce recul devrait aiguillonner l'ardeur de tous ceux et celles qui croient et tiennent à cette langue. Charles Durand nous rappelle que la place d'une langue n'est pas le fruit d'«événements fortuits et aléatoires», mais dépend en grande partie des actions concertées de ceux qui la parlent et la défendent. De nombreuses choses peuvent être faites pour contrer la tendance actuelle, surtout si l'on reconnaît l'importance des facteurs internes comme cause de ce recul. Aux États-Unis, un enseignement du français des affaires et des professions plus ouvert sur la francophonie, et particulièrement sur le Québec, atténuerait les effets de certains stéréotypes et refléterait une image plus internationale de la réalité francophone. Cette action est particulièrement importante alors que l'on parle de plus en plus de marché unique pour les Amériques, un marché où le français, malgré son faible poids démographique, peut et doit avoir sa place. Le projet d'examen nord-américain CCIP/CCQ mérite d'être soutenu, en premier lieu par tous ceux et celles qui enseignent le français de spécialité aux États-Unis. Il faut aussi espérer qu'il ouvrira la porte à des partenariats encore plus ambitieux entre les diverses communautés francophones, tant pour l'enseignement que pour la diffusion de la langue française.

Notes

[1] Joseph A. WIECZOREK, «The Concept of French in Foreign Language Texts», *Foreign Language Annals* 27, no. 4 (1994): 487.

[2] C'est le cas par exemple du livre *French for Business*, un des livres les plus utilisés aux États-Unis (LEGOFF, Claude, 1994. *Le Nouveau French for Business : le français des affaires.* 2e édition, Hatier, Paris).

[3] Mentionnons ici le travail de Steven LOUGHRIN-SACCO qui a créé un cours de français des affaires sur le Québec à Boise State University et a beaucoup contribué au projet d'un examen nord-américain CCIP/CCQ (voir la fin de cet article).

[4] D'après le ministre algérien de l'éducation, la langue seconde que le gouvernement veut promouvoir est l'anglais, non le français. Le Rwanda avait deux langues officielles, le français et le kynyarwanda. Le gouvernement a récemment décidé que l'anglais serait aussi une des langues officielles du pays (*le Devoir*, 3/9/97). Les exemples de ce type se sont multipliés ces dernières années.

[5] Charles DURAND, *La langue française : atout ou obstacle ?* (Toulouse : Presses Universitaires du Mirail, 1997) 14.

[6] Richard BROD et Bettina J. HUBER. «Foreign Language Enrollments in United States Institutions of Higher Education, Fall 1995», *ADFL Bulletin (Association of Departments of Foreign Languages)* 28, no. 2 (Winter 1997) : 55-61.

[7] Denise W. KOCH, «Foreign Languages in MBA Programs», *Journal of Language for International Business* 8, no. 1 (1997) : 53-66.

[8] Samira SADIK, «Le français demeure la langue de travail ou de référence... Entretien avec Margie Sudre, secrétaire d'état chargé de la francophonie», *Point commun — La revue du français des affaires et des professions* 1 (avril 1997) : 4.

[9] Irène FINEL-HONIGMAN, «Perspectives — Le français des affaires: At the crossroads of US/EU trade and language policies», *Journal of Language for International Business* 8, no. 1 (1997) : 79 et 86.

[10] DURAND 425.

[11] «Méditant sur l'avenir du français en Afrique, un commentateur du journal *La Nation*, de Cotonou, au Bénin, écrivait récemment que ce ne sont pas «les discours ni les génuflexions des prébendes de la Francophonie qui feront la pérennité de la langue française en Afrique, mais les œuvres des écrivains africains». Il soulignait hélas que ces œuvres étaient «systématiquement rejetées en France», mais traduites en anglais. «Et si nous sortions de la Francophonie» ? disait-il. Il semble que certains pays soient déjà engagés dans cette voie. (*Le Devoir*, 3/9/97).

[12] Brian BLOH, «The Language-Culture in International Business», *Foreign Language Annals* 29, no. 1 (1996) : 31.

[13] Cet organisme a été récemment créé par le ministre de la Culture de France. Il s'ajoute aux autres organismes du gouvernement français responsables de la préservation de la langue : le Conseil supérieur de la langue française et la Délégation générale à la langue française.

[14] Loïc DEPECKER, *Les mots de la francophonie* (Paris, éditions Bellin, coll. Le français retrouvé, 1990).

[15] Denyse THERRIEN, «État d'urgence. Entretien avec Yves Berger», *Infolangue*, revue d'information sur la langue française de l'Office de la langue française, Les publications du Québec, vol. 1, no. 3 (été 1997) : 24.

[16] BLOH 28.

[17] BLOH 34.

[18] Dans son article «The Cultural Implications of International Business: Three French Experiments in the United States and their Classroom Dimension», (Languages and Cultures for Business and the Professions, Eastern Michigan University, 1992), Françoise WATTS passe en revue ce qui distingue les Français des Américains dans leurs habitudes de travail, dans leurs relations professionnelles et dans le regard qu'ils portent sur leur

environnement social. Ce descriptif met en relief tout ce qui distingue également les Français des Québécois dans leur environnement de travail.

[19] La lecture du livre de Charles DURAND (cité plus haut), et particulièrement du chapitre intitulé «Un espéranglais pour les sciences», est indispensable pour bien comprendre le rôle que jouent les élites françaises dans l'anglicisation des territoires francophones et le manque d'intérêt de ces élites vis-à-vis de la francophonie.

[20] Mentionnons toutefois que pendant plusieurs années, l'American Association of Teachers of French (AATF) a offert des bourses aux professeurs de français du niveau secondaire qui désiraient étudier au Québec. Dans certains cas, les boursiers ont pu orienter leurs recherches sur le français des affaires.

[21] Charles LUSSIER, «Mérites du français 1997», *Infolangue, revue d'information sur la langue française de l'Office de la langue française,* Les publications du Québec, vol. 1, no. 2 (Printemps 1997) : 19.

[22] Damien FERLAND, directeur de l'école de langue française et de civilisation québécoise à Chicoutimi et Hervé de Fontenay, directeur des programmes de français, langue seconde, à l'Université McGill, à Montréal.

[23] Il est vrai que les épreuves orales de ces examens permettent une certaine adaptation puisque les centres d'examen en choisissent les documents-déclencheurs. Aux États-Unis, cela se traduit le plus souvent par des documents portant sur des entreprises françaises installées dans le pays. Les épreuves écrites, elles, sont conçues à Paris.

[24] Il faut ici remercier Emmanuel RIMBERT qui a piloté ce dossier à la CCIP en 1996 et Madame G. MARATIER-DECLÉTY qui, depuis qu'elle est à la tête de la Direction des relations internationales de la CCIP a toujours appuyé ce projet.

[25] Un an plus tard, le Comité-directeur comprenait un représentant de chacun des établissements ou organismes suivants : l'Université McGill, l'Université du Québec à Chicoutimi, la Chambre de commerce du Québec, la

Chambre de commerce du Montréal métropolitain, la Chambre de commerce du Saguenay-Lac-Saint-Jean.

[26] Ce colloque, organisé dans le cadre du 64e Congrès de l'Association canadienne française pour l'avancement des sciences (ACFAS), a eu lieu en mai 1996 à l'Université McGill, Montréal.

[27] Cette acceptation n'était pas acquise au départ. En effet, le rôle et le mandat d'une chambre de commerce au Québec diffère sensiblement de ceux d'une chambre de commerce en Europe. L'actuel président de la CCQ, Michel AUDET, a compris l'importance de ce dossier et a su le défendre auprès de ses membres.

[28] Mission menée par moi-même et rendue possible grâce à l'aide de la coopération franco-québécoise.

MEETING THE NEEDS OF THE NON-TRADITIONAL FOREIGN LANGUAGE PROGRAM

Eileen M. Angelini

"None of us was prepared to deal with the difference between our training and our actual work, teaching French." –
Alice Kaplan, French Lessons: A Memoir[1]

Foreign languages have become more important in the curricula of American colleges and universities as greater emphasis has been placed upon the global environment. Learning a foreign language provides an effective method for introducing and sensitizing students to international and intercultural issues. But are today's graduate programs adequately training their doctoral students in foreign language pedagogy in order to meet the demands of current academic trends? Or is the main focus of these programs still on literature and critical theory? Most graduates strive to teach literature. However, the realities of the job market now demand that recent Ph.D.s be prepared to teach the non-traditional foreign language student: the student who will not major, or maybe not even minor, in a foreign language and yet needs to learn the language for practical purposes to enhance career objectives. What follows is a personal account of the difficult but often rewarding transition I underwent from being a graduate student in French Studies at Brown

45

University to being the only full time foreign language faculty member at a small pre-professional college.

As a grant recipient and participant in the 1994-1995 American Council on Education and National Endowment for the Humanities' Project: "Spreading the Word: Improving Foreign Language Instruction in Colleges and Universities," I was required to give a final presentation on what I had been able to achieve through my participation in the project. It was after this presentation that Dorothy James of Hunter College, a mentor of the above cited project, asked me to be a part of the 1995 MLA session entitled: "Are We Prepared to Teach the Non-Traditional Foreign Language Student?" She also encouraged me to publish my account, so as many people as possible would benefit from my experience.

I completed my doctorate in September 1992 and then immediately left for Lyon to be a visiting lecturer in English for the academic year at the Université Lumière Lyon 2 and at the Université Jean Moulin Lyon 3. Initially intended to help me perfect my French, the year proved to be an invaluable experience for me as I worked to cultivate my teaching skills. My doctorate was based on 20th century French literature, not on teaching English. Even though I was exceptionally armed with three summers of experience of teaching English as a Second Language at Phillips-Andover and Northfield Mount Hermon schools, where I had worked with excellent master teachers and colleagues, I was not prepared to teach in Lyon. I was not prepared for students who had professionally oriented career goals. At Brown, Phillips-Andover, and Northfield Mount Hermon, I had been spoiled by students whose main goal was to learn French or English. Truly, they were gifted language learners and were interested in learning languages for the love of learning languages. I relished the environment of being able to share with them my love for learning languages. But my training at Brown had not prepared me for the type of teaching I was required to do in Lyon. In Lyon, I had to learn what aspects of English the business, law, history, and geography students needed to know in order to succeed in their chosen careers. To say that my year in Lyon was an incredible and culturally rewarding learning experience for me is a major understatement. I spent a good portion of my year in Lyon observing other teachers and learning from their techniques.

Knowing that I only had one year in Lyon, I prepared for job interviews at the 1992 MLA convention in New York City. My dream was to obtain a tenure-track position at a small liberal arts college similar to Middlebury College, where I had done my undergraduate studies. Yet, I knew the job market was tough and I was looking at all possible French positions across the United States. Although I was truly enjoying my year in Lyon and had been offered the opportunity for a second one-year contract, I was anxious to begin my career as a professor of French literature in the United States. I knew I would have to teach introductory language courses, but I was excited about teaching an introductory literature course that stemmed from my graduate training. After fourteen convention interviews and five on-campus interviews, I decided that the best position for me was at the Philadelphia College of Textiles and Science (PCT&S).

However, as in Lyon, I was not prepared to teach PCT&S's students who had professionally oriented career goals. Furthermore, I was to coordinate and develop the school's newly formed foreign language program. PCT&S is known for its curriculum development, in particular for its programs that support connections between liberal and professional faculty, and for its creation of a liberal professional curriculum, all of which have been supported by a US Department of Education Fund for the Improvement of Post Secondary Education (FIPSE) grant. PCT&S is an exciting place to work with a very committed group of supportive people with wonderful intentions. Unfortunately, what I did not properly estimate was the true difficulty of the task that lay before me. In short, I am isolated from other foreign language specialists and I am involved in administrative and teaching tasks that I did not receive training for while I was in graduate school. I am not teaching French literature and I must rely on the services of interlibrary loan in order to attempt to do any type of research. Furthermore, like in Lyon, the majority of my students at

PCT&S are fulfilling a foreign language requirement and many lack the desire to go beyond the requirement. How I strive to foster their interest!

My colleagues in the School of General Studies and the College's administration want and need the foreign language program to work. Yet, they are not foreign language specialists and, therefore, my struggles are not just in the classroom. They have given me a tight time frame in which to develop the program and I am on my own. For example, some faculty advised their students to take a semester of French I and a semester of Spanish I so as to be able to study abroad in both France and Spain. These faculty members had no idea of the class contact time and effort needed to become moderately proficient in a foreign language. To say that I would be able to make students proficient after a fourteen-week semester of a class that only meets three times a week was incomprehensible. Luckily, I had worked with Judith Liskin-Gasparro while at Middlebury College on oral proficiency interview techniques and had some basic groundwork for presenting ACTFL proficiency guidelines to my colleagues. But once again, the training I had received from Liskin-Gasparro was an exception to the norm. Furthermore, one of my first tasks at PCT&S was to develop a system for placement examinations. Without the help of Joan Grenier-Winther of Washington State University, I would have been at a complete loss. Joan provided me with information on how the examinations were run at her school and, most importantly, what the pitfalls could be.

To my school's and college administration's credit, they are aware of just how isolated I am from colleagues in my field. Therefore, they fully support my participation at conferences and workshops. These conferences and workshops are my means of survival. Always carrying a ready supply of business cards, and forever prepared to ask a multitude of questions, I network to build relations with other schools. But while I have learned to network creatively, I lose precious time on my literary research and I must battle with the fear that I get farther and farther away from my original career goals as each day passes. However, I also recognize the need for my work as American colleges and universities move towards internationalizing their curricula and although my primary research had been literary, significant new goals have evolved for me.

My second big means of survival was the "Spreading the Word" project. I applied to be a part of this project in November of 1993 and in February of 1994, I began to work with my two mentors, Jane Harper and Madeleine Lively of Tarrant County Junior College. Their help was the most instrumental component in the development of PCT&S's foreign language program. Their experience and guidance was what I needed most, especially when it came to curriculum development. I needed their prestigious reputations to back me up and to prove that even though I was only a junior professor, I actually did know what I was talking about and that I was serious about how the foreign language program was to be developed. For example, with Jane's and Madeleine's help, I was able to convince the college's curriculum committee that in order to fulfill the college's foreign language requirement, a student should not be allowed to take two different beginning-level languages. That is to say, if a student wishes to attain a desirable level of oral proficiency, they are advised to take a sequence of two levels of the same language. However, if a student is not a talented language learner, she or he still has the option to take one semester of a foreign language and an area studies course.[2]

Even before I received the help of Jane and Madeleine, I knew that if I was going to get the foreign language program to work, I was going to have to be consistent, persistent, and organized. Before I arrived at PCT&S, the school had offered pilot courses in French I and Spanish I. When I arrived at PCT&S in the fall of 1993, I was immediately responsible for coordinating a team of adjunct faculty who would offer courses in French, German, Italian, Japanese, and Spanish. The first thing that I did was to invite all the adjunct faculty to my apartment for a pot luck supper so that we could all get to know each other. At this dinner, we discussed what we saw as necessary for a foreign language syllabus. Realizing that the majority of my faculty were native speakers with little or no training, I knew that I was going to have to impose certain elements of the syllabus. For example, I introduced my adjunct faculty to the idea of in-class and out-of-class journals, the importance of computer and video materials, oral as well as written exams, weekly group skits, objective grading forms and a standardized grading policy. I must admit that it took me three semesters to form a team that knew what ACTFL and oral proficiency guidelines were and how to adapt our courses to be more professionally oriented. I continue to have pot luck dinners once a month with my adjunct faculty so as to facilitate communication among all the instructors who have very different teaching schedules. I have also asked the registrar to sandwich my classes among the adjuncts' classes so that I see them for at least ten minutes every day as we cross paths between classes.

Implementing the ACTFL oral proficiency guidelines was the easy part of my job. I had the help of Judith Liskin-Gasparro and the help of my ACE/NEH mentors Jane Harper and Madeleine Lively. My problem was how to construct professionally oriented foreign language courses. While I was in graduate school, I was mainly trained to teach literature. I had had only one course in methodology and had been part of a supervised team of teaching assistants for three semesters. My junior year in Paris, my senior winter term in Guanajuato, Mexico, and my teaching year in Lyon had provided me with culture and civilization material. But how was I to teach a French or Spanish course for International Business majors? How was I to develop the content materials for the German, Japanese, and Italian courses? Yes, I had minored in mathematics at Middlebury, but I didn't know the first thing about the differences, for example, between corporate structure in the United States and in France. I first turned to the Cultural Services of the French Embassy for help. From them, I learned about the Centers for International Business Education and Research (CIBER), located at various American universities, and the *French for Business and International Trade* newsletter, edited by Maurice Elton at Southern Methodist University. From just these two sources alone, I was able to find out about and receive two scholarships. The first, sponsored by the SDSU CIBER, enabled me to attend the special training program, "Enseignement du Français des Affaires" at the Centre International d'Études de Langues à Strasbourg during the summer of 1994. The second enabled me to participate in "Formation à Distance en Français de la Gestion et du Commerce" from September 1994 to May 1995. The knowledge that I acquired via these two scholarships enabled me to become much more at ease in teaching my students. There is nothing worse than to be in the position of the teacher who knows the foreign language but does not understand the content material that the students need to learn. Furthermore, these two programs showed me how to seek out similar materials for the other foreign languages that my program offers. For example, I now know how to work closely with publishing companies on finding text-specific computer software and culturally authentic materials.

Finally, I have worked very hard to expose my students as much as possible to foreign language outside of the classroom. Foreign language classes only meet three times a week and each class period is only fifty minutes. For example, several foreign movies have been purchased and are currently in the school's audio-visual center. Students wishing to earn extra credit points watch a movie and then make an appointment to meet with their professor in order to have a 20-minute to a half-hour discussion in the target language about the movie. At all levels, students are provided with study guides while they watch the movies. To help satisfy my desire to teach literature, I provide my students with a reading list. Those interested may either do an oral report in class or individually with me or they may do a written composition in order to earn extra credit points. This past semester I was overwhelmed by the number of students who chose to do literary readings. In addition, students are able to earn extra credit points if they find articles concerning current events. (In the spring of 1995, the French presidential election was a popular topic with students.) I have also created foreign language conversation groups that are moderated by students who are native speakers of the language or are advanced-level students. Students attend a conversation group at least once a week for a half-hour period. During the conversation group, they work on class skits for which they are provided with peer feedback and which build confidence in their speaking abilities. At the end of each semester, a dinner is held for each of the foreign languages offered.[3] The class is divided into working groups of three to four students. Each group is given a recipe in the target language and is asked to prepare that part of the meal for the dinner. When we did the French dinner, for example, students were made aware of the differences between how the courses are served in the United States and France, the differences in table manners, and the fact that France uses the metric system. Plans are currently underway to develop foreign language clubs and a chapter of Alpha Mu Gamma at PCT&S. This national honor society would recognize students who successfully achieve an A in two or more foreign language classes. Since PCT&S does not offer a major in any of the foreign languages, I am hoping that the development of foreign language clubs and of a chapter of Alpha Mu Gamma will increase the number of students who minor in a foreign language. Presently, the only major that requires students to take more than the school's requirement of two semesters of a foreign language and/or area studies is International Business. International Business majors must take an additional three semesters and are the largest population of students who minor in a foreign language. My wish is to make a minor in a foreign language popular with other majors, such as Fashion Design, Physician's Assistant, and Architecture. As part of this effort, I directed a study tour to Cannes, France in July 1996. The students attended a four-week summer program with the American Institute of Foreign Study (AIFS). PCT&S wants me to oversee the program, especially as many of the students have never travelled outside the United States and/or come from families that have never travelled outside the United States.

My big future project is the improvement of PCT&S's Language and Culture Center. In support of this project, the college administration has granted the foreign language program a graduate assistant. The graduate assistant, an MS candidate in Instructional Technology, assists me in the development of text-specific software, such as that which was developed to accompany *French in Action*, our French text for the first two semesters. The graduate assistant also ensures that all the Center's computers are functioning properly (the Center currently houses three IBM and five Macintosh computers). In addition, commercially made text-specific software is in use to accompany *Destinos*, our Spanish text for the first two semesters. *Système D*, *Atajo*, and French and Spanish word-processing programs are also available to students so that they may complete their out-of-class journals. These two word-processing programs have proven to be extremely successful: students truly enjoy working with them and consequently the quality of their writing has increased ten-fold. *Power Japanese* helps students to learn Japanese characters. I am now in search of German and Italian software programs.

In conclusion, the foreign language program and my professional experience continue to be in their growing stages. After my two and a half years at PCT&S, the foreign language program now offers five semesters of French, four semesters of Spanish and two semesters each of German, Japanese, and Italian. Furthermore, I am pleased to report that the foreign language program figures prominently in PCT&S's 10-year academic plan and that the Middle States Accreditation Task Forces are giving careful and detailed attention to the needs of the foreign language program. Indeed, nationwide, foreign language programs are shifting gears in order to adapt to the needs of professionally oriented students and I consider myself fortunate to be at the forefront of a successful professionally oriented foreign language program. It is therefore imperative that graduate schools prepare students for the realities of the current job market.

Notes

[1] Alice Kaplan, *French Lessons: A Memoir* (Chicago: University of Chicago Press, 1993) 166.

[2] Please see appendix 1 for a complete list of goals achieved through participation in the "Spreading the Word" project. The following courses are offered under the rubric of Area Studies: Contemporary Europe, East Asia, Africa, and Latin American Civilization.

[3] PCT&S provides small grant of $50.00 for each foreign language dinner.

PART 2

L'INTERCULTUREL DANS LE FRANÇAIS DES AFFAIRES

FAIRE DES AFFAIRES OU
LE COMMERCE DES HOMMES

Fernande Wagman

J e commence par un jeu de mots «faire des affaires ou faire le commerce des hommes», pour reprendre le thème de mon article dans *Issues & Methods in French for Business and Economic Purposes*. Il s'agit d'utiliser le mot affaire ou commerce dans le sens classique du mot, sens beaucoup plus large qui désignait toutes les activités de l'homme dans la société. Durant ces activités, la communication entre les participants est influencée par leur mentalité ou culture. C'est une influence subtile et profonde, dont il est difficile à prendre conscience dans la diversité culturelle internationale.

Une définition de la culture est de rigueur. On a dit : «La culture, c'est ce qui reste quand on a tout oublié». Que reste-t-il ? – Ce qui est invisible aux non-initiés. Il faut donc pouvoir décoder ce qui est invisible pour «comprendre» les autres. J'aime employer l'analogie de l'iceberg, décrit par Nathalie Prime (Département Marketing du Groupe ESCP, Ecole Supérieure de Commerce de Paris) pour donner une autre définition de la culture. La partie de l'iceberg que nous pouvons voir comprend, dit-elle, le langage verbal et non verbal, les types de comportement (les coutumes alimentaires, vestimentaires, d'habitat) divers savoir-faire (depuis les codes de communication aux modes d'utilisation des outils), les produits de l'application de ces savoir-faire (outils, machines, types d'habitat, œuvres artistiques), les institutions et modes d'organisation collectifs (la Famille, l'Etat, la Justice...). La partie de l'iceberg qui est invisible sont les normes (ce qu'on doit faire et ne pas faire), les valeurs (les nuances qui varient suivant le pays), les états mentaux ou opérations cognitives (états affectifs, perception, mémoire, connaissance...), les croyances et les représentations de l'inconscient, de la nature, de la nature, de la justice...). De nos jours, les étudiants de langues étrangères ont des formations diverses et leur intérêt est principalement utilitaire, car ils espèrent utiliser ces langues dans des situations professionnelles et personnelles. Il est donc important lorsque nous enseignons le français, d'introduire la culture sous forme de situations aussi réalistes que possible, de faire comprendre la partie invisible de l'iceberg en donnant à l'étudiant une vision de l'histoire, de la géographie, de la société, de la littérature de la France. C'est ainsi que le texte : *Faisons des affaires* dans ses six chapitres assez généraux, s'applique à faire ressortir la culture de la France. Chaque chapitre suit un plan défini :

- une lecture exposant le thème, avec questions ;
- un peu de grammaire de révision avec exercices ;
- un extrait littéraire et questions s'y rapportant ;
- une activité, «Pour rire un peu», ou expressions idiomatiques ;
- des sujets de conversation et/ou de rédaction ;
- des sujets de rapports oraux.

Le premier chapitre place «la France dans le monde», place historique et géographique qui explique beaucoup l'attitude des Français vis-à-vis de ses voisins et autres pays du monde. La France, du point de vue géographique est un pays comblé, avec son climat généralement doux et la fertilité de son sol. Placée au croisement de plusieurs pays européens avec accès sur l'Atlantique et la Méditerranée, elle attire actuellement de plus en plus l'intérêt commercial international. Polly Platt, dans son livre *French or Foe*, explique avec esprit que pour les Français, le mot «étranger» rime avec «danger» et que par conséquent cela explique leur attitude soi-disant «froide» et «arrogante» envers les étrangers. Le Français ne sourit pas tout de suite parce qu'il se méfie et doit d'abord vous connaître. Ceci surprend les Américains qui sont dès l'enfance à sourire à tous, d'être «friendly». En France «la mine d'enterrement» est de rigueur, autrement le sourire est hypocrite, comme par exemple «le sourire de circonstance». Les invasions de la France depuis les Huns jusqu'à l'Occupation allemande ont nourri cette méfiance vis-à-vis de l'étranger qui ne se relâche qu'après la connaissance de l'individu. L'attrait de la France physique et ses institutions démocratiques ont poussé à l'immigration de ceux voulant échapper à la faim ou à la tyrannie. Au contraire des Etats-Unis qui est un pays d'immigrés, la France se vante de ses racines : être français de vieille souche est un honneur. Il faut donc être catholique, et avoir un arbre généalogique remontant au moins au Moyen-Age. Pays paradoxal, la France se méfie de tout ce qui n'est pas de vieille souche, ce qui explique sa méfiance vis-à-vis des étrangers, des musulmans, des juifs, des noirs et l'influence actuelle de Jean-Marie Le Pen. Les immigrés, en France comme ailleurs, ont toujours été le bouc-émissaire blâmé pour les maux s'attaquant au peuple : de nos jours, voir le chômage.

L'histoire de la France explique aussi son comportement, ses institutions politiques. J'aime donner à mes étudiants une vue globale de l'histoire de France, pour ne pas trop les ennuyer avec des dates ! Les Français ont passé par une Monarchie Absolue se terminant par la Révolution de 1789, cinq Républiques, deux Empires, sans oublier une Convention, un Directoire, un Consulat, une Monarchie Constitutionnelle, deux autres Révolutions, chaque fois établissant une nouvelle constitution et recherchant la balance des pouvoirs. Ceci ahurit les Américains, fiers de leur Constitution établie en 1776 qui n'a pas changé à part quelques «amendements» et les Anglais dont la Monarchie Constitutionnelle existe depuis le XVIIe siècle avec la décapitation de Charles I. Cette vue panoramique de l'histoire de France explique un peu les sentiments mitigés qu'ont les Français vis-à-vis de la dictature et des partis divers, de la centralisation et de la décentralisation, de la hiérarchie et de l'égalité des classes.

La langue française rayonne dans le monde et se parle en quelques pays européens, dans les anciennes colonies françaises de l'Afrique, de l'Asie, de l'Amérique du Sud. La Louisiane et le Québec ont gardé le vieux français et ont confectionné un vocabulaire nouveau sans avoir à obéir aux limitations de l'Académie Française. Un langage et une littérature francophone se sont établis et sont reconnus. Géographie, Histoire et Francophonie sont trois idées développées dans le premier chapitre de *Faisons des affaires*, sous forme de présentations du professeur, de rapports oraux de l'étudiant sur la France, l'Afrique francophone, les Départements et Territoires d'Outre-mer, Haïti, la Louisiane, le Québec, l'Union européenne. Des lectures de journaux français, de littérature francophone renforcent les connaissances culturelles. Ainsi un poème intitulé : «Métisse d'ici» de Virginia Pésémapéo Bordeleau, Québécoise, parle de ses racines indienne et française et peint son monde. Beaucoup de mes étudiants provenant eux-mêmes d'origines différentes sympathisent avec l'auteur et s'identifient avec elle. De même un poème de Léopold Senghor «Joal» présente «le métis culturel» : l'Africain instruit en France. En effet Léopold Senghor est avec Aimé Césaire un des fondateurs du mouvement de la Négritude. D'autres activités intéressantes introduisant la culture francophone comprennent des films documentaires mais surtout long-métrages, tels que «La Rue Case-Nègre» qui peint la place des Noirs dans les Caraïbes, ou «Indochine» qui décrit sous forme de roman d'amour, le rôle de la France en Indochine avant l'avènement communiste.

La langue parlée, populaire comprend des expression idiomatiques parfois pittoresques qui bien souvent s'expliquent par la culture du pays. La section «Pour Rire un peu» de *Faisons des affaires* se charge de présenter ces expressions. Ainsi «laisse les bons temps rouler» qui nous vient de la Louisiane exprime bien la joie de vivre des Cajuns ou Acadiens qu'on retrouve au Québec. C'est aussi une traduction de l'Américain : «Let the good times roll». Aussi l'expression : «lâche pas la patate» ! traduit l'optimisme et la ténacité cajuns. Encourager l'étudiant à écrire un journal et/ou à composer des essais sur des sujets basés sur des citations littéraires, est une autre manière d'attirer son attention sur la diversité culturelle. Ainsi une dissertation intéressante ou une bonne discussion pourrait s'appuyer sur telle citation de Rousseau : «A prendre le terme dans la rigueur de l'acceptation, il n'a jamais existé de véritable

60

démocratie, et il n'en existera jamais», sur telle de Montaigne : «Chaque homme porte la forme entière de l'humaine condition», sur telle de Montesquieu : «La liberté politique ne se trouve que dans les gouvernements modérés... Pour qu'on ne puisse abuser du pouvoir, il faut que, par la disposition des choses, le pouvoir arrête le pouvoir».

Le deuxième chapitre, qui introduit le bureau et ses activités, insiste sur le rôle important de la correspondance écrite, preuve par excellence dans tout litige, qui maintenant ne se fait non seulement par lettre, mais aussi par le courrier électronique, le fac-similé et l'internet. L'étudiant établit le rôle du téléphone et de la vidéo-conférence dans la conduite actuelle des affaires et est initié aux relations de travail entre patron et employés, entre le chef d'entreprise et les clients.

La correspondance écrite est importante dans le fonctionnement du commerce, car elle tient lieu de preuve, elle sert à agir et à réagir. Afin d'atteindre ces objectifs, la communication écrite doit être claire, précise et logique pour pouvoir convaincre. Bien entendu, il faut être soi-même convaincu de ce que l'on veut exposer. La correspondance commerciale est stéréotypée, aussi bien en américain qu'en français. Les tournures américaines sont beaucoup plus directes : «I wish to inform you...», «Kindly let me know whether...», «Yours truly...» or «Yours sincerely...». La syntaxe française a ses racines dans les formules de correspondance des XVIIe et XVIIIe siècles, basée sur une courtoisie très élégante, utilisant le conditionnel et le subjonctif. Pour expédier le travail de correspondance commerciale, on simplifie un peu les formules en France, à l'américaine. Le contentieux garde cependant les tournures de phrases détaillées, voir même compliquées, soit pour embrumer la situation, soit pour l'éclaircir. Commencer par «Nous avons l'honneur de... » ou «Je vous serais très obligé de...» et finir par «Je vous prie d'agréer.... » ou «Veuillez croire à....» sont des formules acceptées qui semblent très ampoulées au non-initié. Je me sers de deux ouvrages pour illustrer les différences culturelles entre Français et Américains : le livre de Polly Platt *French or Foe* et la vidéo de Jo Ann Hinshaw : «Radishes & Butter». Ce dernier a un titre qui ahurit l'Américain : manger des radis avec du beurre ! Choc culturel ! Personnellement le mélange «peanut butter & jelly» a le même effet ! Jo Ann Hinshaw nous montre par exemple la différence entre le Français et l'Américain dans la recherche d'un emploi : l'Américain est un optimiste, c'est un homme d'action, pour qui tout est possible (même aller à la Lune), il contrôle son environnement. Pour le Français, on ne peut prévoir l'avenir, on doit se résigner à l'inévitable. Ce pessimisme se comprend avec l'augmentation du chômage en France. Ecrire une lettre de demande d'emploi est donc différent pour les deux. Un Français doit l'écrire à la main, car son écriture sera analysée pour établir ses qualités de management. «Radishes & Butter» présente aussi une excellente entrevue entre un PDG français et un jeune Américain à la recherche d'un poste en France. Nous pouvons entendre les apartés des protagonistes. Durant l'entretien, nous observons la réserve française et l'enthousiasme américain. La secrétaire du PDG ne sourit pas, croyant se montrer très efficace, alors que l'Américain la voit plutôt «froide».

Jo Ann Hinshaw et Polly Platt nous introduisent aux représentations sociales du temps et de l'espace. Pour l'Américain «Time is money», c'est une vision économique du temps, relié à la machine, défini. L'activité est subordonnée au temps, les individus ne font qu'une chose à la fois. Ils se concentrent exclusivement sur le travail en cours. Ils sont méthodiques et travaillent à un rythme mesuré. Ils estiment devoir respecter les dates, les délais et les programmes. Ils se sentent liés à la tache à accomplir («Business is business»). Pour l'Européen et le Français en particulier, le temps est «humain», c'est le temps des relations aux autres, à la nature. Le temps est subordonné à l'activité. Les individus font plusieurs choses à la fois et se laissent facilement interrompre. Ils passent facilement d'une tâche à une autre. Ils s'impatientent facilement, travaillent de manière intense mais moins soutenue. Ils considèrent que les engagements temporels sont idéaux mais réversibles et non contraignants. Ils se sentent liés aux personnes concernées.

L'interprétation de l'espace est aussi différente aux Etats-Unis et en France. La poignée de main et les embrassades entre femmes et hommes, entre hommes et hommes choquent l'Américain lors de sa première visite en France. «Toucher» une autre personne est tabou, cela est contraire aux préceptes puritains. Marcher dans la rue, main dans la main, pour des copains et copines donnerait toutes sortes de soupçons à l'Américain. Celui-ci aime garder ses distances, même en parlant à quelqu'un durant une réception. Polly Platt nous donne une citation du Duc de Brissac (ancien PDG de Schneider-Westinghouse) : «Vivre en société est un jeu : il faut donc en connaître les règles et les servitudes» et six codes pour réussir en France :

1. ne pas sourire,

2. flirter (avec les yeux),

3. utiliser les dix mots magiques : «Excusez-moi de vous déranger, monsieur ou madame...»,

4. ajouter «Monsieur» ou «Madame» à «Bonjour»,

5. serrer la main,

6. attention à la porte ! «Après vous...».

Pour illustrer les différences culturelles entre la France et les Etats-Unis, *Faisons des affaires* offre aux étudiants des sujets de lettre commerciale, d'entrevues, de discussions, des expressions familières et idiomatiques sur la vie de bureau, un article de journal sur «le harcèlement sexuel» en France et un extrait littéraire sur *Les Liaisons Dangereuses* de Choderlos de Laclos, cas de harcèlement sexuel par excellence, qui se place au XVIIIe siècle. Etant donné l'importance du «flirt» et de «l'espace» en France, il est évident que la conception du harcèlement sexuel diffère en France et aux Etats-Unis. Si un homme interpelle une femme dans la rue, c'est parce qu'il la trouve «séduisante». Le mot «seduce» en anglais signifie tout à fait autre chose : «séduisant» pourrait se traduire par «pleasing» ou bien «appealing».

Le troisième chapitre de *Faisons des affaires* développe le thème du «Marché du Travail». Il semble que la Révolution industrielle de la fin du XVIIIe siècle et début du XIXe nous ait légué non seulement la machine à vapeur et l'électricité, mais aussi l'inégalité sociale. Il est certain que celle-ci existait déjà, mais a explosé par une prise de conscience de la classe ouvrière ou «prolétariat», mot créé par Karl Marx. Dans un monde où il est impossible de contrôler son environnement, le Français demande la protection de l'Etat et son intervention. Les utopistes du XVIIIe siècle et plus tard Karl Marx créent une nouvelle idéologie du travail : le socialisme avec une intervention de l'Etat dans certains secteurs et le communisme où tout est géré par l'Etat. Depuis la Commune de 1870 jusqu'à nos jours en passant par la IIIe et la IVe Républiques, les Partis Socialiste et Communiste se sont souvent alliés et aussi ont souvent lutté entre eux pour obtenir le pouvoir. L'effort commun a eu pour résultat de nombreux changements dans les droits des ouvriers et l'amélioration des conditions de travail. Les syndicats se sont formés pour protéger ces droits : les congés payés, la semaine de 40 heures, les conventions collectives, le SMIC, les assurances médicales, de maternité, invalidité, décès, les pensions de vieillesse, les allocations familiales. Celles-ci avaient été établies après la Deuxième Guerre Mondiale pour encourager les familles à augmenter la population de la France. De nos jours, beaucoup de Français se plaignent de leurs impôts qui servent à couvrir toutes ces dépenses sociales.

Les patrons du XIXe siècle dirigeaient, le plus souvent, des entreprises familiales. Aujourd'hui la plupart de celles-ci sont remplacées par de grandes firmes à la tête desquelles se trouve le PDG. Il existe une hiérarchie : au bas de l'échelle se trouve le manœuvre sans qualifications, puis on passe aux ouvriers aux qualifications de plus en plus spécialisées. Parallèlement se trouvent tous ceux dont le travail n'est pas nécessairement manuel tels que les secrétaires, sténodactylos, techniciens, qui eux-mêmes suivent une hiérarchie et enfin ceux qu'on appelle les cadres. C'est une classification d'individus qui se situerait entre le prolétariat et le patronat. Le cadre est un salarié comme les autres, mais à qui on demande d'exercer un certain pouvoir. Il y a entre le PDG et les cadres toute une série de relations possibles suivant le tempérament du PDG et la conception qu'il se fait de son autorité. Ils peuvent donc se sentir paternalistes et tenir à distance tout subalterne. Chaque membre de l'entreprise est conscient de son rôle et de son échelon et possède le code de toutes les formules de politesse, gestes, attitudes se rapportant à chacun de ces échelons.

Pendant longtemps les hommes étaient les seuls gagne-pain de la famille française. Comme on le sait, cela a beaucoup changé. Les femmes, durant la Première et surtout durant la Seconde Guerre Mondiale, ont démontré leur capacité de gérer leurs biens durant l'absence du gagne-pain traditionnel. Celui-ci était prisonnier, déporté, résistant ou décédé. La fin de la guerre a accordé aux femmes : le droit de vote en 1944. Pays catholique, la France a pourtant concédé aux femmes les droits : à la contraception en 1967, à l'avortement en 1974, au divorce par consentement mutuel en 1975. Finalement, puisque la femme passe plus de temps au travail qu'au foyer, il a fallu établir la loi sur l'égalité professionnelle en 1983.

Les jeunes traditionnellement ne travaillaient pas, à moins que ce ne soit nécessaire. Mais aujourd'hui, cela a changé depuis «la Révolution» de 1968. Les jeunes se sont rendus compte qu'un diplôme n'offrait nécessairement pas un poste.

Comme on l'a vu dans le premier chapitre de *Faisons des affaires* les étrangers sont attirés par la France, et avec l'avènement de l'Union européenne, il est facile pour un Européen de travailler n'importe où en Europe De plus en plus le marché du travail se trouve inondé. Le chômage touche le plus les femmes, les jeunes et les étrangers. Ceci explique la popularité de Jean-Marie Le Pen qui rassemble tous les mécontents de la gauche aussi bien que de la droite. Nous passons par une nouvelle révolution industrielle qui a commencé par l'invention du transistor en 1948, du microprocesseur dans les années 60 et continue actuellement avec le développement de la télématique. Il est probable que de nouveaux métiers seront créés et d'autres éliminés. L'environnement, par exemple, est une grande préoccupation actuelle. Le télétravail semble se développer avec l'internet, le télécopieur, le courrier électronique. En France cela se fait lentement, cela se voit de plus en plus aux Etats-Unis.

Certains exposés oraux du texte *Faisons des affaires* s'addressent à ces questions : ainsi «La Commune et les débuts du socialisme», «le Front Populaire». Des sujets de rédaction ou de discussion se basent sur des problèmes d'importance mondiale : ainsi sur le racisme, l'immigration, ou sur une comparaison de l'intervention de l'Etat en France et aux Etats-Unis ou sur une citation de Simone de Beauvoir : «C'est par le travail que la femme a en grande partie franchi la distance qui la séparait du mâle, c'est le travail qui peut seul lui garantir une liberté concrète». Pour montrer le côté paternaliste et utopique de l'entreprise, *Faisons des affaires* donne un extrait littéraire de *Les Misérables* lorsque Jean Valjean devient M. Madeleine et chef d'entreprise à Montreuil-sur-Mer. Dans ses deux ateliers, pour hommes et femmes, tous peuvent travailler mais il faut rester «sages». «Le chômage et la misère étaient inconnus...», nous dit Victor Hugo. Montrer un film sur le racisme : «Au revoir, les enfants» de Louis Malle, sur la situation des Juifs durant l'Holocauste est une autre activité intéressante. «Pour rire un peu» nous donne des expressions idiomatiques et familières basées sur le mot travail qui expriment la mentalité française, comme par exemple : «tenir le coup», «se défendre». Naturellement, lire le journal et suivre les débats politiques est une activité d'importance.

Le chapitre quatre de *Faisons des affaires* traite des transports en France. C'est un système très développé, sophistiqué qui comprend des réseaux ferroviaires, routiers, aériens et fluviaux. Dans le monde des affaires, les transports sont importants non seulement pour le déplacement des personnes, la distribution des marchandises mais aussi pour le tourisme. Grâce à la voiture, au métro, il est possible de faire ses courses dans un quartier différent de son domicile.

D'après un article paru dans *L'Express* il y a quelques temps, «le fléau tricolore» c'est le record du monde des tués de la route que détient la France, ceci dû soit à la fatigue, à la vitesse ou à l'alcoolisme. Les permis à points sont en vigueur depuis 1992 pour réduire les accidents. On essaie d'introduire les voitures électriques non seulement pour trouver une solution à la vitesse des voitures mais aussi pour résoudre les problèmes de pollution. Les Américains sont très étonnés par le métro, les trains qui sont propres, ponctuels, très rapides comme le TGV et sont beaucoup plus utilisés qu'aux Etats-Unis même pour des voyages d'affaires. Une fois en France et à Paris, il faut s'habituer aux grèves des transports qui arrivent souvent et paralysent le commerce aussi bien que le tourisme.

Le tourisme est important pour les Français qui passent moins de temps à leur travail, vivent plus longtemps grâce aux découvertes médicales et cherchent à avancer l'heure de la retraite. Organiser les loisirs des Français est un commerce considérable. Les transports changent les Français, car ils permettent de développer le goût du voyage, de découvrir les pays voisins, leur culture et leur façon de penser. On fait un voyage pour se reposer, pour s'enrichir culturellement, pour chercher l'aventure. Nous sommes loin des premiers touristes aristocrates anglais, ou des millionnaires américains attirés par la douceur du Midi, de Nice, de Cannes et Juan-Les-Pins en particulier. La nouvelle clientèle, celle des «congés payés», des «jeunes» retraités, des cadres supérieurs et des professions libérales choisit sa saison pour bénéficier de ses vacances. Le mois d'août semble être le mois favori des vacances en France, particulièrement pour les Parisiens qui désertent en masse la capitale. Par contre, Paris en août, devient très cosmopolite, on y entend toutes les langues.

Les sujets d'exposés oraux de *Faisons des affaires* attirent l'attention des étudiants sur une variété de loisirs, tels que la visite des monuments principaux de Paris, de Versailles, tels qu'une recherche sur la Musique, la Gastronomie, la Danse, le Théâtre, le Cinéma, la Peinture, la Sculpture, les Sports en France. Des sujets de rédaction obligent les étudiants à réfléchir et exprimer des sentiments personnels, tels que des citations :

> Jamais je n'ai tant pensé, tant vécu, tant été moi-même, si j'ose ainsi dire, que dans les voyages que j'ai faits seul ou à pied (Rousseau), ou

Le voyage me semble un exercice profitable. L'âme y a une continuelle exercitation à remarquer les choses inconnues et nouvelles (Montaigne), ou

Voyager est un des plus tristes plaisirs de la vie, entendre parler un langage que vous comprenez à peine, voir des visages sans relation avec votre passé ou avec votre avenir, c'est de l'isolement sans repos et sans dignité (Mme de Staël), ou

Le sport devient la plus étonnante école de la vanité (George Duhamel).

Toutes sortes d'expressions familières et idiomatiques sont basées sur le mot «train» : «un train de vie», «un train de maison», «le train-train quotidien», «se manier le train», «dérailler». Un extrait de littérature de *La Bête humaine* écrit en 1889 par Emile Zola montre la fascination de l'auteur pour les chemins de fer. Il compare son héros, Jacques Lantier, le conducteur de train affligé de l'horrible envie de tuer les femmes qu'il désire, au train, brute mécanique. «Comment maîtriser sa machine, si l'homme ne peut pas se maîtriser lui-même» ? Que de fois, à la suite de ses accès, il avait eu ainsi des sursauts de coupable, au moindre bruit ! Il ne vivait tranquille, heureux, détaché du monde que sur sa machine. Quand elle l'emportait dans la trépidation de ses roues, à grande vitesse, quand il avait la main sur le volant du changement de marche, pris tout entier par la surveillance de la voie, guettant les signaux, il ne pensait plus, il respirait largement l'air pur qui soufflait toujours en tempête. Et c'était pour cela qu'il aimait si fort sa machine, à l'égal d'une maîtresse apaisante, dont il n'attendait que le bonheur». Jacques Lantier n'est heureux et calme que lorsqu'il contrôle son train, et comme tout mécanicien se sent tout puissant vis-à-vis de sa machine ou toute personne au volant de sa voiture : la route est la sienne !

L'argent et les ressources monétaires qui sont à la base de toutes les transactions commerciales font l'objet du cinquième chapitre de *Faisons des affaires*. En France, ça ne se fait pas de parler d'argent. «Combien gagnez-vous» ? est une question assez choquante pour un Français, comme d'ailleurs lui demander ses préférences politiques ou ses croyances. Pendant longtemps «faire de l'argent» était considéré comme un péché mortel analogue à l'usure. Bien sûr, le choses ont changé. «Arriver» est un mot acceptable aujourd'hui, et l'argent donne à l'individu une place dans la société parfois jalousé par les autres. Autrefois les premiers banquiers étaient des prêteurs utilisant leurs propres fonds. Ce n'est qu'au XVIIe siècle, avec l'introduction de l'endossement que le crédit est apparu. Au XVIIIe siècle durant la Régence, un banquier écossais John Law, nommé ministre des finances avait pensé réduire le déficit du trésor produit par les guerres de Louis XIV en créant la première Banque Royale. Pour renflouer le trésor, Law avait émit des actions, des certificats en papier monnaie sur la spéculation future dans la Compagnie des Indes en Louisiane dans la région du Mississippi. Les spéculateurs avaient acheté les actions avec de l'or et au bout d'un an, cette affaire ténébreuse avait éclaté et de nombreux investisseurs avaient fait faillite. Les Français avaient perdu confiance dans la monnaie de papier et les opérations de crédit. Lorsque Napoléon a fondé la Banque de France en 1800, les opérations bancaires restaient limitées et la spéculation boursière était découragée. Pour épargner, les Français voulaient de la monnaie palpable qui se transmet de main en main. On se méfiait des banques : une administration, celle des Postes et Télégraphes (PTT) a pris leur place par la création en 1878 du mandat-carte, et surtout, ce qui n'existe qu'en France, de la Caisse Nationale d'Epargne et en 1918, d'un service de comptes courants et de chèques postaux. Il fallait donner le droit au crédit aux petites et moyennes entreprises, alors que la Banque s'adressait aux industriels et gros négociants. Le réseau des bureaux de poste s'est multiplié après la Première Guerre Mondiale et sa popularité vient de la proximité de la plupart des Français qui s'y rendent plus souvent qu'à la Banque. En effet, la Poste a non seulement, celui d'expédier le courrier, les colis, mais aussi on peut y téléphoner, envoyer un télégramme. De nos jours la Poste offre tous les services bancaires, un système d'assurances et même un Publiposte pour «construire une campagne marketing directe». Ce développement de la Poste a donc des sources historiques et explique la méfiance envers la monnaie de papier qu'avaient les Français pendant longtemps. La thésaurisation pendant la Deuxième Guerre Mondiale en est un exemple. Beaucoup de Français se méfiant du Franc, achetaient des Louis d'or. Ce n'est que dernièrement que les Français se risquent à acheter à crédit. Maintenant, les Français se plaignent des queues qui se forment à leur banque pour encaisser un chèque !

Les grandes banques de dépôts, telles que le Crédit Lyonnais, la Société Générale, créées pendant la période économique du Second Empire, ont été nationalisées en 1945. Lorsque François Mitterrand, chef du Parti Socialiste, est devenu Président de la République, celui-ci a nationalisé de nombreuses banques privées. Durant les luttes entre la «gauche» et la «droite» en 1987, les banques sont de nouveau privatisées pour renflouer le déficit de l'Etat. Les revenus des individus et des entreprises sont limités par l'Etat socialiste qui lui aussi a besoin de ressources pour payer ses dépenses : l'Education, les Affaires Sociales, la Santé, l'Emploi et la Défense. Les recettes de l'Etat proviennent des impôts directs et indirects et les Français s'en plaignent car les charges sont lourdes. Un programme de télévision récemment montrait les dépenses que font les Français pour restaurer les vieux monuments de Paris. Peu de Français rechignent car ils apprécient le patrimoine national.

Pour renforcer ces idées, on peut trouver dans *Faisons des affaires* des poèmes de La Fontaine comme «Le Savetier et le Financier», «Le Laboureur et ses Enfants», «La Cigale et la Fourmi» qui soulignent l'importance du travail comme ressource monétaire. D'après La Fontaine, l'argent ne fait pas le bonheur. Voilà donc quelques sujets à discuter pour comparer les différences de conception de l'argent. Balzac est remarquable dans ses romans quand il décrit l'influence de l'argent dans la société du XIXe siècle. Quelques sujets de rédaction ou de discussion orale offrent aussi aux étudiants une occasion d'échanger leurs idées : des proverbes comme : «l'argent n'a pas d'odeur», «l'argent n'a pas de maître», ou des citations comme : «Il n'est pas possible de rire quand on n'a point d'argent» (Roger, Comte de Bussy-Rabutin) ou «L'argent qu'on possède est l'instrument de la liberté, celui qu'on pourchasse est celui de la servitude» (Jean-Jacques Rousseau).

«Pour rire un peu» dans ce chapitre propose quelques expressions familières et idiomatiques amusantes qui décrivent le rôle de l'argent d'une manière pittoresque : «le fric, le flouze, le pognon, l'oseille, le blé», «plein aux as, être une grosse légume», «être fauché, être sans un rond».

Le dernier chapitre ou le commerce intérieur et extérieur montre que la réputation élitiste de la France n'est pas méritée dans son sens péjoratif. En effet, la France est non seulement un pays artistique, célèbre pour sa gastronomie, ses vins, ses fromages, sa couture, mais aussi un pays dont la technologie se fait connaître indirectement dans tous les pays du monde. C'est une conception erronée de la France que les Français ont du mal à changer aux Etats-Unis, mais c'est une conception qui change avec les voyages des jeunes, les échanges commerciaux. Le stéréotype du Français, la cigarette aux lèvres, la moustache, le béret et la baguette sous le bras se transforme lentement en faveur de l'homme/la femme d'affaires aux besoins moins frivoles, sous une influence américaine qui n'est pas toujours accueillie avec plaisir. Dans *Forbes* de juillet 1997, la France est placée dans les sept pays économiques les plus importants : les G7 (Canada, France, Allemagne, Italie, Japon, Royaume Uni, et les Etats-Unis). Parmi les 25 compagnies les plus importantes du monde, la France (AXA-UAP Assurance) est encore citée avec le Japon, la Hollande, le Royaume Uni, l'Allemagne et la Suisse. En ce qui concerne les investissements aux Etats-Unis, les entreprises telles que l'Oréal, Rhône-Poulenc SA, AXA-UAP, Saint-Gobain, Thomson SA, Pechiney, Elf-Aquitaine, SNECMA, Schneider, Renault, ont des intérêts les plaçant parmi les cents premiers. De même les investisseurs américains s'intéressent à une centaine d'entreprises françaises parmi lesquelles Elf-Aquitaine, le Groupe Danone, le Groupe Havas, le Groupe L'Oréal, Le Groupe Total (énergie).

Bien que la France soit un pays capitaliste, et que la plupart des entreprises commerciales fassent partie du secteur privé, les principales industries françaises appartiennent au secteur public. L'Etat français contrôle la Poste, les aéroports de France, la SNCF, la RATP, les Charbonnages de France, le Gaz de France. La nouvelle gauche de Lionel Jospin voudrait privatiser l'assureur GAN et sa filiale bancaire CIC, mais aussi se concerte sur la privatisation partielle de France-Telecom pour combler les déficits publics. En 1993, le gouvernement Balladur avait présenté une nouvelle loi de privatisation : l'Etat veut céder 21 groupes dont trois entreprises appartenant depuis longtemps au secteur public : Air France, Renault et Aérospatiale et 12 groupes que le gouvernement n'avait pu vendre entre 1986 et 1987, sous la première «cohabitation» entre le gouvernement socialiste et une majorité centriste : Elf-Aquitaine, les compagnies d'assurances, les banques (Crédit Lyonnais, et BNF) et Rhône-Poulenc. On voit donc cette lutte entre la gauche et la droite, la nationalisation et la privatisation qui s'expliquent par le passé de la France.

Le petit commerce où l'on allait faire les commissions et où l'on connaissait le patron et même la clientèle, est en voie de disparition. Les supermarchés et les hypermarchés le remplacent lentement, car le Français aime la petite boulangerie ou le petit boucher du coin. Un film français très récent : «Chacun cherche son chat» décrit bien la vie dans un quartier populaire de Paris. Une des «pipelettes» du quartier déplore l'avènement du supermarché et la lente disparition du petit commerce.

La réussite dans le commerce international se mesure par la connaissance interculturelle. Il ne suffit pas de se réunir dans un bureau pour discuter une future transaction. Les affaires en France, comme ailleurs, se font au restaurant, au «coquetèle», et là encore il y a tout un code qu'il faut déchiffrer et qui peut éberluer l'étranger et l'américain en particulier. Polly Pratt, dans *French or Foe,* blâme tout sur Louis XIV, non seulement le style ampoulé de la lettre commerciale mais aussi la communication qui est la forme la plus éclatante de la culture française. Dans la conversation, le Français aime taquiner ou «mettre en boîte», ce qui est difficile à accepter, surtout si l'on n'en a pas l'habitude. Les Français ont parfois «l'esprit gaulois» et de «l'esprit» tout court ! Dans un dîner, un «coquetèle» d'affaires, l'Américain, très direct, pour lequel «time is money» trouve ces échanges spirituels agaçants et une perte de temps. Pour le Français, au contraire, c'est une façon de jouir de la vie, de connaître les autres, et même de se prouver. Un film intéressant sur ce sujet : «Ridicule» montre l'importance de l'esprit dans la conversation dans la France ancienne. Ce trait existe encore de nos jours. Jo Ann Hinshaw dans «Radishes & Butter» nous montre aussi cela : nous pouvons visionner une scène au restaurant où l'Américain est impatient de revenir à ses moutons (ou ses affaires) alors que le Français continue à jouir du déjeuner. Le marketing où la publicité joue un rôle si important doit être exploré. On peut remarquer la différence entre la publicité aux Etats-Unis et en France où la nudité n'est pas un problème, car le corps est quelque chose de naturel, que seul l'hypocrite demande à dissimuler : «Cachez ce sein que je ne saurais voir» dit Tartuffe. Aux Etats-Unis, la publicité cherche à encourager la consommation, et les produits ne sont pas toujours de première qualité justement pour encourager cette consommation. En France, la qualité précède en général la quantité, bien que l'influence américaine se fasse de plus en plus sentir.

Les activités de *Faisons des affaires* permettent d'illustrer ce qui est décrit ci-dessus. Les exposés oraux sur les diverses industries de la France, des sujets de rédaction et de discussion introduisant des pensées plus générales exigent de l'étudiant des recherches approfondies. Enfin, comme toujours les expressions de «Pour rire un peu» amusent d'une façon pittoresque.

Pendant cet exposé, on pourrait se demander quel est le rapport entre ce que nous ressentons lorsque nous conduisons un train ou une voiture et lorsque nous faisons des affaires. Tout ce que nous ressentons se reflète dans nos actions. Tout ce que nous venons de développer fait partie de la culture, cette partie invisible de l'iceberg, si importante dans l'enseignement du français des affaires. Faire des affaires, c'est faire le commerce des hommes ou communiquer. On se croit donc entendu, compris, non seulement dans la langue-outil, mais dans le sens profond, c'est-à-dire on permet à l'autre d'évoquer toutes sortes d'émotions, d'idées, de souvenirs communs. C'est pourquoi les clients de Polly Platt dans *French or Foe* sont si mécontents des Français lorsqu'ils arrivent en France. Ils mesurent leurs attitudes suivant le sens américain, et jugent qu'étant différentes, elles ne sont pas acceptables. Le Président Clinton, par exemple, lors d'un discours, vantait la richesse des Etats-Unis, son taux de chômage de 4%, et donnait conseil aux pays européens de suivre la même politique économique : diminuer l'intervention de l'Etat et par conséquent diminuer les impôts. Ce jugement de M. Clinton a provoqué des protestations et il était intéressant de voir à la télévision la réaction d'un Français qui répondait : «Il y a peut-être moins de chômage, mais en fait la grande majorité des Américains n'ont pas d'assurance médicale». M. Clinton, comme beaucoup d'Américains, avait jugé suivant ses propres normes. Pour avoir du succès en affaires en France ou dans n'importe quel pays étranger, il faut donc non seulement en connaître la langue, mais aussi en comprendre la mentalité, et surtout ne pas la juger.

BIBLIOGRAPHIE

Wagman, Fernande. *Faisons des affaires*. Saddle River, NJ : DEM Publishing, 1995.

Platt, Polly. *French or Foe? Getting the Most out of Visiting, Living and Working in France*. n.p.: Culture Crossings, Ltd, 1995.

Hinshaw, Jo Ann. "Radishes & Butter: Doing Business with the French." Cultural Services of the French Embassy. Cambridge, MA: Schoenhof's Foreign Books, 1996.

TEN "COMPORTEMENTS" APPLIED TO TEACHING A UNIT ON THE FRENCH ECONOMY

Raymond Eichmann

For over a quarter of a century, Wylie and Bégué's classic textbook, *Les Français*, and its 1995 edition, revised with the collaboration of Jean-François Brière, have provided teachers with an anthropological/sociological approach to French contemporary culture. *Les Français* focuses on the daily life, behaviors and attitudes of French people, and provides numerous opportunities for students to compare common French and American institutions to discover how both solve common problems. One senses throughout the textbook the presence of a pattern of behavior and recurrences of attitudes which, although never systematically formulated by the authors, allow the instructor to tie together otherwise isolated classroom presentations of modules on the family, on justice, education, religion, government, politics, and, especially relevant to the present article, on the economy.

Throughout the years, I have been able to identify and articulate a number of patterns of behavior, or "traits de comportements" which provided a sense of continuity among the various components of the course and a sense of what is particularly French about a given institution.[1] The usefulness of these overarching "comportements" in the teaching of French particularities was reinforced by an article which appeared in *L'Express* in 1985. The authors attempted, in a similar way, to identify French ailments and to analyze the collective mentality of French society (Fallot and Pierre-Bossolette). Basing their findings on a corpus of literature on the subject of "Le Mal français" from de Tocqueville to contemporary historians (Th. Zeldin) and journalists (François de

75

Closets), the authors identified 10 spiritual, abstract illnesses afflicting the French, referring to them as "blocages." They proceeded to diagnose for each "blocage" the symptoms, how and why they have evolved to such a serious condition, and to offer a short remedy for the ailment. While the themes created in my class are not as negative or critical as the ones in the article (nor can they be described "blocages"), some are, however, close enough to allow me to borrow some of the terminology provided by the two authors.[2]

I suggest the following ten "comportments" as a global approach to the teaching of French culture and civilization or of Business French. Application of the "comportments" will enable instructors to present cultural topics in a unified, rather than disparate, manner.

I. "L'Harmonie de l'ensemble."

A. "Le Complexe hexagonal,"

B. Emphasis on reason,

C. Emphasis on "équilibre," "balance," "variété";

D. "Repli sur soi."

The contours of their country lead the French to view it in the shape of a hexagon, varied but harmoniously balanced with well-defined borders (with the exception of one border in the northeast), inside which the citizens are given a clear, geographically delineated, and secure national identity. The "complexe hexagonal" refers to the French tendency to consider themselves as the "nombril du monde" and to retrench snugly inside their hexagonal house or in their historical past. This "repli sur soi" may lead not only to an ignorance of the other, but also to a view of themselves as different from the rest of the world, to consider themselves as exceptional ("l'exception française"). The fact that the French see France as a six-sided geometrical figure reveals their ideals of, and taste for, reason, equilibrium, balance, and (measured) variety. A hexagon is an abstract, rational creation, and its six equal sides give the impression of equilibrium and balance, even in their variety.

II. "L'Horreur de l'imprécis."

A. "Demande de clarté." "Intellectualisme,"

B. "Esprit cartésien,"

C. "Prédilection pour le discours."

As Rivarol said, "Ce qui n'est pas clair n'est pas français." This truth does not apply to language alone. The Cartesian mind, which delights in seeing well-defined parameters applied to any subject or question (even to borders in the Hexagon, five of which are clearly defined while the unfortunate other is an undefined, imaginary line between France and Belgium where many battles have been fought), demands clarity of view and of expression. Before undertaking a project on any scale, one must make clear plans like the traveler who consults the *Guide Michelin* before setting out on a trip. A strong preoccupation with a rational approach to any endeavor leads to an intellectualization of discourses. While in most cases intellectualizing is a most desirable quality, it can become what the authors in *L'Express* call a passion for the "situations à angle droit," (32) a "souci de la forme," which at times values abstraction more than the real.[3]

III. "L'Homme n'est pas naturellement bon."

A. "Méfiance de 'l'autre.'"

Nature, botanical or biological, savage and untamed as it is, can and should be domesticated. The beauty of French gardens where no tree, bush, or plant tries to choke others out of its space, contrasts in geometrical design to that of English gardens, which attempt to copy or duplicate nature in its original, wild and virginal form. Likewise, human nature is not originally and naturally good (for example, the Catholic notion of original sin) and, if left unformed will lead to evils such as egotism and greed in constant search for profit, and will ignore the needs of "l'ensemble" and threaten it with disharmony. Therefore, the care of nature, the raising of children, and all other human activities will bear man's imprint and be structured and molded so as to become socialized.[4]

Such a concept helps us understand the French reluctance to accept Anglo-Saxon style capitalism as well as, for instance, their reluctance to respect the cultural diversity of immigrants. In view of the axiom that "Man is often conditioned to do the opposite of what is good,"[5] the other ("l'autre") will be looked upon with suspicion until she or he proves to be acceptable to society, to a group (see the French concept of friendship), or to a family (see the legendary difficulties in being invited to a French family, in entering a French home). In economic terms, "l'autre" will not be identified as a challenging competitor as he would be in American society, but rather as a potential threat to the finely balanced fabric of society.

IV. "L'Homme est un animal social."

A. "Importance de l'extérieur,"

B. "Importance de la société,"

C. "Importance de l'esprit,"

D. "Culte de la forme,"

E. "Tabou de l'argent, du profit."

Parents have a social (and legal) responsibility to "civilize" their children, to provide them with an acceptable outward persona, to teach them to function smoothly in society, and to help them to accept the demands of "l'ensemble." Raymonde Carroll emphasizes the importance of nurturing the child as one would care for a plant in nature (49, 50). A successful socialization will be demonstrated in the offspring's ability to deal with a society that lays great store in the ability to manipulate language with elegance and wit and to converse with articulate, rational arguments. In return for this mature acceptance of society's requirements, the child's interior (i.e., what she or he believes, thinks, and fantasizes) will be respected and be his or hers alone (Carroll 51-53).

Socialization also implies respect for rules (clearly formulated, of course) and must lead to an ability to navigate through society with a minimum of friction. Typical examples of Edward T. Hall's high context culture, French interactions (assuming they are performed among "socialized" people) are "implicit, coded, circular, indirect" (Platt 203) and imply an acquired sense of what to do and not to do (tu vs. vous, letter formulas,...). The sense of what is appropriate is innate and difficult to acquire. One of the most vexing for foreigners is the French "tabou de l'argent." While one does not ask for, or talk about, money, or about how much one makes, one nonetheless never refuses any. Money must be acquired discreetly and without flouting. Individual attitudes toward profit have their implications in the collective attitude toward the economy.

V. "L' Idéal de civilisation."

A. "Civilisation vs. démocratie,"

B. "Esthétisme vs. matérialisme."

There used to be three nations in the world that believed they had global missions. After the disintegration of the Soviet Union, only two remain: France believes it has a civilizing mission, while the US assumes for itself the duty of bringing democracy, along with its political and economic systems, to the rest of the world (Wylie and Brière 44). Grasping these divergent missions is useful in understanding why these two nations clash periodically, more than any two friends should. The sometimes antithetical ideals (democracy and civilization) account for these two countries' divergent views on economic policies: "civilized" policies must emphasize the harmonious, disciplined and rational characteristics of a people (Themes I & II) and are contrary to the more materialistic, "free market," and democratic systems. In this view, market-driven societies are places where every individual is for him or herself and where the opportunity to be materially successful may rate ahead of the social fabric of a community. In this sense, materialism is placed ahead of the aesthetic, the "civilized."

VI. "Le Manichéisme français."

A. "Le Royaume de la subdivision,"

B. "Le contrevers: la réaction anti-manichéenne,"

C. "Tentation sinon monarchique, du moins jacobiniste."

These concepts refer to the tendency of the French to be quarrelsome, as G. Barzini described them (chapter 4), and to split into factions. Pierre Daninos quipped that "La France est divisée en 43 millions de Français" and he further explained this tendency thus: "La France est le seul pays du monde où, si vous ajoutez dix citoyens à dix autres, vous ne faites pas une addition, mais une division" (51). Examples abound in the "royaume de la subdivision": the variety of politicized rival labor unions, feminist movements, political parties, etc. This process of splintering is quite different from the associative powers and energies in the US so well described by de Tocqueville.

This "comportement" has its opposite (réaction anti-manichéenne), which can be called "la manie du sauveur." In times when reforms have exhausted themselves, when they are no longer effective because of over-application, the French will be moved close to insurrection. At that time, a savior is called to deal with the crisis in a reaction that can be named "the Jeanne d'Arc syndrome." The savior will redress the situation and unite the nation momentarily until the French, once again, get weary of him (or her) and revert to their factious tendencies. "How can you govern a country with 246 different varieties of cheese?" De Gaulle is once quoted to have said.[6]

Given their contentiousness, the French have in the past been tempted by, and in the present may dream about, the unifying powers of the monarchy, at least in its political rather than in its literal form.[7] A moderate example is de Gaulle and an extreme one is the often uttered need for a "homme à poigne" like Le Pen. During these times, the French no longer behave like a nation with 246 varieties of cheese and remain somewhat united in purpose. As soon as the danger is over, manicheism reinstates itself as an overriding characteristic.

VII. "La Peur du risque."

A. "Goût de la sécurité,"

B. "Esprit fonctionnaire,"

C. "Absence de mobilité: Attachement au terroir."

Although contentious and individualistic, the French are not risk-takers. France is a nation of "fonctionnaires" where even the private sector supports the practice that the best minds, graduates of the ENA or from the "Polytechnique," opt to work in the public sector,[8] and where over one-fourth of the working population relies on the public sector. Since the State has assumed so many functions which in other countries would be left to the private sector (such as the retirement system in the "Sécurité [a revealing term] Sociale"), the power of the State to attract the best minds is not that surprising. The few true and successful entrepreneurs are at first idolized and then cynically vilified: Dassault was an aeronautical billionaire but his firm was twice nationalized (and now may be merged with Aérospatiale), and Bernard Tapie, once lionized and a cabinet minister, has been sentenced to jail. Very much related to the taboo about money (Theme IV E), this "comportement" (La Peur du risque) may be linked to a Catholic mindset which associates wealth with the deadly sin of greed and does not, like the Protestant work ethic, value material success.

"L'Attachement au terroir" [9] denotes an absence of mobility which, of course, aggravates France's unemployment. The French expect the jobs to come to them instead of moving where the jobs are, as in the US. Critics of American mobility and flexibility point out that a low unemployment rate in the US comes with a heavy social cost to the family and results in "une fracture sociale" and families of "déracinés." John Ardagh chronicles this lack of mobility even among French cadres and blames it for the regional economic imbalance within the "Hexagone" (169-71).

VIII. "L'Esprit de clan."

A. "Féodalités,"

B. "Esprit de citadelle,"

C. "Culte de l'acquis."

The "Vive nous!" syndrome. It denotes the tendency to form small groups who will (momentarily) unite to fight to preserve what can be called their "feudal" rights ("l'acquis," acquired rights) and erect a "fortress" to protect them when they are under attack. Such a mentality will resist new ideas originating from the outside such as the Economic and Monetary Union (EMU) because it requires some sacrifices of assumed privileges. It will also give preference to products that are "made in France," will resist consumerism, and, in its extreme form, will support farmers who block roads and dump vegetables in protest against much needed reforms in the EU's Common Agricultural Program (CAP) or against negotiated agreements in the GATT.[10]

Rights acquired through negotiations turn into entitlements that defy reforms. These entitlements quickly become non-negotiable, and discussions will have to begin with "l'acquis" as the point of departure. When "l'acquis" comes under attack, the wagons are circled and, as a result, reformers will withdraw their attack and will propose a milder reform that acknowledges the "acquis" and will simply be tacked on to the previous one. Changes are thus conceived in terms of "more". As a consequence, "En France, rien ne se perd, tout s'entasse" (*L'Express* 28). As Alain Peyrefitte has pointed out, the mass will increase and increase to a point when it erupts. In such an environment, downsizing and rationalizing the working sector ("dégraissage" in French!) are most difficult and dangerous endeavors.

IX. "Pour le Français, le passé existe."

France's attachment to the past is indeed legendary. For any issue or problem, one only need ask a French person for an explanation to hear "une historique," an historical background of the question. If knowing one's past has the significant merit of anchoring oneself in the present, it can also inhibit useful changes: a family enterprise will be difficult to sell, changing employers will be considered a drastic action, and uprooting one's family and migrating to a new, more promising region in search of a job will be viewed as a personal tragedy. While France is constantly pushed forward by progressive forces, it is also held back by a strong attachment to past traditions. Thus, all changes, reforms, or innovations (unless applied in times of crises) must be carefully negotiated against a background of previously acquired rights ("l'acquis").

X. "L'Etat-Papa."

A. "Interventions et réglements,"

B. "Ambivalence du citoyen: Contre l'Etat-Gendarme mais pour l'Etat-Secouriste."

French "Etatisme" has its roots in royalist and Napoleonic history and denotes the highly centralized, sometimes overbearing, nature of the role of the State. While "Jacobinisme" has allowed for ample examples of foresighted interventions by the State, it is also responsible for breeding apathy and for stunting local initiatives and the development of a civic culture.[11] The State has been so pervasive in its numerous interventions and regulations that a counter-reaction has been developed: the famed French "Système-D" or the capacity for the "malins" and the "rusés" to beat the system. The French will growl when the State interferes too much in their lives ("L'Etat-Gendarme"), but will rise up indignantly when it fails to provide for expected directions or for perceived help. The results of the May 25 elections, which repudiated the Right's attempt to ask the French to give up more privileges now in order to meet the EMU criteria, is but the latest example of this indignant reaction. The electorate has given the very clear message that they prefer a more "secouriste" State.[12]

I will now illustrate the use of these "comportements" and show how their application can help our understanding of the French economy. Because what follows may be construed as a somewhat critical view of the French economy in view of our favorable disposition toward a free market system, it is important to stress some positive data about France's economic standing. France has the fourth largest economy in the world. It ranks third in the world as investor and recipient of investments, fourth as importer and exporter of products, first in export of food ("agro-alimentaire"), and second in export of services. Its economy is therefore very dynamic, but the French economy faces several challenges: it must lower the high unemployment rate, globalize its economy, and meet the conditions for the European single currency.

While summarizing Wylie and Brière's chapter on "L'économie," I shall refer to the "comportements" by number in parenthesis. In chapter 14, Wylie and Brière endeavor to explain the structures and functioning of the French economy by constrasting them with the American economy.

They emphasize the following: the traditional concept of the French economy and the pressures for new attitudes especially during the "Trente Glorieuses," the contrasting roles of the State within the French and the US economies, the notion of "dirigisme" especially evident in the "Planification" of the State's industrial policies, the economic structures of France, the state of the French labor unions, and the new, modern demands imposed by the European Union's Treaty of Maastricht (1993).

Traditional Concepts of the French Economy

The authors emphasize at the outset that the nature of a country's economy is very much determined by its cultural values. They note two fundamental influences on the French economy which help explain its differences with the US economy: the influence of Catholicism and the powerful urge of the State to apply what they call a "rationalisme centralisateur" (196). The former refers to the legacy of a morality which encouraged a spirit of sacrifice during this transitional life, this valley of tears, and has always been hostile to the "profit commercial et financier, car le profit [Theme IV E, "Tabou de l'argent, du profit," and VII, "La Peur du risque"] était signe de l'esprit de lucre (greed), donc du mal" (196). This very morality was also one of the sources of bourgeois attitudes and still produces a certain malaise with the process of money acquisition and individuals feel obliged to hide or suppress their natural taste for profit. If openly indulging in such pursuits, an individual runs the risk of social ostracism (Theme IV E, "Tabou de l'argent"). This bourgeois need to be discreet about money and profit is the opposite of the American capitalistic Protestant values in which materialistic achievements are a source of pride, and perhaps also a sign of having been blessed by the Almighty.

As in the bourgeois family where the happiness of the individual is subordinated to that of the familial entity, this French ideal will dictate that the national interest and the public good are to be placed above the individual's private interests. Capitalism and the free market, unregulated and unfettered, "sauvage," like human nature (Theme III, "L'Homme n'est pas nécessairement bon"), are not wholly desirable: the freedom to be able to do is not enough because the French notion of fairness and justice implies providing the access to what is needed to be successful.[13] Hence, the state must intervene (Theme X, "L'Etat-Papa"), and thus, French politicians find it necessary to repudiate the "capitalisme sauvage" with its overtones of the Darwinian survival of the fittest, and where the "invisible hands" of the market will naturally effect the best of all possible outcomes if left alone because human nature is essentially good. Such a concept is decidedly not French (Theme III, "L'Homme n'est pas nécessairement bon.") for if it creates many jobs, it also creates many bad ones and leaves many "new poor" without social protection. Until recently, when politicians like A. Madelin and (more moderately) A. Juppé stressed the need for less interference and more "natural" selection, even their colleagues from the Right were hesitant to laud the benefits accruing from competition and globalization for fear of causing social disruption: the market should not disturb the social harmony of the "ensemble" (Theme I, "L'Harmonie de l'ensemble").[14]

The "Trente Glorieuses"

The French economy has traditionally been dependent on family businesses, conventional industries, and on state protectionism, analogous to a father who is expected to protect his family. Conditions changed, however, with the advent of the "Trente Glorieuses" (1945-1975) during which France experienced very rapid growth (Ardagh 32-39). The advent of a consumer society ushered in a more individual-centered, freer and more open "libéral" market, i.e., a laissez-faire market, ironically, a French name for an unFrench policy. This change was not undertaken without hesitation as Wylie and Brière point out (199): in 1981, the Mitterrand socialist administration initiated a series of nationalizations (of banks and industries) with the noble aim of putting the State in the position of being able to correct the market's mistakes and inequities.

They abruptly ended this policy in 1983. The Chirac administration, in cohabitation in 1986, privatized again several industries that had been nationalized but when the French voters, very concerned about this bout of "libéralisme," sent back to Matignon a Socialist administration in 1988, the latter stopped all privatization and any further nationalizations as well (Mitterrand's famous "Ni...ni..."). In 1993, the center-right Balladur administration began the privatization process again, a process sure to be stopped in view of the electoral victory of the left in May 1997 and of the campaign promises to stop the planned privatization of France Télécom, Thomson, and Air France. While these economic hiccups show that voters and politicians alike are less than comfortable with the concept of an open and free Anglo-Saxon style market, one must admit that the privatizations that have been carried out do give evidence of a somewhat greater acceptance of profit and of the needs for competitiveness. The results have been, as in Germany and in Japan, the implementation of a "capitalism with a human face."

The Role of the State: "Dirigisme"

The proactive role of the State, unacceptable in the US but promoted in corporatist France, is likened by Wylie and Brière to that of a coach ("un entraîneur," 200). Without this essential actor, the private sector would only look after its own individual interest and ignore the well-being of "l'ensemble." The role of the State is also similar to that of a parent raising children: a child, if left alone, "uncivilized," may become a monster because all nature is not necessarily good (Theme III, "L'Homme n'est pas nécessairement bon"). The parent, "l'Etat-Papa" (Theme X) is an enlightened guide who must direct the economic activities of the country and also protect it against potentially destructive foes. Hence, the term that best describes this role is: "dirigisme." In the US, where nature is seen as essentially good, the market is unerring and interventions by the State are the source of all evil. Here, the State is seen as a mere referee whose task is to ensure that the rules of the game are adhered to. No game plan or "planification" are needed.[15]

Heir to the 17th century traditions of Colbertism and mercantilism, "dirigisme" consists of encouraging and prodding national or private industries through such policies as subsidies, exemptions from taxes, and providing monopolistic status, as well as protecting domestic industries from foreign competition (Theme VIII B, "Esprit de citadelle").[16] Aside from some minor ideological differences, the protective role of the State has bi-partisan acceptance from both the Right and the Left. In the 17th century, the king was not only the protector but also the actual owner of some industries, called "manufactures royales." In modern times, the State is following this tradition (Theme IX, "Le Passé existe") by nationalizing some key industries and banks, as described above. The rationale for such ownership is that the general interest can best be served by public rather than private powers (Theme IV B, "Importance de la société"). If one considers that some 2,750 enterprises are owned in various degrees by the State (strictly public or mixed exploitations), as well as all other concerns under its powers (e.g., doctors, insurance companies, railroad workers, taxi drivers, etc.), one can see the range of the State's potential for intervention.[17] Many salaried people's wages, as well as prices of a number of products (bread, milk, and gasoline), are fixed by the State. Moreover, even private employers must present to the State justifications warranting the firing or the downsizing of their work force. All of these interventions give much powers to the State and are, of course, not acceptable in the US, where they are left to the market place.

Central State planning and its assertive leadership have managed to grant employees generous benefits and protection in the form of social charges to be absorbed by the employers. According to one estimate (Ardagh 51), these programs add 45% to costs and 35% to wage bills (Ardagh 7) and are blamed for inadequate investment in new equipment and for the high unemployment rate. In spite of export profits, an employer is hesitant to hire new employees because of the costs of providing benefits and because of the difficulty of releasing them in economic down times. On the more positive side, the leadership of the State has been directly responsible for such glamorous achievements as the tourist resorts along the Languedoc coast, the TGV, the ambitious nuclear program, the Chunnel, and "planification." Most authorities would agree that without State "dirigisme," these projects would not have been realized because the private sector would not have had the foresight or the capital to support them.

Planification

"Planification," a series of 5-year economic plans targeting sectors for which the State sets targets for growth (Theme II A, "Demande de clarté") and for intervention (Theme X, "L'Etat-Papa"), was devised after World War II by Jean Monnet. The State developed industrial policies, identified sectors for State intervention, and coordinated the actions of various ministries in a non-authoritarian and empirical manner. The direction of these actions was (Theme I B, "Emphasis on reason"; II A, "Demande de clarté") from the abstract to the concrete, thus typically French.[18] "Planification" did, for instance, identify regional imbalances, focus attention on the plight of smaller cities, and propose tax breaks for industries willing to settle or resettle in the less industrialized regions of France by creating the ZUP, the free enterprize zones (Ardagh 68). The Calais-Marseille nexus dividing the country into industry-rich and industry-poor regions represents an unacceptable imbalance (Theme I C, "Equilibre, balance, variété") for the French, which can only be redressed by a commission like the Commissariat-Général du Plan. The planification for the regions is mostly controlled by the *Délégation à l'aménagement du territoire* (DATAR). This body attempted to equalize the imbalances between industrial zones as well as between densely and sparsely populated regions. It also addressed the lack of mobility of the worker (Theme VII C, "Absence de mobilité: Attachement au terroir"), and the age-old problem of decentralization, the movement away from Paris toward what was hoped to be a more balanced hexagon (Theme I,

"L'Harmonie de l'ensemble"). Nowadays, DATAR's role has waned because of the Socialists' devolution reforms in the 1980s as well as the European Community's Single Market Program and Regional Aid Fund, which assumed most of DATAR's functions on a European level (Ardagh 168-81).

Economic Structures

Although French industries showcase some impressive achievements on the world market, they still suffer from their narrowness in specialized sectors and are ill-equipped to confront the competition with lower-wage countries. The 80s and the 90s have witnessed an impressive economic movement of liberalization. Yet the economic sector is still experiencing periods of protectionism in certain sectors (agriculture, fishing, trucking, and lately the "fonction publique", the "fonctionnaires") which, when under duress, refuse to give up what they consider entitlements (Theme VIII C, "Culte de l'acquis").

One criticism of French industries in the past has been what Wylie and Brière call "une passion pour les projets audacieux et grandioses qui mettent en valeur la prouesse technologique, mais dont les gains sont discutables" (208), such as the SST, the Rance tidal dam, the Superphénix fast-breeder reactor, and the Chunnel. The authors (as well as Ardagh 76) account for this passion for flair and brilliance as evidence of the French "éthique de l'honneur" (208). Certainly, the preference for esthetic values over material ones (Theme V B, "Esthétisme vs. matérialisme") fits into this "éthique."

Ardagh identifies a similar problem: the failure to marry industry and pure science. The French, in their desire to make a clear separation between the two different worlds of academia and business (Theme II A, "Demande de clarté"), have led the world in research innovations but have neglected to apply them. American undergraduates who have studied in France and who wished to take courses that would transfer to their home university know that courses in applied science classes with laboratory are very rare in French universities. "Abstract" (see above), empirical, theoretical courses abound but, as Ardagh notes, "public opinion tended to regard discovery as its own reward"(56). The chasm between industry and academic research is worsened by the fact that some pure science researchers situate themselves on the political Left and do not willingly cooperate with those of opposite convictions. Such a dichotomy is not all too rare in France (Theme VI, "Le Manichéisme français") and has, until recently, denied the French economy the benefits of its own pure research. Most authoritities agree with de Gaulle when he mused about the CNRS: "Je vois beaucoup de chercheurs, mais où sont les trouveurs?" (Ardagh 57).[19]

Taxation

Unlike in the US where taxation is based directly on property, revenue, and capital, the French, along with most European nations, prefer taxing consumption through a scaled system, called the TVA ("Taxe à valeur ajoutée") which taxes minimally (0 to 5%) some necessary items and more heavily (up to 25%) luxury ones (e.g. cars and furs). The preference for this taxation over direct taxation is that the former has a voluntary aspect to it and thus seems fairer (albeit regressive) and thus more acceptable. In fact, as Wylie and Brière note, the historical and more profound reason for this choice seems more likely to be the propensity of the French for fiscal fraud which is lessened through this more open manner of taxation (208). One could argue that, even more profoundly, the source of this policy is the French definition of human nature: since Man is not naturally good and cannot always realistically overcome "le mal" (Theme III, "L'Homme n'est pas naturellement bon"), the indirect TVA taxation system may be the only viable one.

Labor Unions

Although labor unions were legalized in France over a century ago, they have proportionately fewer members than US labor unions. Strikes, which in the US are seen as acts of last resort after negotiations have failed, are all too often used in France as warnings, as preliminary pressure tactics before negotiations even start. Such overly used strategies may account for the lack of seriousness employees perceive in the labor unions and, as a result, account for smaller membership. One distinctively French characteristic is the large number of labor unions. Fragmented along political, professional and ideological lines, unions experience difficulty in producing effective concerted actions. This situation reflects the anti-collective nature of the French where group initiatives are, for the most part, short-lived (Theme VI, "Le Manichéisme français"). Ardagh notes that the leaders of the main labor unions of the Left, the CGT (Communist) and the CFGT (Socialist), "contrive a façade of comradely unity when they do meet in public but when apart they denounce each other's policies" (110). The basis for this fragmentation is the tendency to intellectualize every issue (Theme II B, "Esprit cartésien"). Because differences must be clearly delineated and "le flou" is unacceptable (Theme II A, "Demande de clarté"), it follows that there will be numerous political battles over ideologies as well as a lack of interest in more practical issues.

The European Union

Wylie and Brière's chapter ends with a brief overview of the European Union's impact on France. The French have already experienced the traumas caused by the adjustment of certain social laws providing closer harmonization with European standards and by a forced uniformity of the TVA across the EU. They also fear very much the dismantling of customs borders, as required by the single European market which went into effect on Jan. 1, 1993. France's fear stems from the globalization of markets which, in the eyes of many, has forced French businesses to trim down in order to remain competitive and from the EU Commission which has not allowed the French government to intervene with subsidies for sectors of the economy that have experienced difficulty.

The French are ambivalent about Europe: they are enthusiastic about the opportunities that the breaking down of trade barriers may offer, but also fearful of what this will do to their cherished harmony (Theme I, "L'Harmonie de l'ensemble"). This dualism is perhaps best exemplified by two recently published books.[20] The best-selling *L'Horreur économique*, savagely attacks the political elite who have promoted a transnational capitalism, and denounces the opening of borders and the resulting competitiveness. Globalization is characterized as a sinister plot devised by a handful of capitalists who force industries to engage in "social dumping" and in downsizing ("dégraissage"). The perception of the presence of a global plot to attack the French way of managing their economy can be cited as an example of *Le Complexe hexagonal* (Theme I A). As a result of this perceived foe, the majority of the French group together (Theme VI B, "La réaction anti-manichéenne") in order to preserve their entitlements (Theme VIII C, "Culte de l'acquis"), as in 1995 when hundreds of thousands took to the streets to demonstrate against the Juppé administration's attempt to challenge the entitlements of "la fonction publique." The challenge to these entitlements was again prompted by the need to cut budget deficits in order to satisfy the criteria for membership in the European single currency. The mandate here is for a French exception, shielded from outside influence (Theme I D, "Repli sur soi") and from free market requirements of Anglo-Saxon origin. The French model, with its proud, State-led administrative record and of its dirigistic achievements, is under attack. This assault causes citizens to withdraw into their own hexagon whose shape, on second look, may also resemble that of a house, comfortable as well as comforting.

A world-class economic power, however, cannot isolate itself. Another book with the revealing title, *Ce Monde qui nous attend*, invites the French not to reject "le libéralisme économique" but rather to accept enthusiastically the challenges posed by globalization. The work bemoans the hesitant attitude of the French to modernize themselves, as exemplified by the slow pace of their acceptance of the personal computer. The author also bemoans the French tendency, when it feels threatened by the rest of the world, to attempt to impose its own civilizing model (Theme V, "L'idéal de civilisation") in order to tame this "capitalisme sauvage." While the rest of the world moves inexorably forward toward globalization, French politicians must accept, and indeed promote, changes in attitudes and endeavor to develop new markets and new technologies.

The French "comportements" that I have noted are the result of centuries of steady development, but, as human dynamic structures, they are not invulnerable to change, and change causes anxieties. Such fears are far-reaching because France is undergoing deep changes in its traditional culture: the social classes are blurred (running counter to Theme II, "L'Horreur de l'imprécis"), and the centralized dirigistic State is under attack from those seeking more regional autonomy (reaction against "L'Etat-Papa", Theme X). France's integration with Europe destabilizes the dirigistic tradition since more and more national powers have been devolved to technocrats in Brussels. Moreover, France's "civilized" culture is threatened: the media and language are perceived to be overwhelmed by American mass popular culture, an unacceptable turn of events for a nation that has assumed a mission of civilizing the world (Theme V, "L'Idéal de civilisation"). These two rival missions clearly explain the failure of France and the US to come to an agreement on French-led European restrictions on US audiovisual services under the GATT negotiations.[21] The US consider audio-visual products (e.g. movies and TV programs) as mere commercial commodities and could not understand the insistence that it was one's cultural identity that was on the negotiating table.[22] In view of its assumed mission, France, through President François Mitterrand, responded very succinctly: "Nos cultures ne sont pas à négocier,"[23] and refused to accept the notion that the identity of a nation could be dictated by an economic agreement. The entire audiovisual sector's negotiations were taken off the table and left for future post-Uruguay Round discussions.

Globalization and integration within Europe are eroding national particularities. The particular brand of French capitalism (sometimes referred to as Latin capitalism)[24] is under attack. Thus, we can predict the reaction of the French who, under siege (Theme VIII B, "Esprit de citadelle"), unite to resist change (Theme VI B, "Réaction anti-manichéenne"). The question remains whether the European Union can eventually force a new model of capitalism to emerge in the future in France and thus modify French "comportements."

The ten "comportements" have, I believe, helped to explain France's particular economic model. They can be used as references to explain most of the other cultural practices encountered in courses on contemporary France. While the "comportements" could be applied to any textbook, clearly, Wylie and Brière's work is the most appropriate in view of its authors' approach. Although not all ten themes can be appropriately used for every topic, they have been successfully used to explain French expectations of the government ("L'Etat-secouriste," Theme X B), attitudes toward immigrants (Jacobinist assimilation), the importance of the family (human nature, Theme III: children must be molded, formed), the French view of history (Theme IX, "Le Passé existe"), geography (Theme I, "L'Harmonie de l'ensemble"), human nature (Theme III A, "Méfiance de l'autre": why it is so difficult to be invited in a French home, the demanding nature of French friendship), and the functioning of the educational, administrative, and legal systems (Theme II A, "Clarté" in their highly organized, systematic, and rigid states). I have, of course, presented very schematic and brief examples of how the "comportements," as a free-standing system can be applied across topics.

During this brief overview of the French economy, I have made 40 references to the "comportements" and have referred to each one at least twice. Constant references to the themes during courses on contemporary France and on Business French will help students compare them to American behavioral characteristics and help them to look more deeply at their own institutions. During the course, such constant references will help the student to become familiar with them. After a few weeks of reinforcing the concepts, the instructor, at some appropriate point, should ask the students to apply the "comportements" to a given topic. The students will also quickly learn that US "comportements" are often the opposite of France's: the US, for instance, does not overly stress the need for an harmonious home where balance and equilibrium must rule, and certainly does not conceive of itself as having an hexagonal shape. Americans value practicality and more readily accept that which is "flou" as long as it gets the job done. They also feel that human nature is better than the French believe, so "l'autre" is more easily accepted in the inner circles of family or friends. If such comparisons are challenging, they are also enduring. Students will be able to refer to the themes in order to account for any future actions, predictable or surprising, taken by the French.

WORKS CITED

Ambler, John S. "Educating Pluralism in the French Fifth Republic." *Searching for the New France.* Eds. James F. Hollifield and George Ross. New York and London: Routledge, 1991.

Ardagh, John. *France Today.* New York: Penguin Books, 1995.

Barzini, Luigi. *The Europeans.* New York: Simon & Schuster, 1983.

Carroll, Raymonde. *Cultural Misunderstandings. The French-American Experience.* trans. Carlo Volk. Chicago and London: The University of Chicago Press, 1990.

Corbett, James. *Through French Windows. An Introduction to France in the Nineties.* Ann Arbor: The University of Michigan Press, 1994.

Daninos, Pierre. *Les Carnets du Major Thompson*. eds. Andrée M.L. Barnett and Robert E. Heibling. New York: Holt, Rinehart and Winston, 1959.

Finel-Honigman, Irène. "French/US General Agreement on Tariffs and Trade Impasse: 'Négociations à la Française.'" *Contemporary Issues in Commercial Policy*. Ed. Mordechai E. Kreinin. NY: Pergamon, 1995: 33-40.

Fallot, Evelyne and Sylvie Pierre-Brossolette. "Les Dix Blocages de la société française." *L'Express* March 1, 1985: 21-33.

Geertz, Clifford. *The Interpretation of Cultures*. London: Hutchinson, 1975.

Hostede, Geert. *Cultures and Organizations: Software of the Mind*. London and NY: McGraw-Hill, 1991.

Hoffmann, Stanley. "Look Back in Anger." *The New York Review of Books* 44.12 (July 17, 1997): 45-50.

Lapeyre, Elisabeth. "Robert Sabatier's Novels and the Teaching of French Culture." *The French Review* 62.1 (Oct.1988): 67-76.

Peyrefitte, Alain. *Le Mal français*. Paris: Plon, 1976.

Pitts, Jesse. "Les Français et l'autorité: la vision d'un Américain." *Français, qui êtes-vous?* Ed. J-D. Reynaud and Yves Grafmeyer. Paris: La Documentation française, 1981: 285-300.

Platt, Polly. *French or Foe? Getting the Most out of Visiting, Living and Working in France*. n.p.: Culture Crossings, Ltd, 1995.

Rhodes, Martin, Paul Heywood, and Vincent Wright, Eds. *Developments in West European Politics*. NY: St. Martin's Press, 1997.

Steele, Ross and Andrew Suozzo. *Teaching French Culture: Theory and Practice*. Lincolnwood, Illinois: National Textbook Company, 1994.

Wylie, Laurence, and Jean-François Brière. *Les Français.* 2nd ed. Englewood Cliffs, New Jersey: Prentice Hall, 1995.

Notes

[1] Several terms have been used to describe patterns of behavior: "whole pattern of living" (Wylie VI), "pattern of meaning embodied in symbols" (Geertz 89), "themal descriptions" by Nostrand (Steele 181), "values" (Hofstede). "Comportements" or themes are more efficient for our purposes. I wish to thank my colleague, James N. Davis, for his thoughtful suggestions about this article.

[2] The ten "blocages" are 1) "Le Complexe hexagonal," 2) "Le Syndrome du topinanbour," 3) "L'Esprit de clan," 4) "La Trouille du risque," 5) "Le Culte de l'acquis," 6) "Le Tabou de l'argent," 7) "L'Etat-Papa," 8) "Le Fétichisme de la botte," 9) "La Méthode du discours," 10) "La Tentation monarchique." Elisabeth Lapeyre made a similar application of patterns of culture to literature and argued that they have been very useful in helping students understand French values embedded in literary works. In her view, the use of literature for this purpose is an appropriate one since a "good writer will have extracted the essence of what deserves to survive as the expression of a time and place" (75).

[3] This passion is noticeable in the "jardin à la française": harmonious, elegant, and characterized by geometrical figures (Theme I).

[4] Carroll 47 and 49.

[5] See the famous quote from Pascal: "L'homme n'est ni ange ni bête, et le malheur veut que qui veut faire l'ange fait la bête" (Wylie and Brière 52).

[6] Corbett 216.

[7] Referring to a poster celebrating de Gaulle's 100th anniversary which said: "Rien n'est si grand qu'un peuple gouverné," Stanley Hoffmann remarked: "Can one imagine, in the Washington subway, a poster telling Americans that a firmly ruled people is the greatest thing on earth? As a former Gaullist minister put it: 'France is still a monarchy, and when the monarch is bad, France is sick' " (49).

[8] It seems that power is more attractive to French than money, although the latter is no disincentive either. See Platt (143, 44) and Ardagh (90). Stanley Hoffmann numbers civil servants at five million, proportionately five times as many as in the US (45).

[9] The authors of the *L'Express* article call it "Le Syndrome du topinambour" (i.e., Jerusalem artichoke, which has numerous underground roots).

[10] In general, the French do not like to sense weakness. When during the strikes and protests that have rocked France, the administration is seen as capitulating to demands, the French seem to lose respect for their elected officials and to side with the malcontents. Jesse Pitts sees a similar disgust on the part of students which leads to a "chahut" in schools when the instructor is perceived to have lost control because of lack of "style" or weakness (287-89).

[11] "...Jacobinism means a strictly hierarchical structure in which decisions and personnel assignments are made from the center, with very little local authority" Ambler (194). This concept of a centralized state will, of course, be hostile to diversity in the name of unity and equality of opportunity.

[12] For a deeper analysis of this complex relationship between governmental authority and the citizen who continuously oscillates "entre la passion pour l'Etat et la passion contre le gouvernement," see Pitts (285).

[13] "...être libre, c'est pouvoir exister en tant qu'identité distincte, protégé de tout risque de disparition,..." (Wylie and Brière 58). Thus, supermarkets are seen as enemies of freedom since they tend to crush small store owners. As

Wylie and Brière put it (58): "La conception française traditionnelle de la liberté s'accorde mal avec celle du système capitaliste."

[14] Such concerns are probably responsible for a backlash of voters against the Right: at present, Socialists boast nine prime ministers out of fifteen in the EU. Yet socialists are not all alike. The French brand of socialism is quite different from "New Labour" Tony Blair's, for instance. While the latter calls for flexibility in the labor market, less regulations, and a less interventionist State, Lionel Jospin speaks revealingly in old-fashion terms: "If market forces are allowed to rip, it will spell the end of civilization (Theme V) in Western Europe" (Quoted in *Financial Times,* June 7/8, 1997: 1).

[15] Lester Thurow Laments This Lack of National Game Plan. See, *Head to Head. The Coming Economic Battle among Japan, Europe, and America* (New York: Morrow, 1992) 290-97.

[16] On Colbertism and Mercantilism, see G. de Bertier de Sauvigny and David H. Pinkney's *History of France* (Arlington Heights, Illinois: The Forum Press, 1983) 156-60.

[17] For a succinct account of the nationalization-privatization debate, see the Chambre de commerce et d'industrie de la ville de Paris' "Le Français commercial," *Bulletin de Liaison* (Spring 1983): 3-18.

[18] Wylie and Brière trace the same movement, starting from the abstract and going to the concrete, in the field of education (chpts. 1 & 2), in law and justice (chpt. 9), and in raising children (chpt. 5).

[19] In the late 80s, a part of the CNRS budget was reallocated in the form of incentives to private industries to encourage them to develop more Research and Development programs. Another good example of "dirigisme" (Theme X).

[20] Viviane Forrester, *L'Horreur économique* (Paris: Fayard, 1996) and Eric Izraelewicz, *Ce Monde qui nous attend* (Paris: Grasset, 1996).

[21] A European Commission directive requires all television channels to broadcast at least 60% European programs. The US claimed that such a

directive was incompatible with a free market. France countered that since 70% of movies in France are American and only 2% in the US are French, the imbalance is evident.

[22] For a deeper look at the cultural component of these negotiations and how much the French and the US were on culturally different planes, see Finel-Honigman.

[23] On Antenne 2 on October 15, 1993.

[24] As opposed to Atlantic capitalism (Thatcherite) and Rheinish (German), see Rhodes and Van Apeldoorn.

[25] Over the past few years, many studies, published by ASHE-ERIC *Higher Education Reports*, discuss the challenges to higher education. They emphasize the need to improve learning experiences, add experiential learning, and engage in curriculum reform to prepare students more effectively for the global community.

LE FRANÇAIS DES AFFAIRES AU NIVEAU «GRADUATE» : UNE PEDAGOGIE MULTIDISCIPLINAIRE ET INTEGREE

Michel Gueldry

Le français des affaires est un champ universitaire encore relativement fluide, dont la pédagogie est loin d'être entièrement fixée. Cela tient à deux faits au moins. D'abord, il s'agit d'une discipline assez récente, puisque son apparition date du milieu des années 1970, suite aux efforts de Jacques Cartier au sein du «Service des Examens pour Etrangers» de la CCIP. Ensuite, la plupart des enseignants viennent d'horizons extérieurs à cette matière, avec une dominante de littéraires et de linguistes, et pour le reste des historiens ou des politologues, et peu d'économistes proprement dit. Le français commercial, s'il ne rencontre plus de problème de légitimité universitaire, a encore de grands besoins en matière de «formation des formateurs».

Ainsi, pour satisfaire à la perspective du présent volume, nous présentons ci-dessous sinon un «modèle» pédagogique global (un objectif désirable mais difficile), du moins une méthodologie développée depuis quatre années au *Monterey Institute of International Studies* (CA), et appuyée sur des matériaux appropriés, pour enseigner cette discipline au niveau de la maîtrise (*graduate*). Ce type d'enseignement semble avoir moins retenu l'attention des chercheurs et des enseignants. En effet, si l'on considère trois indicateurs professionnels importants: la substantielle bibliographie rassemblée par Maurice G.A. Elton dans le premier volume de cette série (29-42), les articles de la *FFBAIT Newsletter* et les manuels disponibles sur le marché, on constate que notre discipline est essentiellement orientée vers un public de *colleges*, avec de nombreuses ramifications en direction

103

des *high schools*. C'est à juste titre, parce que les «gros bataillons» sont là, et parce que le français commercial voulut dès le départ répondre aux besoins d'étudiants désirant un enseignement concret, remédiant par là à une certaine désaffection pour les cours traditionnels offerts par les départements de français.

On voudra donc ici combler une lacune pour le niveau *graduate* en proposant une approche à la fois *multidisciplinaire, intégrée et pratique*. Multidisciplinaire, dans la mesure où le français commercial faisant partie d'un tout, les étudiants francophones de MIIS apprennent bien sûr son vocabulaire et ses pratiques spécialisés, mais abordent aussi l'économie politique, les sciences politiques et même les relations internationales contemporaines. Intégrée, en ce sens que les niveaux microéconomique et macroéconomique sont abordés : le cycle de vie d'un produit spécifique, démarche typique de *marketing*, ou l'enregistrement d'une SARL (société à responsabilité limitée) au RC (registre du commerce) de la CCI (Chambre de Commerce et d'Industrie) locale, mais aussi la planification nationale ou la monnaie unique. Pratique, en cela que l'enseignement est fonctionnel et *task-oriented* : se débrouiller dans le métro, écrire une lettre de réclamation, mais aussi faire des exposés publics en français via l'outil informatique.

Avec l'espoir d'apporter par la description de cette approche quelque bénéfice à nos collègues, nous commencerons par identifier ses caractéristiques, avant de présenter ses trois axes principaux. Cela mènera à s'interroger sur les limites de cette méthode, pour terminer en suggérant des *exemples précis de transposition* de cette expérience par d'autres enseignants. Ces exemples concrets et détaillés constituent la partie la plus longue du présent article.

Spécificités de cet enseignement au niveau maîtrise

Une partie de l'originalité de ce cours tient à la nature de l'institution où il est offert et au parcours universitaire de l'instructeur. MIIS est une école professionnelle au niveau de la maîtrise, dont la mission est d'intégrer les langues à des disciplines (relations internationales, commerce international, études environnementales, etc.) traditionnellement enseignées en anglais après les quatre premières années universitaires (*college*). C'est pourquoi le département de français s'efforce de développer des cours avancés (3ème et 4ème années de français) dans le domaine de la civilisation, des sciences politiques et économiques pour un groupe hétérogène d'étudiants venant de quatre écoles : gestion des affaires (MBA), politique internationale, traduction et interprétation, et enseignement des langues. L'enseignant a une double formation d'historien et de politologue, et approche le français commercial dans une perspective de sciences sociales, ce qui permet de présenter aux étudiants des notions relevant de :

- L'histoire de la pensée et des théories économiques. Par exemple, nous étudions la théorie de la valeur (rareté, travail, capital ou utilité),

- La science politique et la macro-économie. Par exemple, les modes d'intervention de l'Etat dans la vie économique et financière de la France sont abordés: politique monétaire, budgétaire, réglementaire, planification, ainsi que service public et monopoles,

- Les relations internationales. Par exemple, les institutions de l'Union européenne, ses 2ème et 3ème piliers sont survolés. Nous étudions plus longuement son 1er pilier, c'est-à-dire, l'union économique et monétaire, et notamment les implications de la monnaie unique, des critères de convergences et de la dérégulation européenne pour l'économie de la France.

Il s'agit là d'un vaste programme, et il est évident qu'on ne peut l'étudier de manière exhaustive. Son caractère ambitieux se justifie néanmoins par la qualité des étudiants au niveau de la maîtrise. Leur niveau général de grammaire et de vocabulaire est déjà avancé, dans la mesure où ils ont au minimum quatre semestres universitaires de français et très souvent plus, combinés avec des séjours plus ou moins longs en France ou en pays francophone, et des expériences professionnelles. Donc, ils doivent utiliser la langue d'arrivée (*target language*) dans des situations intellectuelles vraisemblables, complexes et constamment renouvelées. Le curriculum ainsi modelé par les préoccupations professionnelles de cette «clientèle» étudiante vise 1) à enrichir leur vocabulaire utile, 2) à leur faire comprendre le capitalisme français dans ses dimensions nationales ainsi que dans son insertion dans l'économie européenne et globale.

C'est pourquoi nous avons fusionné deux cours, le premier portant sur la langue et les pratiques des affaires, le second portant sur l'économie politique de l'Hexagone. Cette classe est structurée en deux fois deux heures chaque semaine, sur une durée de quinze semaines. Une session hebdomadaire est consacrée exclusivement à l'étude du vocabulaire, des pratiques commerciales et de la microéconomie (lettres, CV, nature juridique des entreprises, statuts, éléments de mercantique ou de gestion du personnel...), l'autre session est réservée spécifiquement à la macroéconomie, aux théories économiques, aux relations internationales et à l'enseignement des logiciels de présentation.

Etant donné le haut degré de motivation et de curiosité de ses étudiants, l'enseignant est ici à mi-chemin entre un coordinateur et un mentor. Les erreurs de date, de détail, de forme, de mémorisation sont considérées comme moins importantes que celles de fond, de substance et de compréhension. Les considérations institutionnelles évoquées *supra*, liées à des priorités budgétaires et à une mission educative spécifique, ont, beaucoup plus que des a-priori pédagogiques, modelé le cours présenté ci-dessous.

Plain French : le vocabulaire, étape incontournable

Nous abordons ici quatre questions essentielles : quel vocabulaire enseigner, comment le communiquer, le tester, et enfin, comment le mettre en pratique et en perspective ? (Pour cette dernière question, on se référera aussi au dernier chapitre *infra*.) En faisant la part des anglicismes acceptés ou tolérés, nous distinguons cinq familles de mots, ce qui mène naturellement, sinon aisément, à une réflexion sur la culture économique hexagonale et, par *l'intégration des mots aux concepts*, à une démarche globalisante.

Nous soulignons que cette culture est une culture dite de «haut contexte», largement auto-référentielle, d'où la nécessité d'un certain décryptage du vocabulaire économique et social. A côté de nombreux mots généraux, sans référant social ou historique particulier (investir, antidater, liquidités, détaillant, PIB...) et dont on peut souvent inférer le sens par le contexte, prolifèrent des expressions liées à des événements précis (les Trente Glorieuses, le colbertisme, le jacobinisme...) que le contexte n'explique pas, et dont on ne trouve pas d'équivalent direct en anglais. Une troisième sorte de vocables comprend les termes techniques et sans jugement de valeur, très liés à une profession en particulier, et aisément traduisibles, par exemple CAC 40, zinzins, SICAV, chevalier noir, second marché, MATIF et bulle financière... Nous insistons par ailleurs sur le fait que le vocabulaire socio-économique n'est pas toujours neutre, mais qu'il exprime parfois des jugements sur l'argent, l'entreprise, etc. Ceci permet de distinguer une quatrième catégorie de mots politiquement chargés : dire ploutocratie ou 200 familles, spéculateur ou financier, flexibilité du travail ou atteinte aux droits acquis, ne communique pas du tout la même impression ! Cinquièmement, des mots tels que socialisme, social-démocratie, ou Etat-Providence sont expliqués en fonction de l'expérience profonde de la nation, parce que, même traduits en anglais, ils n'ont pas le même sens dans la société américaine. Ils expriment une *Weltanschauung* (une vision du monde totalisante) française spécifique, souvent différente de celle des Etats-Unis.

Par exemple, «Sécurité Sociale» ne peut être simplement traduit par «Social Security», car ce n'est pas du tout la même chose au quadruple plan économique, social, politique et affectif. Pour simplifier à l'extrême ces traductions :

France	Etats-Unis
Sécurité Sociale	pas d'équivalent bref
dont : assurance maladie	Health benefits, fringe
	Benefits, benefit package
Retraite	pension, social security
Allocations familiales	«welfare»
	(conditions d'allocations et philosophies très différentes)
Accidents du travail	Workers' compensation, disability

Pour en rendre compte, il faut aussi expliquer l'œuvre de Pierre Laroque, la retraite par capitalisation et par répartition, les valeurs de solidarité issue de la Résistance, et lier tout ceci au Front Populaire et au troisième mot de la devise de la République sociale : «fraternité» (article 2 de la Constitution de 1958). Il faut aussi lier ces considérations historiques au débat contemporain : l'élection de Lionel Jospin, les propositions de

Claude Bébéar sur les fonds de pension, le monétarisme, la pensée unique, l'autre politique de Philippe Séguin, voire *L'horreur économique* de Viviane Forrestier, dont le succès de librairie en dit long sur le malaise français.

La «francité» des mots des catégories un et trois tient exclusivement à la combinaison des lettres et aux règles de grammaire et de prononciation. Ce vocabulaire «objectif» et pragmatique est donc orienté vers la résolution de problèmes (*problem solving)* quotidiens (poste, banque, assurances...) ainsi que vers la connaissance des professions (pour CAC 40 et les autres : la Bourse). Alors, les étudiants sont testés à la manière éprouvée des examens de la CCIP. Un bon dictionnaire économique et un minimum d'explications permettent de couvrir ce champ lexical. Mais pour les mots plus conceptuels de la seconde catégorie, en plus de la disposition lexicale, existe un riche substrat économico-historique, qui implique une certaine connaissance de la matrice culturelle dont ils sont issus. Celle-ci est acquise par les présentations de l'instructeur, et à travers la lecture de la presse économique, (*Le Monde-Economie, Le Figaro* (cahier saumon), *Le Nouvel Economiste, L'Usine Nouvelle, et L'Expansion, Le MOCI* et *La Tribune Desfossés*, et dans une moindre mesure *Le Point, L'Express, Le Nouvel Observateur* et *L'EDJ*). Elle est aussi testée à travers elle, en demandant d'expliquer ou de traduire des passages à fort référant socio-culturel. Pour éviter une acquisition mécanique et répétitive de mots, et la fragmentation entre vocabulaire spécialisé et économie générale, il est enfin demandé aux étudiants de consulter, en vue d'un court rapport oral, des sites Web en français, par exemple la riche revue de presse, à jour et archivée, du Ministère de l'Industrie (http://www.ensmp.fr/industrie/sy) ou les dossiers du Ministère de l'Economie et des Finances (http://www.tresor.finances.fr).

La production et la distribution sociales des richesses n'est pas libre de jugements de valeur (*value-free*), tout au contraire. C'est pourquoi nous considérons comme incomplet tout enseignement au niveau de la maîtrise qui n'en appellerait pas au sens critique et politique *largo sensu* des étudiants. Dans le but d'éviter une acquisition purement quantitative du vocabulaire et pour en intégrer les différents niveaux, les étudiants doivent, après étude commune en classe, écrire des essais sur la conception du travail, du capitalisme, de l'Etat, etc., qui se dégage d'expressions telles que : technologies de pointe, corporatisme, planification, ENA (énarques, énarchie), grandes écoles, ou comité Colbert. Ceci permet d'inclure les expressions des quatrième et cinquième catégories.

Deux exemples. 1) Quand Michel Albert, dans son livre célèbre, distingue le «capitalisme rhénan» du «capitalisme libéral», de quoi parle-t-il au juste, et que vaut sa théorie ? 2) Un mot aussi simple que «patron» révèle, lui aussi, un riche filon d'histoire économique : il a un sens général plutôt neutre, mais en plus, pour la gauche, il a longtemps fleuré bon l'atelier, la lutte des classes et le Front Populaire. Or, à partir de 1983-84, avec le Thatcherisme, le Reaganisme et la vulgarisation du libéralisme économique en France, «entrepreneur» (positif) ou «employeur» (le summum, en cette période de chômage) lui furent préférés par les socialistes alors au pouvoir. Ce glissement sémantique s'accompagna d'une modification profonde de leur perception de l'entreprise privée, du profit et de la compétition économique. En abandonnant le mot «patron» et ses connotations poussiéreuses et militantes (exploiteur, mur d'argent, Grand soir) vers 1983-84, les socialistes se sont ainsi réconciliés avec l'entreprise privée, aux dépens de leur programme (d'avant 1981) de «rupture avec le capitalisme». Voici deux mots simples en apparence, mais dont l'explication mène à un intéressant puzzle linguistique, conceptuel et économique. Le dernier chapitre de cet article fournit deux exemples d'activité intégrée pour le vocabulaire et les concepts.

No Self-Evident Truths : Comparer deux systèmes et deux cultures économiques

Les désaccords franco-américains en matière de relations commerciales, parfois vifs, tiennent moins à la malice ou à la mauvaise volonté qu'à deux types de divergences objectives : de fortes luttes d'intérêts et des référents culturels dissemblables. Faute de le comprendre, bien des personnes, de chaque côté de l'Atlantique, continuent de porter un jugement hâtif, négatif et, surtout, *mal informé* sur le partenaire. Donc, si dans un premier temps on veut communiquer aux étudiants un vocabulaire et des concepts appropriés, un second objectif du cours est d'expliquer ces désaccords, ce qui permet d'aborder l'économie française (macro) au sein de l'Union européenne (UE), et de sensibiliser le public aux valeurs françaises sous forme d'un atelier interculturel.

Pour faire comprendre la compétition entre ces deux pays, et en supposant que les étudiants connaissent quelque peu l'économie américaine, il faut leur apporter des informations sur le capitalisme français : secteurs économiques, liens entre l'Etat et le *big business*, rôle de l'Afrique et des DOM-TOM, impact de l'UE surtout. Ici, la meilleure démarche est d'offrir un tableau cohérent et équilibré des faiblesses et des forces de l'économie nationale. Les premières (chômage, omniprésence de l'Etat...) sont amplement soulignées, et le plus souvent condamnées, par la presse des USA, en l'espèce d'un grand mimétisme — encore faut-il les expliquer ! Par exemple, la fréquence des mouvements sociaux (grèves, manifestations de rue) est moins un signe de déliquescence économique ou de pagaille méditérranéenne qu'une indication des rapports de force entre capital et travail, Etat et syndicats, une méthode de négotiations et un mode de régulation systémique accepté. Par contraste, on invitera les étudiants à s'interroger sur l'atonie du mouvement syndical américain (*labor*), sur les rapports entre classes sociales et le discours «consensuel» qui domine aux Etats-Unis, sur la mobilité individuelle, et à comparer les rôles respectifs des tribunaux aux Etats-Unis et des syndicats en France pour la défense des droits sociaux.

Parler des forces de l'économie française est encore plus indispensable car les medias américains se concentrent sur le *Pacific Rim* et l'Allemagne, et façonnent la vision du monde des Américains, notamment des plus jeunes. L'image flatteuse mais réductrice et passéiste de la France des châteaux doit être fortement nuancée. Il y a en la matière un vaste travail d'information à faire. La France est bien la quatrième économie mondiale, un pays de science et de haute technologie, le second investisseur financier *per capita* aux Etats-Unis depuis plusieurs années, et bénéficie de services publics (les transports par exemple) de qualité. Les dysfonctions du système ne doivent pas être ignorées ou sous-estimées, mais ses performances doivent être évoquées sans complexe d'infériorité ou de supériorité. Ici, les nombreux documents diffusés par *Invest in France* (la DATAR aux Etats-Unis) et par la *French-American Chamber of Commerce*, dans le cadre de leur campagne *France Technology* sont des plus utiles. On y ajoutera les documents spécialisés des postes d'expansion économique.

A partir du moment où l'audience comprend qu'il y a une lutte d'intérêts, et non antiaméricanisme (cela existe aussi, mais on ne peut tout ramener à des mouvements d'humeur), on peut mieux faire comprendre les positions françaises dans cinq domaines de haute compétition franco-américaine : aviation, agriculture, langue, «produits culturels» (exception culturelle), et ventes d'armes. Nous n'évoquerons ici que les deux premiers.

L'opposition entre Airbus, le consortium européen (Allemagne, Espagne, France et Grande-Bretagne) et Boeing est bien couverte par les media des deux côtés de l'Atlantique. Elle retient l'attention des étudiants américains, et peut faire l'objet de *dossiers de presse comparatifs* des plus intéressants. On soulignera qu'Airbus est né, dans les années 1970, du désir des dirigeants européens de ne pas laisser à l'industrie aéronautique américaine le monopole du marché mondial. Volonté politique en Europe contre logique du marché aux Etats-Unis, accusations réciproques de subsides, lutte âpre qui associe entreprises privées et politique industrielle des Etats : tout ceci passionne les étudiants.

L'agriculture constitue aussi une pomme de discorde franco-américaine, comme on l'a vu lors de la conclusion du cycle d'Uruguay des accords de l'AGTDC (GATT). Paris, accusé de vouloir continuer les subsides à son agriculture dans le cadre de la PAC (politique agricole commune), était accusé de bloquer unilatéralement la finalisation des accords de Blair House. C'est simplifier les choses : vraiment seule, la France aurait peu obtenu. Voilà pourquoi il importe de montrer aux étudiants que Paris était discrètement, mais efficacement, soutenu par Helmut Kohl, parce que celui-ci, au sein de son gouvernement de coalition, avait (et a toujours) besoin du soutien politique de la CSU, la branche bavaroise de la CDU, qui entendait bien que l'agriculture bavaroise continue de bénéficier de certaines des dispositions de la PAC, menacée par le libéralisme de l'AGTDC. En outre, plusieurs pays de la périphérie de l'UE soutenaient aussi discrètement la position française, de peur de voir leur agriculture relativement peu performante menacée par le retrait du FEOGA (le budget de la PAC), sans aucune compensation des fonds structurels de l'Union.

Voici deux exemples qui révèlent à nos classes comment l'économie nationale s'insère, ici pour son profit (mais ce n'est pas toujours le cas), dans un ensemble régional qui détermine ses rapports avec l'économie globale. On pourra aussi faire le lien avec la section «vocabulaire» en parlant, par exemple, d'un *colbertisme high-tech* pour l'UE. Tout bon manuel sur l'économie française sera utile ici. Mais aussi des ouvrages compacts comme *Que Sais-Je* (P.U.F), les *Guides pratiques* chez Nathan ou la collection *U* chez Armand Colin. Il s'agit d'ouvrage brefs, clairs et structurés, genéralement pour classes terminales, dans la perspective du Bac.

Restent les différences culturelles : ces «évidences invisibles» (Raymonde Carroll) font l'objet d'un atelier interculturel d'une semaine, présenté avec PowerPoint. Son format est un tableau comparatif commenté des valeurs françaises et américaines, composé de valeurs politico-historiques et d'attitudes socio-culturelles. Son but est de faire comprendre de l'intérieur une logique nouvelle. Ces valeurs étrangères, perçues comme fantasques, bizarres, arbitraires ou dérangeantes quand les Américains les rencontrent socialement, perdent de leur pouvoir de choquer quand elles sont intégrées dans un cadre explicatif cohérent.

Valeurs politico-historiques	Attitudes socio-culturelles
Histoire	Temps
Religion	Espace (public et privé)
Etat	Relations hommes-femmes
Constitution	Individu et groupe
Classes sociales	Hiérarchie et protocole
Race	Pensée et communication
Capitalisme	Structures familiales
Libéralisme	Succès et pouvoir
Socialisme	Compétition et action
	Langage corporel
	Langue et humour

Ces deux listes ne sont pas exhaustives, loin s'en faut. On pourra bâtir un tel atelier interculturel grâce aux manuels présentés dans la bibliographie déjà mentionnée de Maurice G.A. Elton. Trois exemples d'application pratique de cette comparaison des économies et des cultures sont présentés dans le dernier chapitre du présent article.

The New Frontier : présenter avec l'ordinateur

Troisièmement, notre cours prépare à des exposés professionnels et au discours public (*public speaking*) en français avec intégration de

PowerPoint et d'Excel. Le premier logiciel est une banque d'images, de symboles et de figures géométriques, le second sert pour les chartes, courbes et autres graphiques. Connaître PowerPoint est une chose relativement aisée, l'intégrer dans un exposé professionnel en est une autre.

Pour ce faire, on communique aux étudiants le vocabulaire approprié : logiciel, progiciel, moteur de recherche, page d'accueil, serveur, écran, clavier, touche, courriel, bale (boîte aux lettres électronique), télécharger... Ensuite, on les sensibilise aux critères à respecter : temps (dont on dispose pour la préparation), durée (de présentation), nature du sujet (plus ou moins technique), et de l'audience, buts recherchés...

Après instruction en laboratoire, chaque étudiant présente deux exposés, pour permettre une progression. Le premier porte sur une entreprise française dont la page d'accueil sur le réseau mondial (WWW) doit être consultée et des éléments (logo, organigramme) téléchargés. Le site <http:www.expansion.tm.fr> fournit un classement des 1000 premières entreprises nationales. Le second exposé, lui doit comporter des tableaux statistiques et graphiques, obtenus par Excel ou Microsoft.

Le problème essentiel du monde du travail n'est pas le manque de renseignements, mais leur pléthore, et le manque de temps pour les assimiler et les mettre en perspective. Donc, on doit apprendre la concision sans dommage pour la précision. Le dernier chapitre résume les conseils pratiques donnés aux étudiants dans ce but. Avec cet exercice pratique et non simulé, on donne aux étudiants un argument pour parler en public, obtenir un stage en entreprise ou même un emploi. Il est à noter que cette partie du cours s'inspire de deux *stages pour professeurs* organisés à MIIS avec l'aide du BCLE du Consulat de France à San Francisco : «Ressources françaises sur Internet» (février 1996) et «Français des affaires et Internet» (février 1998).

Quelques contraintes pédagogiques

Premièrement, l'enseignant est sollicité par les attentes contradictoires de ses élèves, notamment celles des étudiants de MBA, des étudiants de l'école d'interprétation et de traduction, et enfin celles des futurs enseignants de langue. Alors que les premiers voudraient des cours plus techniques, (comme la comptabilité en français), les seconds mettent plus l'accent sur la langue elle-même, et les derniers sur la pédagogie. Deuxièmement, le caractère interdisciplinaire de ce cours et son ouverture en limitent la profondeur. Mais il nous semble plus profitable de donner une vision cohérente *et intégrée* du vocabulaire, de l'économie, et du *public speaking*, qu'une présentation plus approfondie (en terme de contenu), mais plus déséquilibrée, d'un seul de ces trois domaines aux dépens des deux autres. Au demeurant, à temps égal, mieux vaut, par exemple, faire comprendre tel comportement français, ce qui exige la participation de la classe, qu'étudier un chapitre supplémentaire de vocabulaire, tâche à laquelle un bon dictionnaire peut en partie pourvoir. «Mieux vaut une tête bien faite qu'une tête bien pleine», disait justement Montaigne.

Troisièmement, cette approche intègre l'Union européenne, dont l'étude exige beaucoup de temps, mais passe sous silence l'expérience commerciale du Québec ou d'autres pays francophones. On le regrette, mais ce choix se justifie par l'importance de l'UE pour la France et les Etats-Unis. Quatrièmement, pour intégrer les étudiants linguistiquement les plus faibles, il est nécessaire de rappeler périodiquement bien des règles de grammaire et/ou de composition, ce qui diminue le temps consacré aux autres activités. Une solution consiste à associer ces étudiants avec des assistants ou des logiciels de grammaire — si on dispose de ces ressources et s'ils peuvent effectuer ce travail supplémentaire. Cinquièmement, la diversité de cette approche exige du doigté : la transmission du vocabulaire, de l'économie politique et de l'informatique, leurs méthodes d'exercice, de contrôle et de notation sont bien différentes. Pour utiliser ce différentiel au profit de tous, l'instructeur doit alterner diverses tactiques, combiner une pédagogie directrice avec une *hands-off approach*, et communiquer la logique du tout — un exercice de précision, s'il en est un ! Enfin, et ce n'est pas là le moindre problème, la préparation d'un tel cours exige beaucoup de travail, de recherche de documents et de mise à jour de la part de l'enseignant.

Suggestions concrètes pour la transposition

Intégrer le vocabulaire et les pratiques spécialisées

On utilisera le maximum de documents originaux et primaires : billet de train, lettre de banque, bail, formulaire de location... Par exemple, remplir un constat amiable et composer une lettre explicative constituent d'excellentes activités pour étudier le vocabulaire et les pratiques des assurances dans l'Hexagone. On développera aussi les activités établissant des liens directs avec la France : écrire une lettre d'opinion à *Libération* sur son site Web, demander au Premier Ministre des informations économiques, puisque Matignon a établi un service de questions-réponses via «Sourignon»... Enfin les deux activités suivantes pourront conférer à cette classe réalisme et fonctionalité.

Première activité intégrée : discussions et jeux de rôles

La méthode est classique. Après constitution spontanée ou dirigée de groupes, on établit un temps-limite et un scénario : confrontation sans résolution du conflit ou négociation avec élaboration d'un compromis, qui est rédigé. En début de semestre, on préfère la discussion libre où la seule règle du jeu est le respect de l'alternance et du temps de parole. Cette formule autorise plus de spontanéité et permet (on l'espère !) de souder la classe en laissant se dégager une dynamique de groupe. Par la suite, on peut canaliser les efforts dans le sens de la résolution de conflits, exercice plus exigeant. Le choix des sujets dépend du but recherché et du niveau

117

linguistique général : plus «polémique» pour la confrontation (une publicité de cigarettes qui proclame qu'il est plus dangereux pour la santé de boire du lait que de fumer, avec des représentants de l'industrie et des anti-tabagistes...) et plus «complexe» pour la résolution (un article sur les «Tamagotch», ces gadgets électroniques dont le programme simule la vie d'un petit animal domestique virtuel, gadgets fort populaires au Japon).

<u>Seconde activité intégrée : les dossiers d'entreprise</u>

Les étudiants constituent des groupes stables pour le semestre et vont créer une entreprise fictive (avec raison sociale, domiciliation, distribution des parts, nature juridique, rédaction des statuts...) et l'animer (rédiger une offre d'emploi pour un VRP (voyageur, représentant, placier), répondre à l'offre d'emploi d'une autre entreprise fictive par un CV et une lettre manuscrite...). Pour ces derniers, les *Bulletins de liaison* de la CCI de Paris constituent une excellent source. L'enseignant animera cette entreprise par divers incidents : tel désaccord avec tel fournisseur, des agios à négocier, un article du journal local qui accuse l'entreprise de polluer... Autant de scénarios auxquels les étudiants devront répondre par lettres, fax, au téléphone ou oralement. L'enseignant peut aussi notifier ces «entreprises» par courriel et demander une réponse électronique ou traditionnelle. On peut transposer les dossiers d'entreprises sur la page d'accueil du professeur ou du département de français (via *Internet* ou *Intranet*), en articulant les débats menés en classe avec des devoirs à effectuer par courriel.

Comparer les économies et les cultures

En plus de la presse, les étudiants pourront interroger le Consulat de France ou les services culturels français à New York, par fax ou courriel ou en consultant leur page d'accueil. On notera aussi le serveur du CNRS qui inclut des centaines de sites francophones, ou encore *Yahoo France* qui fait de même. Pour étudier les deux cultures, on peut intégrer vocabulaire, concepts interculturels et littérature par un exercice globalisant comme la lecture commentée d'un roman à clefs, comme *Le Salon de conversation* de Catherine Hermary-Vieille et Michèle Sarde.

Enfin, les trois activités suivantes lieront comparaison des économies et des cultures.

<u>Première activité intégrée : comparer les Etats</u>

Parmi la liste (non exhaustive) des valeurs et attitudes présentées au chapitre trois, nous comparerons l'approche française et américaine de l'Etat. Commençons par une affirmation engageante : «Les Américains ont créé l'Etat, mais l'Etat a créé les Français». Décrypter ce paradoxe livre la clef des comportements nationaux envers cette entité essentielle pour la vie socio-économique.

D'abord, on fera un commentaire évident : en France, on dit l'Etat (non l'état), mais le peuple (non le Peuple), ici ce sont les *Etats Unis* (que signifie cette expression ?). Ensuite, on rappellera que l'Etat est apparu tard dans l'histoire du Nouveau Monde, et que selon la mythologie américaine, ce sont les pionniers, individus audacieux et familles dures au labeur, qui ont créé la nation américaine *from the bottom up*. Cette conception est en partie fictive, car elle omet le rôle du gouvernement central dans la conquête territoriale, la lutte contre le Mexique, les Indiens et le Sud sécessionniste. Mais elle correspond à une auto-représentation puissante et est en partie vraie. Par exemple, l'Etat fédéral a affirmé son rôle dans l'économie et le domaine social tardivement : avec Theodore Roosevelt, et plus encore par le *New Deal* des années 1930 et la *Great Society* de LBJ. Et l'unification politico-légale est encore plus tardive : elle remonte aux années 1960, quand Washington imposa sa volonté aux Etats ségrégationnistes du Sud, et permit enfin (contre le pseudo-droit des états du Sud) l'inclusion des Africains-Américains dans le régime de droit national. Avant cela, il existait bien deux Amériques, avec un Sud en état de sécession *de facto* sinon *de jure*. De ce point de vue, l'Amérique moderne date des années 1960.

Au contraire, dès le Xème siècle, c'est la volonté monarchique des Capétiens aux Bourbons, qui créa le royaume de France contre la féodalité atomisante et les autres puissances européennes. Sans cette monarchie centralisatrice, il existait des «pays» avec des langues, des monnaies, des coutumes et des lois très différentes, et sans aucun sens national. D'où l'intérêt de connaître le rôle de Jeanne d'Arc, du catholicisme unificateur et la thèse de Tocqueville sur la Révolution qui compléta l'œuvre centralisatrice des Bourbons. On comprend mieux l'exaltation de l'Etat en France quand on considère les forces centrifuges : la boursouflure de Louis XIV s'explique par les guerres de religion et la Fronde, celle de de Gaulle par la guerre civile de l'entre-deux-guerres (une expression révélatrice) et sous Vichy, etc.

Donc, les immigrants américains ont chronologiquement précédé l'affirmation de l'Etat fédéral, mais l'Etat parisien a rassemblé par la force des groupes divers pour en faire le peuple français, *from the top down*. Ainsi, les étudiants perçoivent de l'intérieur le colbertisme, la protection sociale, le service public, le poids de Paris...

<u>Seconde activité intégrée</u> : *Money Talks !*

L'importance symbolique et pratique de la monnaie pour un cours de *Business French* n'échappe à personne. Alors, on étalera les billets sur les tables, et on posera deux questions : qui figure sur les billets, et pourquoi ?

	Etats-Unis		**France**
1:	G. Washington		
2:	T. Jefferson	50:	A. de Saint-Exupery
5:	A. Lincoln	100:	G. Delacroix
10:	A. Hamilton	200:	G. Eiffel
20:	A. Jackson	500:	P. et M. Curie
100:	B. Franklin		

La conclusion, simple à exprimer, est essentielle à comprendre. Aux EU, on peut célébrer les *Founding Fathers* parce qu'existe depuis 1776 un accord universel et permanent sur les institutions : la démocratie, la république, la constitution, le capitalisme. En France, au contraire, la modernité a été source de guerres civiles, et ce n'est que très récemment qu'un accord transpartisan sur les formes de gouvernement et d'économie est apparu. C'est pourquoi pas un seul homme politique ne figure sur les coupures nationales. On pourra parler de la longue lutte entre démocrates et royalistes, entre républicains et catholiques, entre réformistes et révolutionnaires... La culture, elle, permet d'unifier les Français dans l'admiration patriotique pour les arts, les sciences et les lettres. Voilà qui éclaire d'un autre jour les projets, très mal perçus aux USA, de défense de la langue, ou un certain ethnocentrisme culturel hexagonal, etc. Le même exercice sera fait avec d'autres symboles : Jean Moulin sur les nouvelles pièces de 2 francs, Marianne, le Génie de la colonne de la Bastille sur celles de 10 francs, une affirmation religieuse : *In God We Trust* (curieuse pour un Jacobin laïc) sur les coupures du Trésor américain, etc. Les timbres pourront aussi être mis à contribution.

Troisième activité intégrée : comprendre les publicités

La publicité, surtout télévisuelle, est une mine d'informations. Sous une forme concentrée et distrayante, elle transmet maints messages et jugements de valeurs conscients et inconscients. Une analyse multiforme doit donc en être faite : linguistique (niveaux de langues, vocabulaire spécialisé, accents locaux), esthétique (couleurs, formes, rythmes, sons), sociale (rôle de la famille, des femmes, de la jeunesse), marchande (type de consommation, place du crédit, importance de l'ostentation), etc.

Cette analyse développe le sens critique des étudiants vis-à-vis de toute manipulation commerciale et leur apprend à décrypter les valeurs profondes d'une société à travers la «persuasion invisible». L'enseignant détournera alors la didactique intéressée des publicités au profit d'une pédagogie ludique et lucide. *French in Action* (chapitre 37) présente un intéressant échantillon : Nescafé, Bic Marine (Planches à voile), Rasoir

Bic, Vittel, Cognac Rémy Martin, Brother (machine à traitement de texte), La Pie qui chante (bonbons), dont chacune suscite maintes comparaisons avec le système américain. A cet égard, on peut demander à des groupes d'étudiants d'établir des comparaisons raisonnées entre marques, objets, valeurs, bref d'avoir une *perspective de mercantique* (public ciblé, émotions et valeurs sollicitées, message apparent et implicite, système symbolique, etc.).

Présenter avec PowerPoint : la règle des 12

PowerPoint est aisé à apprendre et à utiliser mais c'est un outil utile seulement si on suit les règles de l'exposé professionnel. L'ordinateur est le moyen, la communication est le but. Donc, l'ordinateur doit être utilisé pour servir les objectifs définis à l'avance par le présentateur : informer, convaincre, réfuter, plaire, etc. Aucun logiciel ne peut remplacer les qualités humaines du présentateur : clarté, concision, respect de l'audience, etc. Il s'agit là d'une compétence professionnelle essentielle, dans un monde où il y a trop d'informations et trop peu de temps pour les assimiler.

Donc, nous présentons en douze diapositives adaptées les douze règles suivantes :

1 - La première diapositive doit être neutre : nom, prénom, titre et lieu de la présentation. Cela permet d'intégrer l'audience dès le tout début, d'attendre les retardataires, de faire un peu de *small talk*, et de ménager une transition tandis que le silence se fait progressivement dans la salle (on n'a pas toujours des salles silencieuses avant de parler !). En plus, si on est nerveux, on peut se tourner vers l'écran et lire ces choses indispensables...et évidentes. Leur simplicité permet un début naturel et aisé à ceux que les exposés en public paralysent.

2 - Quatre principes universels, quels que soient le sujet, le but, l'audience, le niveau, etc. : simplifiez, structurez, progressez, répétez. Etre complexe est facile, mais bien vulgariser exige beaucoup de travail de filtrage et de sélection. «Ce qui se conçoit simplement s'exprime

aisément». Le présentateur doit à la fois connaître parfaitement son sujet et se mettre à la place de l'audience qui ne le connaît pas ou peu. D'où l'utilité d'une répétition des éléments importants ou difficiles, en respectant la progression.

3 - Présentez votre plan et vos objectifs clairement. Le temps de votre audience est précieux. «Je vais vous présenter ceci dans tel ordre». «Mon but est de…». Soyez naturel et sans rigidité : «Il faut beaucoup de travail pour effacer les traces du travail».

4 - Utilisez des visuels adaptés. Si vous parlez de justice, montrez la balance. Utilisez les cartes, drapeaux, etc, à votre disposition.

5 - Couleurs et dimensions : attention aux combinaisons trop pâles, difficiles à regarder, aux couleurs sombres et tristes, etc.

6 - Il peut être utile d'interrompre votre présentation, surtout si elle est un peu longue, par un temps pour les questions. En ce cas, utilisez une diapositive adaptée, marquée d'un grand «?», et demandez «Vos questions, s'il vous plaît».

7 - Créatif ou sobre ? Adaptez vos aides visuelles, votre vocabulaire, et vos concepts à votre audience. Ce qui marche ici ne marche pas là. Il n'y a pas de *one size fits all*. «Cent fois sur le métier remettez votre ouvrage».

8 - Utilisez le réseau mondial (WWW) mais avec prudence : on peut télécharger les informations d'une page d'accueil sur une présentation, mais attention aux droits déposés (*copyright*).

9 - Chartes et organigrammes enrichissent votre exposé, mais trop fatiguent.

10 - N'écrivez pas trop sur la diapositive. Autrement, l'audience va lire, au lieu de vous écouter. En ce cas, l'aide visuelle remplace le présentateur comme centre de l'attention, l'outil se substitue à l'homme. N'écrivez pas des phrases trop structurées : le style écrit est une chose, le style oral en est une autre. Vous risqueriez d'être prisonnier de l'écrit, au

lieu de pouvoir improviser, changer de registre, retenir votre audience, faire de l'humour, etc. Simplifiez.

11 - Concluez en répétant votre plan et vos objectifs («Je vous ai présenté ceci... de telle manière...»). Répétez.

12 - Votre dernière diapositive doit être neutre, identique peut-être à la première. Ceci permet de terminer l'intervention de manière cohérente, et de donner une impression de sérieux de bout en bout. Evitez de montrer une page *at ease* en fin d'exposé.

En conclusion, pour relativiser les suggestions présentées ci-dessus, il faut souligner que la pédagogie adoptée pour tout cours de français des affaires dépend de trois facteurs principaux. D'abord, les conditions institutionnelles dans lesquelles cet enseignement est exercé : mission éducative de l'école, population étudiante, ressources budgétaires (et autres) disponibles. Ensuite, la formation et l'orientation professionnelle (éducation et recherches) de l'enseignant. On enseigne ce que l'on sait et aussi ce que l'on est. Enfin, la réponse apportée à la question de la définition du français commercial en tant que champ académique. Dans la mesure où la pédagogie du français des affaires n'est pas rigidement définie, et que, contrairement à d'autres disciplines, elle n'est dominée par aucune «école» ou «orthodoxie», il existe un vaste espace d'expériences diverses, auquel cet article espère contribuer.

BIBLIOGRAPHIE

Albert, M. *Capitalisme contre capitalisme.* Paris : Le Seuil, 1993.

Carroll, R. *Cultural Misunderstandings : The French-American Experience.* Chicago : University of Chicago Press, 1988.

Cummins, P.W. *Issues and Methods in French for Business and Economic Purposes.* Dubuque : Kendall/Hunt/AATF, 1995.

Cohen, E. *Le Colbertime High Tech.* Paris : Hachette, 1992.

Hermary-Vieille, C. et Sarde, M. *Le Salon de conversation.* Paris : J.C. Lattès, 1997.

PART 3

L'UTILISATION DES CAS
PRATIQUES DANS LE FRANÇAIS
DES AFFAIRES

L'UTILISATION DES CAS PRATIQUES DANS LA CLASSE DE FRANÇAIS DES AFFAIRES

Salvatore Federico & Catherine Moore

Introduction

Les cas pratiques sont utilisés pour l'enseignement des affaires depuis de très nombreuses années. L'université Harvard en a répandu l'usage il y a plus de soixante-dix ans (Uber Grosse 131), mais dans des disciplines aussi variées que la médecine ou le droit, l'utilisation de cas pratiques remonte à plusieurs siècles (Merriam xi). Valdivieso nous indique même que dans les domaines de la religion, de la morale et de la politique, les cas pratiques, sous la forme d'*exempla*, ont été utilisés depuis le Moyen-Age (Valdivieso 24). En ce qui concerne l'enseignement des langues, et plus spécialement le français des affaires, l'utilisation de cas pratiques est extrêmement récente. Après avoir acquis de solides bases en vocabulaire et en grammaire, après avoir développé son expression orale et son expression écrite, l'étudiant qui veut poursuivre son étude de la langue s'oriente généralement vers la littérature ou vers la linguistique. Le français des affaires, discipline bâtarde, est souvent relégué au rang de cours optionnel dans de nombreuses universités, et n'a suscité de recherche que depuis une période très récente, sous la poussée de la globalisation des marchés. Le professeur chargé du cours de français des affaires, outre son manque de formation dans les disciplines techniques, n'a en général que peu d'expérience professionnelle dans le monde de l'entreprise, et se contente d'enseigner le français des affaires à travers le vocabulaire technique de manuels peu créatifs et de quelques articles de vulgarisation trouvés dans la presse.

Après avoir défini les cas pratiques, nous tenterons d'examiner comment cette méthode peut être utilisée de manière efficace pour l'enseignement du français des affaires, quel est le rôle du professeur, et quels sont les avantages pour ce dernier à utiliser les cas pratiques.

Qu'est-ce qu'un cas pratique ?

Un cas est un texte plus ou moins long présentant une situation généralement économique, commerciale ou administrative, qui pose un problème de gestion, d'organisation, de communication, de décision, et qui demande un diagnostic ou une décision. Charles Gragg, pionnier de la méthodologie des cas à la Harvard Business School, précise qu'un cas est l'exposé d'une situation devant laquelle se sont réellement trouvés des décideurs, avec les faits, opinions et préjugés essentiels qui sont entrés en jeu au moment où il a fallu prendre une décision (*Teaching with Cases* 10).

Les cas pratiques, utilisés couramment pour l'enseignement de la gestion, constituent donc une approche pédagogique efficace pour la formation des futurs praticiens. Même si la méthode est inadaptée dans les domaines de l'érudition pure et du savoir faire technique (Pointet 2), elle est fortement recommandée pour la formation au diagnostic et à la décision. La méthode des cas requiert l'aptitude de l'étudiant à mobiliser l'ensemble de ses connaissances acquises, à exploiter une documentation, et à proposer une stratégie cohérente après avoir analysé la situation et précisé les objectifs à atteindre (Milon et Saint-Michel 9). Dans le cadre du français des affaires, les cas pratiques constituent une méthode active, où l'étudiant s'investit dans son rôle de preneur de décisions.

Il existe une grande variété de cas pratiques. Tout d'abord, un cas peut être réel ou basé sur une situation réelle, ou bien il peut être fictif. Il peut également être narratif, et décrire une situation en la racontant (Yin 21), ou bien encore se contenter de poser les questions à résoudre en ne donnant pour toute description de la situation qu'une série plus ou moins longue de documents à analyser. Pour les enseignants du français des affaires, il est bon de savoir que les cas américains sont en général narratifs, alors que les cas français ont tendance à être extrêmement analytiques et à donner une quantité parfois déroutante d'annexes, de statistiques, de schémas et d'autres documents se rapportant, de près ou de loin, à la situation. Enfin, les cas pratiques peuvent être quantitatifs (ou «fermés») : ils seront alors précédés ou suivis d'une liste de questions auxquelles correspondent des réponses précises ; ou bien les cas peuvent être «ouverts» : il n'y a alors ni bonne ni mauvaise réponse, mais plusieurs décisions possibles qui seront discutées en classe. Les cas utilisés dans les écoles de commerce françaises ont tendance à être quantitatifs et spécialement portés sur les formules mathématiques. Les annales que l'on peut trouver dans le commerce sont d'ailleurs accompagnées de corrigés où figure la solution aux questions posées. Il est intéressant de noter que ces annales sont formées de cas pratiques donnés aux étudiants comme épreuve finale écrite d'un examen (BEP, BTS, etc.). Les cas utilisés dans les universités américaines ont en revanche la discussion en classe comme but principal. Ces cas sont en général plus courts que les cas français, avec peu ou pas d'annexes. On ne cherche pas à piéger l'étudiant ni à tester ses connaissances quantitatives. Alors que le cas quantitatif se résume à une opération mathématique plus ou moins complexe, le cas «ouvert» est plus proche de la réalité de l'entreprise en demandant un effort de réflexion et d'analyse de la part des étudiants. Le cas «ouvert» stimule également la créativité des étudiants qui vont proposer toutes sortes de solutions au problème, sans avoir peur de commettre une erreur. Dans le cadre du cours de français des affaires, il est plus important pour les étudiants de parler et d'utiliser activement leur vocabulaire technique, que d'avoir la réponse correcte. D'autant plus que la plupart des étudiants qui hésitent à participer activement à une discussion en classe invoquent «la peur de dire une bêtise».

Utilisation des cas pratiques

Une fois qu'il a décidé de centrer son cours sur l'étude de cas pratiques, le professeur de français des affaires se trouve confronté à une première décision : sélectionner les cas pour le semestre. Il lui faut probablement offrir un éventail assez large de cas couvrant les principaux domaines du monde des affaires ; le marketing, la publicité, le management, l'import-export, les finances et l'interculturel. Cette dernière catégorie occupera sans doute une place primordiale dans une classe constituée principalement d'étudiants en langues étrangères puisque, a priori, c'est le sujet qu'ils connaissent le mieux et qui les intéresse le plus. Les étudiants sont généralement fascinés par le rôle de l'interculturalité dans les négociations commerciales. Forts du bagage reçu dans les cours de civilisation et de langue, ils se sentent moins intimidés car ils ont déjà le vocabulaire et les connaissances nécessaires pour débattre des sujets proposés. En revanche, le professeur pourra limiter le nombre des cas de finances, qui sont très techniques et difficiles d'accès pour les néophytes. En mélangeant les catégories, le professeur peut exposer ses étudiants à un grand nombre de sujets différents ce qui leur permet d'enrichir leur vocabulaire tout en maintenant leur attention et leur intérêt dans le cours (Westerfield 76). Le professeur veillera également à offrir aux étudiants une perspective globale du monde francophone, en ne limitant pas les cas à la France, mais en incluant l'Afrique francophone, la Belgique, la Suisse et le Québec. Une fois sur le marché du travail, les élèves auront acquis des connaissances qui leur permettront de briguer des postes tournés vers l'Union européenne, mais aussi vers le marché nord-américain de l'ALENA ou vers les économies les plus performantes de l'Afrique. Il existe d'ailleurs des différences culturelles de taille entre le monde des affaires québécois et français.

Le professeur doit probablement limiter la longueur des cas à quatre ou cinq pages, il vaut mieux choisir des cas clairs et concis qui utilisent un minimum de chartes et de diagrammes afin de ne pas décourager les étudiants. On peut commencer le semestre avec les cas qui présentent le moins de difficultés linguistiques et techniques (Valdivieso 26), puis progressivement, au fur et à mesure que les étudiants acquièrent les connaissances requises, intégrer des cas de plus en plus complexes.

Les cas pratiques offrent au professeur l'opportunité d'utiliser des documents authentiques, c'est-à-dire de confronter les étudiants à des situations réelles et ordinaires du monde des affaires (Uber-Grosse 132). Les élèves devront littéralement se mettre à la place d'un cadre ou d'une société et apporter leur propre solution pour résoudre un problème qu'ils auront analysé au préalable. Lors de la lecture du cas, l'élève ne doit pas se limiter à une compréhension passive, mais aussi utiliser son esprit critique et ses capacités de raisonnement. Il faut donc bien connaître son auditoire (étudiants de langue, de l'école de commerce, etc.) afin de choisir les cas les plus pertinents et les plus intéressants pour chaque groupe.

Le professeur peut sélectionner une douzaine de cas, un pour chaque semaine du semestre, et alterner ces exercices pratiques avec des textes théoriques quand il a une classe de non spécialistes ; en revanche, face à un public plus averti, tout le cours peut être centré sur l'étude de cas pratiques dont le nombre sera alors plus élevé.

La méthode des cas pratiques va donner l'occasion aux étudiants de pratiquer tous les aspects de la langue de manière active et créative grâce aux exercices variés qui suivent généralement les cas : la compréhension écrite (lecture des cas, exercices de vrai ou faux) et orale (analyse et commentaires du professeur et des autres élèves), l'écriture (rédaction de compositions, réponses écrites aux questions) et la discussion (jeux de rôles, débat, explication de la portée culturelle du texte) (Uber-Grosse 134). La lecture et l'étude approfondie du texte lui-même favorisent l'acquisition de vocabulaire technique ainsi que d'expressions idiomatiques d'usage courant. En effet, comme il ne s'agit pas de caser un maximum de mots techniques dans un dialogue artificiel qui sonne faux, les cas restent naturels, réalistes et recouvrent un vocabulaire plus général que dans les méthodes traditionnelles. Les élèves ne sont plus assaillis par une avalanche de termes spécialisés et de concepts ésotériques ; ils se sentent davantage disposés à participer en classe et à s'intéresser à la leçon.

Avant de commencer une leçon axée sur un cas pratique, le professeur et les étudiants doivent bien se préparer à l'avance, car il leur faut connaître le texte à fond avant de pouvoir l'analyser et le discuter en classe. Le premier jour, le professeur s'assure que les étudiants ont bien lu et bien compris le cas, et qu'ils ont étudié et mémorisé le vocabulaire en faisant des exercices pratiques. En fait, le travail de préparation que les étudiants ont dû terminer au préalable à la maison est un élément essentiel du succès de la méthode. Tout d'abord, «l'étudiant analyse par une lecture rapide la structure du cas qui lui est proposé» (Pointet 16) tout en soulignant les mots et les idées clés (Westerfield 77).

Ensuite, il lui faut relire le cas lentement et attentivement en s'arrêtant sur chaque détail et en prenant des notes. Il doit arriver à le connaître parfaitement et à comprendre la problématique posée (Pointet 17). Si un concept lui échappe, il est parfois souhaitable que l'élève fasse une recherche en bibliothèque sur l'entreprise étudiée ou sur les facteurs théoriques sous-jacents.

Il est essentiel que l'étudiant maîtrise le vocabulaire du cas. La liste de mots et d'expressions idiomatiques qui lui aura été distribuée ne doit plus avoir de secret pour lui. Afin de s'assurer qu'il a mémorisé les mots nouveaux et qu'il a saisi les subtilités du texte, l'élève prépare une série d'exercices ; par exemple, il peut compléter des phrases avec le vocabulaire de la leçon, répondre à des questions de vrai ou faux, associer des termes français à leur traduction anglaise et vice versa, associer des mots avec leur synonyme ou leur définition, ou faire une traduction soignée des passages les plus difficiles.

De son côté, le professeur est obligé de préparer consciencieusement le plan de la leçon, car, de par sa nature, la discussion de cas n'a pas de structure rigide et peut donc s'orienter de manière imprévisible. Son but est d'éviter que le cours ne s'égare en discussions stériles ou ne provoque pas le débat attendu.

Avant le cours, le professeur lit le cas en profondeur, puis il s'assure qu'il maîtrise et peut expliquer les concepts qui y sont exposés. Ensuite, il prépare sa propre analyse, et choisit la solution qui lui paraît la meilleure, tout en faisant une liste des autres possibilités. Pour chacune, il mesure les avantages et les inconvénients afin d'être prêt à corriger les élèves et, éventuellement, à les orienter vers un meilleur choix. Il doit, par ailleurs, penser aux questions que ne manqueront pas de poser les étudiants et pouvoir y donner une réponse. Le professeur garde en tête la composition de sa classe (niveau, préparation, formation des divers élèves) et il réfléchit à la manière dont il pourra s'assurer le maximum de participation de la part de chacun. Il prépare des exercices qui faciliteront l'interaction des étudiants y compris les plus timides d'entre eux, et des questions qui stimuleront le débat (Uber-Grosse 134-135). Bref, le professeur de cas pratiques ne peut pas se reposer entièrement sur un manuel de classe, il doit utiliser les ressources de son imagination, et posséder de bonnes bases théoriques. En outre, il est préférable qu'il ait un style d'enseignement dynamique et énergique, et qu'il sache déléguer ses pouvoirs aux étudiants, puisque le but de la méthode est de les faire participer le plus activement possible.

En classe, la leçon commence par un résumé rapide du cas à l'étude, ce qui permet de cerner le problème. Un élève choisi au hasard accomplit cette tâche en deux ou trois minutes. Le professeur vérifie, ensuite, si les élèves ont appris le vocabulaire de la leçon. En effet, ils devront utiliser (recycler) les mots nouveaux pendant toute la discussion et il n'est pas question qu'ils perdent leur temps à vérifier leur signification. Il n'est pas besoin de répéter les exercices de vocabulaire que les étudiants ont préparés à la maison ; le professeur peut cependant relever certaines copies pour les noter afin d'inciter les élèves à ne pas négliger les devoirs. En outre, il est parfois souhaitable que l'enseignant demande aux étudiants d'éclaircir le sens de quelques expressions idiomatiques ou de définir les mots techniques en donnant des exemples d'utilisation. Les élèves peuvent également faire des phrases où ils utiliseront le nouveau vocabulaire. Enfin, une fois par semaine, le professeur peut donner aux étudiants un petit examen de vocabulaire pour évaluer leurs connaissances. Cette épée de Damoclès ne manquera pas de motiver la classe.

Dans un deuxième temps, le professeur vérifie les connaissances culturelles générales des élèves sur la vie en France ou dans un autre pays francophone. Ainsi, par exemple, s'il s'agit d'un texte consacré aux petits commerces parisiens, il peut revoir les différents commerces de quartier, le concept d'arrondissement, le plan de la capitale, etc.

Un cas consacré à l'Afrique permet de rappeler le nom des pays francophones et de leur capitale ainsi que leur situation géographique et économique.

Ensuite, l'enseignant choisit des jeux de rôles qui s'apparentent au cas et qui permettent de recycler une nouvelle fois le vocabulaire de la leçon dans une atmosphère détendue. On donne aux étudiants (divisés en groupes de deux ou trois) la description d'une situation dans laquelle on leur assigne des rôles ; par exemple, ils doivent recréer un entretien professionnel pour un poste de cadre ; un élève joue le rôle du recruteur et un autre celui du candidat. Ils devront respecter les différences interculturelles et conduire une entrevue à la française qui inclura des questions personnelles ou agressives. Dans un autre cas, on peut imaginer une situation où un cadre américain serait confronté à des problèmes interculturels dans ses rapports avec son supérieur. Cet exercice donne aux élèves une véritable expérience pratique, bien que simulée, d'un aspect du monde des affaires français. Il n'est pas question pour eux de porter un jugement de valeur sur la manière dont les négociations ou l'entretien se déroule, mais plutôt de découvrir, par eux-mêmes, les différences de style entre leur pays et la France. Pour que l'exercice soit valable, il faut que les étudiants prennent leur rôle aussi sérieusement que possible (Wilson 101-102). Les groupes joueront leur situation devant la classe qui choisira la meilleure interprétation. Grâce à ces jeux de rôles où ils créent eux-mêmes au lieu de lire passivement des dialogues peu réalistes, les élèves se souviennent mieux de la leçon et des défis de l'interculturalité. Pris par le jeu, ils perdent souvent leurs inhibitions linguistiques et parlent de façon libre et spontanée. En général, ils sont friands de cet exercice qu'ils notent positivement dans leurs évaluations (Wilson 104). D'après Hubert Kratiroff, «la bonne étude de cas commence par l'implication dans un jeu de rôle» (20).

Enfin, la partie la plus importante du cours, c'est la discussion du cas avec l'ensemble de la classe ou en petits groupes. Dans les deux cas, le professeur pose une question ouverte qui introduit le problème à résoudre. La classe doit s'efforcer d'y répondre soit individuellement, soit en groupes de deux ou trois élèves. Les étudiants prendront le rôle de consultants. Ils devront présenter une analyse du problème dans laquelle ils identifieront sa nature ; puis, mobiliser leurs connaissances acquises pour proposer une stratégie, c'est-à-dire un plan d'action qui aboutira sur une résolution du cas. Les étudiants ne peuvent pas se contenter de donner des solutions possibles, il leur faut être capables de défendre les tactiques employées pour atteindre leur objectif (Kratiroff 21) et de répondre aux objections que le professeur et la classe ne manqueront pas de soulever. Il n'existe probablement pas de solution miracle ou de véritable «bonne réponse», seulement différentes possibilités qui présentent chacune des avantages et des inconvénients. Il est certain que le professeur peut sélectionner celles qu'il juge préférables (Westerfield 78). Mais, face à une classe composée d'étudiants d'origines et de nationalités diverses, il est probable que le professeur n'arrivera pas à un consensus. Une telle situation peut irriter les élèves qui viennent de pays où normalement, l'étude de cas pratiques débouche sur un diagnostic unique. Les pays anglo-saxons mettent l'accent sur l'art de débattre, de discuter et de défendre ses idées car le but est d'apprendre à négocier et à travailler avec les autres.

Le travail en petits groupes permet de créer un esprit de coopération entre les étudiants qui devront s'entendre entre eux afin de proposer une solution collective au problème (Cooper 157). La discussion se fera à deux niveaux ; dans le groupe, où les élèves, qui s'y sentent probablement moins intimidés, discuteront avant de s'accorder sur une solution commune ; puis, avec l'ensemble de la classe où chaque groupe présentera sa décision.

Le professeur peut également choisir d'élargir tout de suite le débat à l'ensemble de la classe. Dans ce cas, chaque étudiant aura analysé individuellement le problème au préalable (Paquin 400) et sera prêt à défendre sa position devant ses camarades. Au départ, les élèves hésitent à s'exprimer et à défendre leur choix en public ; mais, petit à petit, ils s'enhardissent, et ils s'engagent dans la discussion. Après quelques semaines, les élèves commentent et critiquent les propositions des autres, ils leur donnent des suggestions constructives, ils répondent aux critiques qu'ils reçoivent, ils s'expriment plus librement, le débat devient animé (Desbiens 395). Les étudiants notent une nette amélioration de leur capacité de communication et de négociation dans la langue étrangère (Jennings 234).

Certes, les élèves qui attendent toujours que l'ultime décision, la seule réponse correcte vienne du professeur, risquent de se sentir déçus et frustrés. Le professeur, lui, doit s'habituer à un certain manque de structure, puisqu'on ne peut jamais prédire à l'avance la direction que va prendre la discussion. En fin de compte, on observe souvent un regain d'intérêt pour le cours de français des affaires ; les étudiants se sentent plus motivés car cet enseignement pratique les prépare mieux pour le monde professionnel.

Avantages de la méthode des cas pratiques par rapport à la méthode traditionnelle

La plupart des professeurs de français des affaires utilisent aujourd'hui des manuels dits 'traditionnels' qui ont pour but principal d'augmentation de vocabulaire technique des étudiants et qui ont aussi, parfois, comme objectif secondaire, la préparation au Certificat pratique ou au Diplôme de la Chambre de Commerce et d'Industrie de Paris.

On peut reconnaître facilement ce genre de manuel. Leur table des matières inclut des chapitres sur «la banque», «la bourse», «le Minitel», etc. Les dialogues manquent souvent de naturel et sont éloignés de la vie réelle. Ils semblent parfois même dénués de logique. Le texte de lecture est généralement suivi d'une longue liste de vocabulaire à mémoriser. Les mots ne sont pas nécessairement des mots courants, parfois ils sont même archaïques (utilisés dans le monde des affaires du XIXème siècle).

Le cours n'est guère dynamique. Les discussions en classe sont rares et les étudiants ne s'identifient pas aux personnages des lectures et des dialogues trop artificiels. Le français acquis est de la langue écrite plutôt que de la langue parlée, car les étudiants pas plus que le professeur ne savent utiliser le vocabulaire de manière vivante.

Les cas pratiques, en revanche, servent de répétition à la vie active. Les étudiants sont exposés à des situations réelles où ils sont directement impliqués (Federico and Moore v). C'est à eux de faire les choix, les analyses et de prendre les décisions. En outre, ils peuvent profiter des connaissances de leurs camarades de classe lorsqu'ils travaillent en groupe ou lors du débat final avec le professeur et tous les élèves. Ils corrigent et se font corriger, ils présentent et défendent, ils critiquent constructivement, bref, ils apprennent à débattre, à discuter et à résoudre des problèmes collectivement. Ils font des activités qui correspondent à des situations qu'ils rencontreront fréquemment dans le monde du travail, à travers, par exemple, les jeux de rôle.

La classe est extrêmement flexible et le professeur peut choisir d'approfondir le côté culturel ou l'aspect technique du cas selon les besoins et les intérêts de son groupe (Stake 4).

Les cas pratiques constituent une méthode dynamique et directe où les étudiants ont le sentiment de contribuer, et surtout, d'apprendre activement en utilisant un vocabulaire technique qu'ils auront préalablement travaillé. Il est certain qu'ils se souviendront mieux du vocabulaire et des concepts pour en avoir fait l'expérience pratique eux-mêmes.

Il est à espérer que les futurs manuels de français des affaires s'orienteront vers cette nouvelle méthode d'enseignement.

BIBLIOGRAPHIE

Cooper, William and Charles Malone, «Improving Case Discussion Through Cooperative Learning». *A Case for the Case Study*. Chapel Hill : University of North Carolina Press, 1991.

Desbiens, Danielle. «Teaching Case Writing and Case Method Teaching in a Different Cultural Environment : A Challenging Experience». *A Case for the Case Study*. Chapel Hill : University of North Carolina Press, 1991.

Erskine, James and Michiel Leenders. *Teaching With Cases*. London, Canada : University of Western Ontario Press, 1981.

Federico, Salvatore and Catherine Moore. *Cas Pratiques pour le Français des Affaires*. 2nd Ed. New York : McGraw-Hill, 1997.

Jennings, David. «Strategic Management : Evaluating the Case Method». *A Case for the Case Study*. Chapel Hill : University of North Carolina Press, 1991.

Kratiroff, Hubert. *Dix Cas de Stratégies Marketing*. Paris : Les Editions d'Organisation, 1994.

Merriam, Sharan B. *Case Study Research in Education*. San Francisco : Jossey-Bass Publishers, 1990.

Milon, Alain and Serge-Henri Saint-Michel. *Etudes de Cas de Stratégies Publicitaires*. Rosny-sous-Bois, France : Bréal, 1992.

Paquin, Michel. «The Case Program of the *Ecole Nationale d'Administration Publique*». *A Case for the Case Study*. Chapel Hill : University of North Carolina Press, 1991.

Pointet, Marc. *Etudes de Cas Corrigées de Marketing*. Paris : Eyrolles, 1994.

Stake, Robert E. *The Art of Case Study Research.* Thousand Oaks : Sage, 1995.

Uber-Grosse, Christine. «The Case Study Approach to Teaching Business English». *English for Specific Purposes* 7 (1988) : 131-136.

Valdivieso, Jorge. «The Case-Study Method in Business Language Teaching». *Journal of Language for International Business* 4-1 (1992) : 24-29.

Westerfield, Kay. «Improved Linguistic Fluency with Case Studies and a Video Method». *English for Specific Purposes* 8 (1989) : 75-83.

Wilson, Timothy. «Role Playing : An Intercultural Example». *A Case for the Case Study.* Chapel Hill : University of North Carolina Press, 1991.

Yin, Robert K. *Applications of the Case Study Research.* Newbury Park : Sage, 1993.

Steven J. Loughrin-Sacco & Michael P. Fronmueller

Introduction

Despite its increasing visibility in the global business arena, its membership in NAFTA, and its common border with the US, Quebec continues to be a non-entity in most postsecondary Business French programs. Since the Quiet Revolution of the 1960s, Quebec has transformed itself from a 19th century rural and agrarian society into one of the world's top 20 economies and one of the major trade partners of the US. Today, Quebec makes up ¼ of Canada's gross domestic product, is rich in natural resources, and is a world leader in aeronautics, aerospace, and transportation (Bombardier), forest products (Cascades), brewing (Molson), distilling (Seagram's), publishing (Quebecor), engineering technology (Lavalin-SNC), and pharmaceuticals (BioChem Pharma). Quebec's economic juggernaut is fueled by an educated workforce, entrepreneurial spirit, inexpensive investment capital from Quebec's financial community, and the availability of inexpensive hydroelectric energy. These assets paint a bright economic picture for Quebec as she enters the next millennium.

Quebec's continued exclusion from US Business French programs has become untenable. Quebec is an integral part of Canada, our largest trading partner. US-Canada trade is at a rate of $1 billion per day, the largest volume of trade between two nations in the world (Campbell). US trade with its NAFTA partners surpasses US trade with EU countries. Additionally, trade between the US and Quebec is more prolific than trade between the US and France, i.e., approximately $45 billion versus $33 billion in 1996 (US Department of Commerce, no page provided). Because of NAFTA, American companies have fewer trade barriers with Quebec than with France. Given Quebec's proximity to the US, it is much cheaper for our students to study or participate in internships there than in France. It is also much easier for our students to find jobs related to trade with Quebec than with France. Consequently, the continued exclusion of Quebec in US Business French programs can only hurt our students as they plan careers in international trade.

One cannot totally fault US Business French educators for the exclusion of Quebec in Business French programs. Until recently France held a monopoly on Business French workshops, materials development, and testing. Today, Quebec is challenging France's monopoly on Business French with its own workshops, scholarship programs, materials development, and testing. Recently, the Quebec Chamber of Commerce and Industry and the Paris Chamber of Commerce signed an accord for joint projects including the development of a North American option within the Paris Chamber's testing program (see de Fontenay, this volume). Much work remains to be done to help US Business French educators incorporate Quebec into Business French programs.

Our Case-Study Project

To facilitate the inclusion of Quebec in US Business French programs, the lead author and Robert André Gagnon from the Université du Québec à Chicoutimi have launched a project to present an overview of Quebec's economy through a series of case studies. The case studies, entitled *Québec Inc.*, focus on companies representing key industries such as banking, energy, transportation, forest products, pharmaceuticals, and brewing. *Québec Inc.* frames these case studies between an introductory chapter and a conclusion which present contextual information on Quebec's history, political situation, and economic emergence. [1,2]

The goal of our project is to 1) prepare advanced learners of French to better understand Quebec's economy, business practices, and role within NAFTA; 2) hone French-language skills of advanced non-native learners of French; and 3) enhance learners' analytical and critical-thinking ability for use within a business context. *Québec Inc.* prepares learners to better understand Quebec's economy and role in NAFTA through profiles of key Quebec businesses, industries, and government agencies; newspaper and magazine articles on issues such as NAFTA, nationalization vs. privatization of companies, trade disputes, entrepreneurship, emerging industries, management styles; and through interviews with entrepreneurs. Our Internet homework activities within each case study introduce learners to ample electronic sources on Quebec. *Québec Inc.* strengthens learners' French-language skills through lexically rich readings, authentic reference materials found on the Internet, vocabulary enrichment activities, stimulating discussions, role playing, and in-class and out-of-class activities. Learners enhance their analytical and critical-thinking skills by role playing as consultants, analyzing the financial and economic status of companies and industries and by critiquing the arguments found in the text. All three goals of *Québec Inc.* contribute to the development of oral skills. Every activity in the text is designed to facilitate small-group or whole-class discussion. *Québec Inc.* has been written for students having an intermediate high (1+) or above rating on the ACTFL Oral Proficiency Guidelines.

Québec Inc.'s Case-Study Approach

Case studies take many forms depending upon the profession using them or an author's philosophy. What they share in common is their realism, interactivity, practicality, problem-solving nature, and flexibility (Federico & Moore, see this volume; Dolan, preface). The case studies within *Québec Inc.* possess all of these components. Our case studies are real, i.e., they involve the study of existing companies and industries in Quebec. They are interactive, involving students in stimulating group assignments, provocative discussions, crosscultural study, and opportunities to communicate with representatives of the companies under study. *Québec Inc's* case studies are practical, offering information on NAFTA, language laws as they pertain to conducting business in Quebec, innovative management practices, and the status of key industries. They involve problem-solving activities, requiring students to formulate and present plans to resolve a particular problem within a company. In the Hydro-Québec case study, for example, students work in groups to propose a new public relations campaign to repair Hydro-Québec's damaged reputation. Finally, the case studies are flexible in format. Most of their activities can be expanded into larger projects or reduced to smaller tasks. They can be used individually in a variety of French classes or used as the primary text in a Business French course.

Our case studies are not of the classic style found in business courses.[3] Our focus in *Québec Inc.* is wide-angled in scope, presenting an overview of Quebec's economy through the study of representative companies and industries. We have not used a telescopic lens to study particular problems as Federico and Moore have done in their fine work, *Cas Pratiques pour le Français des Affaires*. As for content, the case studies contain not only business and economic information, but also historical, political, geographical, and cultural content. Our goal is for learners to understand Quebec and Quebec's economy, companies, industries, and business practices more thoroughly. As for text types, our case studies not only include text written by the case study authors but also media articles, homepage information, and excerpts of interviews with business practitioners. They are longer than average cases: 12-15 pages, accompanied by activities. Each case study has three parts: 1) the company's profile, 2) a profile of the industry in which the company under study is a part, and 3) controversial topics involving the company or some aspect of Quebec's economy. As in most French textbooks, we involve learners in vocabulary enrichment activities, comprehension checks, class discussions, role playing, and writing. However, we extensively involve learners in one activity absent from current foreign language textbooks, the use of the Internet for information gathering and problem solving. What we hope to have accomplished is the publication of an exciting and stimulating collection of case studies.

Case-Study Content

The companies or organizations that we included in the case-study project are the following:

1. Hydro-Québec (Quebec's state-run power company),
2. Le Mouvement des caisses populaires Desjardins (Quebec's financial giant),
3. L'Office de la langue française (Quebec's French-language watchdog),
4. Chlorophylle (a midsize company specializing in winter clothing),
5. Bombardier (Quebec's high technology, transportation, aeronautics leader),
6. Cascades Inc. (Quebec's forest products leader),
7. Les Brasseur de L'Anse Saint-Jean (a micro brewery),
8. BioChem Pharma (Quebec's pharmaceutical leader).

Our series of case studies begins with an introductory chapter "L'Historique économique du Québec." The introduction traces Quebec's historical, political, and economic evolution from Champlain's colonization of Quebec in 1608 to the interminable discussions of sovereignty in the 1990s. Within this time frame, we discuss the effects of the Conquest in 1760 on the survival of the French language and *Québécois* culture during the last two centuries; Quebec's transformation from a non-industrialized society to its current status as the world's 17th leading economy; the *francisation* of the government and business; and the decline of the English-speaking minority as a result of the sovereignty movement. The introduction ends with speculation on Quebec's future within the Canadian confederation or as an independent nation.

Our first case study begins with Hydro-Québec, Quebec's state-run giant and one of the largest electric power companies in the world. Hydro-Québec motors Quebec's economy by providing abundant and inexpensive electric power to Quebec's manufacturing companies. Without Hydro's cheap rates, Quebec's aluminum companies and paper mills would be hard-pressed to compete successfully in the global marketplace.

Recently, Hydro has expanded its role by exporting energy to the Northeastern US and neighboring Canadian provinces. Not all is rosy, however, with Hydro. The company has come under attack because of a series of disputes with Quebec's aboriginal peoples on whose lands many hydroelectric power stations have been built. In addition to studying Hydro's impact on Quebec's economy and disputes with Amerindian peoples, learners debate the pros and cons of the nationalization versus privatization of key companies in today's global economy.

Our second case study focuses on Quebec's unique and powerful financial conglomerate, Le Mouvement des caisses Desjardins. Desjardins was originally founded in 1900 by Alphonse Desjardins to provide investment capital to Francophone businesses and individuals that were largely ignored at the time by English-dominated financial institutions in Quebec. Desjardins has grown from a conglomerate of credit unions into a financial empire that dominates Quebec's financial sector. Considered an icon like Hydro-Québec, Desjardins helps to fuel Quebec's economy through low-cost loans, especially to French-speaking entrepreneurs and companies. Like Hydro-Québec, Desjardins has been embroiled in controversy due in part to its CEO's pro-sovereignty stance during the Referendum campaign of 1995. In addition, English-speaking Quebecers generally avoid placing their investments in Desjardins because of its nationalist philosophy. In studying Desjardins, learners will capture the essence of the unique nature of Quebec's financial sector and the continuing friction between Francophones and Anglophones in the *Belle Province.*

Our third case study involves a non-business: l'Office de la langue française, considered the protector of the French language by some and the infamous "language police" by others. Since 1977, when French became the official language of government and business, the OLF has served as a lightning rod for the linguistic debate in Quebec. In this case study, learners will examine the functions of the OLF, trace the myriad of language-oriented legislation, analyze the latest legislation describing the use of French in business situations, critique the arguments of Francophone and Anglophone advocate groups, and debate the pros and cons of French-only legislation.

In our fourth case study, we switch gears from the linguistic debate to one of Quebec's most exciting midsized companies: Chlorophylle Haute Technologie. Chlorophylle specializes in the manufacture of over 145 outdoor clothing products such as ski jackets, back packs, and sleeping bags. Chlorophylle tests its products in exotic expeditions, ranging from the Arctic to the Antarctic. Within a decade, Chlorophylle has become the leader in this sector in Canada and is challenging prestigious companies such as Patagonia and Columbia Sportswear. In addition to studying the innovative nature of this young company, learners explore the rise of entrepreneurship in Quebec.

From Chlorophylle, we leap to the highest echelon of Quebec companies: Bombardier, a world leader in transportation, aeronautics, and aerospace. A family-owned company, Bombardier is known worldwide for its snowmobiles and jet skis (Ski-Doo and Sea-Doo), its airplanes (Learjet), and its light rail cars and locomotives for the Chunnel and the TGV. Bombardier is involved in a cooperative effort with the French company, GEC-Alsthom to build the TGV in the US. Bombardier is an excellent point of departure for the study of multinational companies and their ability to procure government contracts.

A world leader in the forest products industry, Cascades Inc. has transformed itself from a small family-run business into a multinational company within a generation. The forest products industry in Quebec generates more than $10 billion in revenues annually and is responsible for more than 250,000 jobs in Quebec. Commercial forests cover 1/3 of Quebec or the equivalent of France and Great Britain combined. What separates Cascades from other multinationals is its participative management style in which Cascades' workers possess significant autonomy for strategic planning and production. Workers' loyalty and productivity are also enhanced through a profit-sharing plan which was established before profit sharing gained popularity in other companies.

Les Brasseurs de l'Anse Saint-Jean, a Quebec microbrewery, serves as an excellent starting point for the study of Quebec's and Canada's brewing industry (represented by Molson and Labatt), as well as the dispute between Canadian and American brewers during these early years of NAFTA. Like Chlorophylle, les Brasseurs de l'Anse have gained celebrity quickly because of their innovative marketing and product excellence. Learners will enjoy studying the strategies the Canadian brewing industry is implementing to fend off threats from US and international brewers.

In our final case study, we present BioChem Pharma, a pharmaceutical company that has made a major impact in the pharmaceutical industry worldwide. Founded in 1986, BioChem Pharma is best known for the development of 3TC, an anti-AIDS drug. BioChem Pharma is an interesting study in Quebec's financial support for fledgling small companies. BioChem Pharma has received significant financial support from la Caisse de dépôt et placement and le Fonds de solidarité des travailleurs du Québec, two pension funds that assist Quebec companies in economic development. Since 1992, its revenues have leaped from $33 million to $200 million, largely because of this unique financial support.

In our concluding chapter, "Le Québec de demain," we summarize the contributions of Quebec's companies and entrepreneurs with a look toward Quebec's political and economic future. Learners have the opportunity to critique Quebec's economy and speculate as to Quebec's future.

Inside Each Case Study

Each case study is divided into three parts. Part I, "Profil de l'entreprise," introduces learners to the company under study and prepares them to analyze the company and the industry. Part I covers several subjects. "D'un coup d'oeil" bullets summary data such as the headquarters location, the year the company was established, number of employees, the company's markets, etc. "L'historique de l'entreprise" traces the birth and development of the company. Each profile also includes the study of the company's entrepreneur or key official. "La société de nos jours" brings the company's current activities up-to-date (up-to-date as of the writing of the case study).[4] In "géographie économique," learners explore (through the Internet) and describe (in a short writing assignment) one of Quebec's regions from an economic perspective. Finally, in "décideurs de la société," learners study and document the contribution of a key figure in Quebec economic or political history. All three parts of each case study end with vocabulary enrichment activities, comprehension checks, discussion topics, and mini-research projects. The length of the company profiles in Part I range between three and five pages.

Part II, "Regard sur l'industrie" offers learners an overview of the industry to which the company in question belongs. For example, in the Bombardier case study, we report the status of the aerospace and aeronautics industry in Quebec. We do likewise with the other industries we study such as banking, forest products, brewing, and pharmaceuticals. In three case studies, we diverge from the study of a particular industry. In Hydro-Québec, we present an overview of the conflict between the utility company and the native peoples on whose lands the hydroelectric power plants are built. In l'Office de langue française, we present the answers to FAQs on the specifics of French-language regulations as they pertain to conducting business in Quebec. In Chlorophylle, learners look at the spirit of entrepreneurship in Quebec. As in part I, the length of the texts in Part II range between three and five pages.

In Part III "Perspectives," learners examine current Québécois economic issues as they appear in the press and other authentic sources. The readings are generally controversial and are excellent sources for discussion and debate. The economic issues include the pros and cons of NAFTA, the linguistic debate on the francization of business, the need for state-run companies, alternatives to downsizing, strategies for total employment, the development of the TGV along the Windsor-Quebec corridor, global challenges to Quebec's industries, and crosscultural advertising in Quebec. At the end of each perspective, learners analyze arguments and defend or attack points of view.

Québec Inc.'s Pedagogical Philosophy

We have worked hard to craft pedagogical activities carefully for *Québec Inc.* We believe that French-language development necessitates heavy doses of rich and interesting texts (authentic, for the most part) to read, ample opportunities for oral commmunication, and intensive purposeful writing. In addition, we believe in independent learning through mini-research projects, practical and problem-solving activities, and vocabulary enrichment. Below is a breakdown of the pedagogical strategies found in each case study.

Pre-reading section

The pre-reading section serves as an advanced organizer, linking readers' prior knowledge of the subject matter to new information from the case study. Readers begin with the abstract of the case study, followed by bulleted information highlighting key information about the company. Next comes "Avant de lire" in which we 1) question readers about their prior knowledge, 2) assign readers to begin constructing a lexicon of words and phrases pertaining to the industry under study, and 3) present key vocabulary, accompanied by their English translation. To illustrate, in the Desjardins case study, readers are asked to list the services offered by banks and credit unions, and the names and types of financial institutions where they live. Next, readers begin constructing a lexicon of terminology pertaining to finance. The authors suggest categories (types of institutions, services, nouns, verbs, adjectives, etc.) and provide examples for each category (*la caisse populaire, les prêts, le réseau, emprunter, coopératif*). During the case study, learners can exchange their lexicon and discuss their entries in class or simply turn them in to their instructor. The lexicon grows throughout the case study until a finished copy is presented in class or to their instructor. Finally, in the Desjardins case study, readers are presented with key vocabulary to assist them in their reading. Words and expressions include *la caisse populaire* (credit union), *succursale* (branch bank), *épargne* (savings), *le rendement* (yield, output) as well as several others.

Post-reading activities

Post-reading activities include "enrichissement lexical," "à discuter," and "enquêtes et découvertes." In *Québec Inc.*, vocabulary acquisition and use are crucial to the linguistic and cultural development of readers. Readers also need a strong business vocabulary to pass the Paris Chamber of Commerce and Industry examinations and function successfully in job-related situations. Vocabulary activities can be found in each of the three sections of each case study. In "enrichissement lexical," readers recognize, manipulate, generate, and use vocabulary acquired in the case study in context. Specific activities include updating their lexicon, discussing unknown words and expressions in class, generating antonyms, synonyms, and word families; recognizing semantical matches ("cherchez l'intrus"), and generating sentences using key words and expressions. While reading a case study, readers are expected to look up some words in their dictionary as they would when reading a literary text. *Québec Inc.* presents no large-scale vocabulary lists such as those found in other Business French texts.

The second type of post-reading activity ("À discuter") verifies comprehension and provokes discussion through the use of lower- and higher-order questions, summaries, the analysis of arguments, comparisons and contrasts, hypothesizing, and the stating of opinions. In the Desjardins case study, readers compose a summary of Desjardins' founding and development in their own words, state the differences between credit unions and banks, identify reasons for the popularity of the Desjardins credit unions in Quebec, and describe Desjardins' political involvement in Quebec's sovereignty movement.

"Enquêtes et découvertes" take readers a step further in their study of a company and industry. In Part I of each case study we included "géographie économique" and "décideurs de la société québécoise." In these two activities, learners provide one-page summaries on a geographic region of Quebec and a key figure in Quebec history, politics, or business. We have included these two activities to ensure that learners come away with a solid understanding of Quebec's history, geography, and politics. In Parts II and III of the case study, learners conduct a variety of interesting mini-research projects. For example, in the Desjardins case study, learners work in small groups or individually on providing a profile of major Canadian and Quebec banks, an update on NAFTA, and a comparison between NAFTA and the European Union. Much of the mini-research projects that the authors assign in "enquêtes et découvertes" can be done on the Internet; for most activities, the authors provide Internet site addresses as a starting point for learners. Instructors can assign these activities as small-group projects or individual work. Most of the activites within "enquêtes et découvertes" can be expanded into major research projects or papers.

Conclusion

Quebec's exclusion in US Business French programs is no longer tenable given Quebec's proximity to the US and its emergence as an economic power within NAFTA. In our defense of the inclusion of Quebec within US Business French programs, we are promoting an additive model that includes Quebec and France, as well other

Francophone nations. As Hervé de Fontenay has brilliantly argued in this volume, French must change its status as a "langue hexagonale" if it is to become the second global language as Finel-Honigman argues. Because of Quebec's economic stature and job opportunities, we present our students with an additional reason for studying French.

Numerous obstacles must be overcome in order to effect the inclusion of Quebec in US Business French programs. Quebec universities need to offer high-quality Business French workshops for US secondary and postsecondary educators.[5] The Quebec government must expand its scholarship program to defray the costs of US educators who attend Quebec-oriented Business French workshops or develop teaching materials. More textbooks and teaching materials must be developed for use in Business French classes.[6] Most importantly, many US Business French educators must overcome their elitist attitude in which they view France as the only Francophone country worthy of study.

Québec Inc. is a solid first step toward providing Business French materials to US postsecondary educators. *Québec Inc.* provides an overview of Quebec's economy and NAFTA through eight case studies framed between an introductory chapter and a conclusion. The case studies describe each company or organization within its operating environment, i.e., background, update, customers, competitors, business practices, etc., its industry, and within its remote environment, i.e., social, technological, political, economic, and ecological contexts (Pearce & Robinson 63). In addition to strengthening French-language skills and illustrating business lexicon, our case studies put learners in touch with many important trade issues within NAFTA, business practices, sociocultural disputes, and geopolitical realities. In addition to reading the case-study materials, learners are required to offer suggestions for resolving problems facing a company, an industry, or Quebec's economy.

Finally, we support Federico and Moore's call (in this volume) for the use of case studies in Business French programs. Case studies represent a break from current pedagogical materials and methods which focus almost exclusively on business lexicon, commercial correspondence, and stylistics. They are worthy of study but are insufficient by themselves as aids for developing successful international business practitioners. Federico and Moore point to the need for studying business practices and business-oriented crosscultural differences, as well as providing students with practice in problem solving. Many current Business French materials lack the treatment of current socioeconomic and geopolitical perspectives realities, crosscultural comparisons of national economies, and the study of key businesses and industries, government policies, business practices, and business culture. Case studies present subject matter that our students need to know to succeed as employees or entrepreneurs in a global society. Additionally, case studies provide students with needed practice at resolving the types of problems they will face in the future.

WORKS CITED

Besnard, Christine and Charles Elkabas. *Pratique des affaires et correspondances en français*. Toronto: Canadian Scholars' Press, 1990.

Campbell, Kim. "The North American Free Trade Agreement: What It Does and Does Not Cover." *Symposium on NAFTA in the Twenty-First Century: The Impact on Free Trade in the Americas*, October 15, 1997.

Fontenay, Hervé de. *Français Inc*. Montréal: Editions Etudes Vivantes, 1990.

_____. "Le Français des Affaires et des Professions: Langue 'Hexagonale' ou 'Internationale'"? *Making Business French Work: Models, Materials, Methodologies*. Loughrin-Sacco, S. and J. Abrate, Eds. San Diego: SDSU CIBER Press, 1997: 35-57.

Federico, Salvatore and Catherine Moore. *Cas Pratiques pour le Français des Affaires*. The McGraw-Hill Companies, 1996.

_____. "L'Utilisation des Cas Pratiques dans le Français des Affaires." *Making Business French Work: Models, Materials, Methodologies.* Loughrin-Sacco, S. and J. Abrate, Eds. San Diego: SDSU CIBER Press, 1997, 171-185.

Loughrin-Sacco, Steven J. and Robert André Gagnon. *Québec Inc.: un manuel de français des affaires.* San Diego: SDSU CIBER Press, 1998.

Pearce, John A. & Richard B. Robinson. *Strategic Management: Formulation, Implementation, and Control.* Homewood, IL: Irwin, 1997.

Quelch, John A. & Robert J. Dolan. *Marketing Management: Text and Cases.* Homewood, IL: Irwin, 1997.

The US Department of Commerce, October 15, 1997, http://www.ita.doc. gov/industry/usfth/france.e-i

Notes

[1] For more information on *Québec Inc.*, contact the lead author at (619) 594-3008 or e-mail him at loughrin@mail.sdsu.edu.

[2] The authors of *Québec Inc.* are deeply indebted to Damien Ferland, Pierre Lincourt, and their staff at the *Ecole de langue* at the *Université du Québec à Chicoutimi* for their support in planning, writing, and publishing the text.

[3] In spite of our unorthodox style of case studies, Mike Fronmueller, the second author of this paper, guided us in the development of our case studies.

[4] Because case studies become dated as soon as they are written, we have included in each case study an activity in which we ask students to update the case study by examining the homepage of the company in question, as well as other Internet resources.

157

[5] One high-quality workshop is offered at the *Ecole de langue* by my *Québec Inc.* co-author, Robert André Gagnon, at the *Université du Québec à Chicoutimi*. For more information on their Business French workshop, contact UQAC at (418) 545-5301.

[6] Two Business French textbooks focusing on Canada are worthy of mention. Hervé de Fontenay's *Français Inc.* is the best stylistics manual the lead author has seen on the market. We currently use Besnard and Elkabas' *Pratique des affaires et correspondances en français* in one of our Business French classes at San Diego State University.

PART 4

INNOVATIVE METHODS AND MATERIALS IN FRENCH FOR BUSINESS

NEGOTIATING LITERATURE IN THE BUSINESS FRENCH CLASS

Allen G. Wood

It is vitally important in the Business French class, at both the intermediate and advanced college levels, to supplement textbooks with supporting materials and documents which reinforce basic vocabulary and concepts. Various authentic, current texts can be taken from the print media and combined with video, audio, and electronic material in order to present students with an accurate depiction of financial situations in France. Many fine articles have appeared in the last few years, describing different kinds of materials (realia, video, Minitel) which can be successfully incorporated into the Business French curriculum to expand and enrich the learning process. Students can read, see and hear about recent business issues, and perform many business functions (write a check, fill out a form, respond to a letter). As useful as these current documents are, however, it is also important to provide a broad cultural and historical dimension to French business practices, which can be found in literary texts portraying people engaged in economic transactions. French literature has much to offer to the Business French curriculum, and a synthesis of interconnecting business and literary issues is long overdue. We can, and should, teach students about *la Bourse* and Balzac in the same class.

As teachers of Business French, we need to negotiate the role of literature and come to an agreement as to its role in our class. The texts we select will relate to business themes, establishing a corpus of "negotiating" or business literature. Finally, we need to negotiate, or make our way through, literary texts as a means to teach business terms and concepts. In

161

these negotiations, we find four main reasons for including literary texts in a Business French class: 1) reinforcement, 2) variety, 3) contextualization, and 4) cultural competence. Certain key business terms and concepts contained in the textbook or other materials can be found in the literary passage and reinforced, although from a varied perspective contrasting with that of factual documentation. Peter Prince's article on vocabulary building emphasizes the fact that "systematically meeting new words in context underlines the fact that words are indeed used in discourse for purposes of communication" (489). Unlike a word in a list, a term in a literary passage has a context that provides connotative cues, which may differ from the same term contained in a more factual document. Finally, a literary passage can build general cultural competence. We must also not forget that French businessmen and businesswomen read and allude to their own literature for significant examples and comparisons, and that our students need a broad cultural base, including general literary knowledge, in order to understand and communicate effectively. If a business partner is teased for being like Harpagon, our students should know what this means.

In contrast to other kinds of texts used in the Business French class, the literary text would seem, at first, to present two disadvantages. It is outdated, and it is fictive. Both of these indicate that a literary passage presents inaccurate information. While this may indeed be true on a literal, factual level, we must remember that this is not the main reason for reading it, and that its value lies primarily at another level. Although the specific details of business transactions can change daily, like *la Bourse*, many general situations, as well as human actions and reactions, remain similar over time. The fifteenth century *Farce de Maître Pathelin* does not convey currently accurate information about currency and pricing, but the general issues of price bargaining, delayed payment, and trying to get out of a deal are still pertinent, understandable, and funny. Literary passages are also rich in interpersonal, psychological details, mirroring reality (which includes financial transactions) in a complex representation of human experience. They give greater meaning and context than a vocabulary list, or even a magazine article.

In order to incorporate literary texts into the Business French course, with care given to the relative emphasis and linguistic/semantic difficulty of the material, a semester-long module consisting of a sequence of texts is both appropriate and effective. This sequence is comprised of between five and ten passages, each a few pages in length. It is not possible, for example, to read an entire novel, nor would it be advisable, since economic and financial matters are usually discussed in isolated, episodic sections of long works. Short passages are easier to read, give students a sense of comprehension and mastery of the material, and allow for a greater variety of authors, periods, and business situations than if only one long text were used.

The corpus of texts that we will examine can certainly be modified according to teacher and student preferences, interests, ability levels, and time constraints. By way of a sample and example, the following sequence, which has been successfully used at both intermediate and advanced-level Business French courses, will be considered: passages from Saint-Exupéry's *Le Petit Prince*, Molière's *L'Avare*, Pilhes' *L'Imprécateur*, and Ousmane's *Xala*. These texts provide a general gradation from easier to more difficult texts, in terms of lexical items and content. In addition, they provide a good variety period and geography, from Molière's 17th century France to Sembène Ousmane's 20th century Senegal. Novels and plays are represented in order to provide generic diversity. Also, the sequence begins with humorous texts (*Le Petit Prince*, *L'Avare*) and progresses to more serious works.

It is essential, as Harper, Kramsch, Montfort and others have suggested, to teach literature using student-centered approaches that develop communicative skills. Reading itself needs to be considered "an active construction process" (Kramsch, 357), and this process needs to be continued in classroom discussion. Because of the diversities within the form and content of the textual passages, it is also important to establish a constant and predictable pedagogical framework so students have a clear set of expectations as they read and consider each work. Following each text, a list of vocabulary items is divided into **general vocabulary** and

163

more specific **business lexicon** citing terms that are used in the text. Usually an English equivalent is provided, although at a more advanced level, French synonyms or definitions can be used. While preference is given to French expression and discussion, it is crucial that basic terms and concepts be understood, which is often faster and more sure when done in English, before progressing to exercises, discussion and interpretation in French.

A set of exercises requires students to review the material in the passages in order to better retain and understand issues of character, setting, plot, time and action, as well as some factual detail relating to the business materials or transactions. A **matching vocabulary** section involves choosing the correct English synonym or definition for approximately one dozen French words and serves to reinforce through practice the vocabulary lists. Then, about ten or fifteen **fill-in-the-blank sentences with choices** in French involve choosing the correct term or expression from three listed after each sentence. Rereading the passage allows students to find the sentence and the missing item. Although this is relatively simple as an exercise, it does require students to focus on certain sentences and it reinforces key terms or concepts. The fill-in-the-blank sentences cover the entire passage and are arranged in order from the beginning to the end of the text. This arrangement is followed for all the exercises, in order for them to be clearer to students, who can more efficiently progress through the exercises. Next comes a series of **fill-in-the-blank sentences without choices**. Students need to reread the passage in order to find the missing word or words. Finally, a dozen **true and false items** call for a fairly basic understanding of the text. In some cases, the answer is rather evident in the text, while in other cases some inference or conclusions need to be drawn from the literal level of the text. All answers must be justified from the text, especially in the case of false items, so that students can rewrite them into true statements. Whenever possible, ambiguous or "tricky" items are avoided. These exercises are all somewhat mechanical, but provide an impetus to reread the passage several times and recall important bits of information. Certain details from the text may be repeated in different exercises, while other answers are unique, an approach which furnishes a good blend of old and new material. The exercises are graduated in difficulty, and lead to more general, analytical activities.

Comprehension questions have as their objective greater student production of language and communication of content. Answers explain who characters are, what their relationship to one another is, where the action takes place, and other issues on the literal content of the passage. Some basic questions, which call for reasons why a particular statement, action, or reaction occurred, require more analysis and synthesis of the material. A set of **discussion questions** and **role-playing scenarios** complete the activities and create an opportunity for students to explore concepts raised in the text in fairly open-ended formats. Good discussion questions and methods can "break the sounds of silence" as Martin writes, especially when questions are asked at an appropriate linguistic and cognitive level, are clear, and sufficiently broad in scope. And, as Vande Berg indicates through a number of role-play activities, "the teacher can make classroom discussion of a literary passage one of the most valuable means of achieving communicative competence" (665). Of course, depending upon the time available and the skill levels of the students, more general activities can be abbreviated or lengthened. Students can also write an essay outside of class based on an item in the general activity section, or prepare an oral debate, dialogue, talk or skit on their own for classroom presentation.

As part of the general comprehension and more comprehensive activities, a set of thematic issues that recur in the different passages in the sequence was established. They also appear in a graduated structure:

1. repetition: both lexical items and concepts are often repeated, with an effect of emphasis or ridicule.

2. circulation: the extent to which exchanges are made, money is circulated or withheld. Power relationships among the characters are examined.

3. social position: the links between individual and society are studied, and the asocial, marginal position of characters is

165

seen. The value of money and business as presented in the text is addressed.

4. satiric, ironic tone: many texts convey a satiric or ironic tone in their critique of dehumanizing aspects of business or people engaged in business. The subversion of business by characters for selfish goals is analyzed.

Although it is not practical to describe all the pedagogical exercises, comprehension questions, and thematic issues pertaining to each text in the sequence proposed, a brief examination of each one will reveal the particular characteristics of that work and its appropriateness for inclusion in a course on Business French. Greater emphasis will be placed on the pedagogical exercises in the discussion of the first text, a chapter taken from *Le Petit Prince*, in order to explain more fully the nature and scope of the different items. It could, however, be tedious and repetitive (one of the thematic issues) to continue this presentation throughout the rest of this discussion.

Le Petit Prince, published by Antoine de Saint-Exupéry in 1943, is a charming and simply written novel, familiar to many students at the university level. The work seems like a good place to start, since its language and plot are easily understood even by elementary students of French, and since it requires little introduction or explanation. The naive and child-like prince leaves his tiny planet in search of adventure and experience and, in his unscientific, intergalactic travels, he meets a wide range of people. In chapter 13, in a passage about five pages long, after having met a drunk on the third small planet he visited, he encounters a "businessman" on the fourth.

The man is so preoccupied with a series of seemingly simple addition calculations, which he makes out loud, that he does not notice the little prince's arrival. It turns out that his final figure of 31 is part of a much larger sum, 501,622,731. But when asked what he is counting, he has a harder time remembering the name of the little "petites choses dorées," or stars, which he claims to own. The little prince proceeds to ask a set of naive questions that deal with issues of the purpose of ownership and wealth. The businessman, who continues to repeat that he is "homme sérieux," seems lost in a circuitous argument, as he states that he owns stars in order to be rich so that he can buy more stars. He counts them and recounts them, writing down the number of stars he owns and putting this information in the bank. At this point, the little prince thinks to himself that this is not such a serious idea. He explains that back on his home planet, he owns a flower, and that he waters it every day, but he cannot imagine how the businessman is useful to his stars. For once, the star counter is left speechless, and the little prince, perplexed at the odd behavior of adults, leaves the businessman behind.

The basic vocabulary requiring explanation in the chapter is not very lengthy. It involves such terms as *balivernes* (nonsense), *fainéants* (do-nothings), and *grincheux* (grumpy), which refer to the businessman's attitude toward others, or describe his own character. Once, twenty-two years previously, a *hanneton* (may bug) had fallen onto his planet and caused him to make four errors in calculation. The little prince's arrival is only the third interruption he has had in his continual counting, and the businessman is not very gracious or welcoming. As for business vocabulary, the verbs *posséder, acheter, breveter, gérer, compter, and placer en banque* all describe financial transactions, although all in a somewhat abstract context, given the fantastical situation of a businessman owning and dealing in stars.

The first fill-in-the-blank exercise involves the very first sentence, and the significance of the man who is identified and defined (in narration and not by the man himself) totally by his occupation:

La quatrième planète était celle _____.

a) de l'homme d'affaires   b) du businessman   c)   du comptable

Certainly items like this can reinforce terms already learned in the Business French class, such as "comptable." While it is true that the man seems to act a lot like an accountant, the answer is "b) du businessman" and not the French equivalent of the term. Students may begin to realize, or it may be pointed out to them, that the use of the English terms may be quite significant, representing a cultural component to the story as an early (1943) critique of the "américanisation" of French business and society. It would be best to delay this kind of discussion until later, even though some of the objective exercises are already laying the groundwork for a better comprehension of the general content and tone of the text.

Yet not every item is as significant, nor does it need to be. Other fill-in-the-blank sentences can refer to the businessman's cigarette being extinguished, to the final calculation of 501,622,731, to the fact that he has been on the planet for 54 years, or that he has only been bothered three times in that period (22 and 11 years before, and now). A number of these items indicate the mathematical precision with which the businessman measures his stars and his life. Some facts could be required as answers in different formats, such as fill-in-the-blank items calling for precise information:

Le businessman habite la planète depuis _____ ans.

a) 44   b) 54   c) 64

or entail a little more processing of information

Le businessman habite la planète entre _____ ans.

a) 30-40   b) 40-50   c) 50-60.

In addition, a true-false statement may deal with the same fact: "V F 1. Le businessman habite la planète moins de trente ans." While the fact that he has lived on the planet and counted his stars for 54 years may not be the most crucial item in the text to comprehend, students who become well aware of this numerical fact after a couple of different kinds of exercises realize the incredibly long duration of the businessman's calculations, and the sense of a life wasted on such an absurd "business."

The chapter is primarily structured by the various questions which the little prince asks followed by the businessman's answers. When the man cannot really recall the name of what he has spent his life counting, his young visitor suggests first "mouches," then "abeilles," before finally getting the correct name: "des étoiles." But the most important and longest series of questions relates to the details and rationale of the businessman's actions. He owns stars in order to be rich so that... he can buy yet more stars, if any can be found. Like a miser whose gold coins sit uselessly in a trunk, the businessman is content to obsessively count and recount his treasure. He emphasizes the difference between "posséder" and "régner," pointing out that kings merely rule, while he is able to possess the stars. True-false questions and even a separate exercise requiring students to place in chronological order the steps in the businessman's "logic" are useful for greater examination and comprehension of this section of Saint-Exupéry's text.

Comprehension and discussion questions may appear quite similar, although the intent of the comprehension question is to focus upon particular material found in the text, while discussion questions are based on the text but expand in scope to cover the entire text, business or literary issues, or student interpretations and analyses of cultural matters. Comprehension questions based on this chapter of *Le Petit Prince* ask students to identify the moment when the businessman realizes he cannot ignore the little prince and so resigns himself to answer his questions, as well as that question which finally leaves him speechless. These questions can be answered by referring to the text, although the answer might not be as readily apparent as for a fill-in-the-blank or true-false kind of item. Facts or details not already covered in previous exercises can also be elicited at this point. These details include the fact that both characters "tutoient" each other, that the businessman once had rheumatism due to his lack of physical exercise, and that the little prince mentally compared the businessman's logic to that of the "ivrogne" on the third planet. A comprehension question also requires students to find textual support for a general contention, such as that the businessman is egotistical, or that the little prince is not as naive as he may appear. Of course, such a comprehension exercise can lead to discussion based on the answers that students provide.

Discussion questions center on such issues as the use of the English term "businessman," the fact that he does not really know what he counts, and that he claims to own the stars. He bases this last claim on his argument that diamonds and islands can be owned, and even ideas can be "brevetée" (patented), which initiates class discussion on the limits and uses of owning natural objects, land, and commonly held things, like ideas. Students are asked what they count, and why, what they own, and what they think they will never own, or that nobody will ever own, and why — and this can all be compared with the businessman's ideas and actions. The importance of the little prince's final question concerning the usefulness of the businessman for his stars can be discussed, and students can even move into the final activity of role playing by imagining a possible answer the businessman could give. Among other role-playing activities, students recreate the scene with a businesswoman, rather than a businessman, imagine what the next interruption will be, or pretend that the businessman finds himself in competition with somebody on another planet. Any of these discussion questions or role-playing activities can also be turned into a written exercise to develop writing skills. In addition, students can be asked to rewrite the dialogue into indirect discourse, or give a summary of the chapter in one or two paragraphs. While students should be encouraged to incorporate business vocabulary and concepts into their discussions and role playing, whether oral or written, they should also be allowed a great amount of liberty to express their ideas and imagination.

Finally, the four thematic issues need to be raised and discussed, which should be facilitated by all the previous exercises and activities. These thematic issues take on greater resonance as more texts are studied, but even in the beginning some basic concepts can be established. Repetition can be found in the prince's repeated questions, in the constant recounting of the stars, and in the repeated insistence (5 times) on the businessman's part that he is "un homme sérieux." In terms of circulation, the man is a virtual prisoner on his planet, and he is unable to circulate his stellar "money" in any useful or real way. As for social position, the businessman is marginalized on his planet, and has no social or family contacts. He is barely civil to the little prince in the beginning, and he does little more than answer the questions from his young visitor. Contrasted with the dozens of questions he is asked, he asks none himself of the little prince. All of this leads to a rather strong satiric condemnation of the businessman, whose megalomaniac desires to possess all the stars are couched in business terms but represent a very poor concept of business realities and transaction. He is a hypocrite, a pretender, a would-be businessman.

Molière's *L'Avare*, first performed in 1668, is a comedy which tells the story of Harpagon, a miserly father, who has secretly buried 10,000 *écus* (about $30,000 today) in his backyard in a vain attempt to keep his money safe. Yet while Harpagon lives very frugally, and gives his son and daughter little, his son Cléante enjoys spending money, which he claims to win at gaming. In the opening scenes of Act II, however, the truth is revealed, as we learn that Cléante borrows the money he spends on clothing and courting. His servant has just arranged for him to accept a loan from an unknown and unscrupulous lender, who turns out to be none other than his own father, Harpagon. The language of borrowing and lending is found in this passage, which can be read fairly easily and independently from the rest of the play.

The general vocabulary in Molière's play is not particularly difficult, although a few expressions and constructions reveal language of the 17th century: *aboucher* (*mettre en relation*), *mémoire* (*liste*), *céans* (*ici dedans*). The most difficult section to understand, due to its many references to objects and goods from the time of Louis XIV, is undoubtedly the list of items which are substituted for part of the money to be lent. These include beds, wall hangings, a table, muskets, a brick furnace, children's games, and a lizard skin. While it is tempting to eliminate this section for linguistic reasons, it is important that students read all the items to get the full impact of the kind of loan being proposed, as well as to see Cléante's reaction as each new item is mentioned, as his anger and disbelief increase. Most editions of the play provide adequate explanations of the various items, and, although the students' reading is slowed at this point, it seems preferable that they read the entire passage as it was written.

As for the financial vocabulary, there are not only money terms that need to be explained, but also the whole currency system and method of calculating interest at the time. The basic monetary unit was the *livre* (pound sterling), having the same value at the time as the *franc*, and allowing for an interchange of the two terms. The coins that circulated ranged in value from the *denier* (about a penny or less) to the silver *écu* (3 *livres*) and the gold *pistole* and *louis d'or* (each about 11 *livres*). Interest was expressed as a relationship of one *denier* interest for every x number of *deniers* borrowed. Cléante is led to believe at first that he is borrowing "au denier dix-huit," a ratio of one to eighteen, or a little more than 5% interest. He finds this, quite naturally, to be acceptable. However, when he learns that his lender has been obliged to borrow the money himself "au denier cinq" (20%) and that this cost will be passed on to him, he explodes in anger at the thought that he will need to repay the loan "au denier quatre" (25%), a usurious rate then and now. As if this is not bad enough, he will not even receive all the loan in money, since 1000 *écus* (3,000 *livres* of the 15,000 total) has been substituted with the list of items (beds, wall hangings, etc.) just discussed. And, to make matters worse still, when Cléante unexpectedly finds himself face to face with his lender, he turns out to be his very own avaricious father, Harpagon.

The general information which can be elicited from fill-in-the-blank and true-false exercises pertain to some of these issues of currency and interest, as well as other details in the text. The relationships among the characters is of critical importance, such as the fact that La Flèche is Cléante's servant, that Cléante is Harpagon's son, and that Maître Simon represents Harpagon in the deal. La Flèche and Maître Simon had begun negotiations, without revealing the identity of the person each represented, which leads to the surprise in the scene when Harpagon and Cléante confront one another.

Although they are father and son, they have few kind words or sentiments for each other. Cléante had stated that his father would be dead "avant qu'il soit huit mois" in his attempt to show he could repay the loan. Harpagon may be upset that his son now knows that he is a usurer, but he is angry that Cléante resorts to loans. As for Cléante, he is both embarrassed to have his father learn that he is borrowing money, and shocked to discover that his father is a loan shark. All this leads to their brief accusations:

> Harpagon: Comment ! pendard, c'est toi qui t'abandonnes à ces coupables extrémités ?

> Cléante: Comment ! mon père, c'est vous qui vous portez à ces honteuses actions ?

At the end of the scene, Harpagon is so angered that his son has resorted to taking out loans that he orders him out of his sight.

Discussion questions focus on the actions of both father and son, as students compare their deeds to determine which, if either, of the characters is more justified in his conduct. In other words, students are asked to reflect upon and answer Cléante's final question in the scene: "Qui est plus criminel, à votre avis, ou celui qui achète un argent dont il a besoin, ou bien celui qui vole un argent dont il n'a que faire?" In many ways both father and son talk, act, and react in similar ways, even though they find themselves at opposite ends of this business deal. Issues of borrowing and lending can be discussed and, even though some of the general and financial language has changed in the last three hundred years, many of the basic concepts remain similar to those currently in use. Differences between borrowing and usury need to be explored. Although questions of collateral and ability to repay are not directly raised in the passage, the social status of the family is an important factor, as is the father's supposed ill health, in the negotiations. Students may talk about credit and borrowing in general in the United States, in France, and more specifically in their own lives, and whether they prefer to borrow from parents or a bank (banks did not really exist in Molière's time in France). Students can be asked their reactions to the part of the loan comprised of the different items, mostly junk really, and whether they would proceed with such a deal, even if desperate. They can speculate as to whether they think this incident has caused Harpagon to stop lending, or Cléante to avoid borrowing money. Also, a discussion of the comic elements in the scene is useful, and students can decide, if they were directors of the play (a kind of transition to role playing), whether to emphasize the humorous aspects, or the serious parts, of the text.

Role playing activities can be based on a number of imaginative variations and extensions of the scene. Students can create the dialogue for subsequent interchanges between Cléante and La Flèche, Maître Simon and a friend, or Cléante and his sister (not present in the passage read in class). A scene of reconciliation between father and son can be created, with each explaining his actions. Finally, the text could be rewritten so that Cléante pretends that the loan is not really for himself, but for somebody else. These are just a few of the many situations that can be derived from Molière's scene.

With regard to the general thematic issues raised in all the texts in the course, the use of repetition is not that noticeable in this passage from *L'Avare*. Certainly, when in a preceding scene Harpagon continues to respond "Sans dot" many times to proposed plans to marry his daughter with a dowry provides a well-known example of repetition. Yet even in the scene under discussion, several replies use parallel constructions, and certain terms are repeated. The issue of circulation is central to the passage, as both borrower and lender are engaged in movements of money in a deal which would have transferred money from Harpagon to Cléante and then on to his creditors. But the deal falls through, and in reality no money is circulated. This monetary stasis can be compared to some extent to Harpagon's more purposeful blocking of monetary circulation by his miserly action of burying money in his yard. In terms of asocial behavior, Cléante falsely claims (but perhaps truly wishes) his father will soon die, while Harpagon has no compassion for the moribund father until he realizes that the reference is about him. He banishes his son, and later in the play states in a fit of anger that he would have been better off without any children. Harpagon is a miser, while ironically his son is a spendthrift, and neither is engaged in sound financial activities. In addition to the irony of the opposite attitudes towards money, father and son are both targets of ridicule and criticism for the dishonor they bring upon themselves and their family. All these themes can be readily found and discussed in *L'Avare*. And even though Molière's play does not describe business practices today, it does provide both useful vocabulary and good insights into different attitudes about money.

Both *Le Petit Prince* and *L'Avare* are well-known texts. Students may already have some familiarity with them before they arrive in a Business French class, where they can read literature from an economic and financial perspective. The last two texts we will examine, *L'Imprécateur* and *Xala*, are not as well known, but provide more realistic and current details in their presentation of the business world.

René-Victor Pilhes' novel *L'Imprécateur* (1974) chronicles the events leading to the collapse of Rosserys and Mitchell, the largest company the world has seen. It is part detective story, part fantastic vision of a company gone wild with a desire for world domination, told from the viewpoint of Pilhes, a middle manager. Cracks develop in the building, the director of marketing dies unexpectedly, and messages on strange roles of paper appear on employees' desks warning of a curse. Although in the final pages of the novel we learn that the narrator had slipped in the basement of the building and been hospitalized in an unconscious dream state, the director of marketing then does die unexpectedly, closing the novel with questions about reality and fantasy, fact and fiction.

The general vocabulary items that are matched with their English definitions deal with the decay, collapse and destruction of the building, (*effondrement, fêlure, affaissement du sol*, and *fourvoyé*), terms of menacing threats (*imprécateur, imprécation*), jurisprudence (*procès, estimer les préjudices, fixer les indemnités*), and religion (*le peuple élu, les*

Tables de la nouvelle Loi, hérétique). Several of these latter terms require some cultural contextualization as well. In addition, a simplified and enlarged map of Paris showing the real locale of the fictional company in the *11e arrondissement*, with the intersection of the Avenue de la République and the Rue Oberkampf and the nearby Métro station of the Filles du Calvaire, provides useful factual, cultural material. Students can trace the route of the narrator on his trips in the neighborhood. Once these general terms and concepts are examined, the business language in the text can be handled. There is a wealth of business vocabulary in the opening five pages of *L'Imprécateur*, referring to company hierarchy (*cadre supérieur, directeur adjoint, directeur général, un poste, ouvriers*) and the activity of the firm (*filiale, compagnie multinationale, fabriquait, emballait, vendait, engins, état-major, siégeait, société de placement*).

The content material which is emphasized and reinforced with fill-in-the-blank and true-false exercises involves the basic descriptions and situations stated in the passage. The company, Rosserys and Mitchell, is located at the junction of the Avenue de la République and the Rue Oberkampf. The narrator is the Associate Director of Human Relations and the General Manager's name is Saint-Ramé. The headquarters of the firm is located in Des Moines. From the vocabulary and the content exercises, students should realize the kind of business in which the firm is engaged, i.e., the making, selling and exporting of farm engines and machinery, as well as the fact that they have grandiose ideas to enlarge their business and diversify.

The six-phase project for enlarging the firm furnishes a good transitional point in the movement from content exercises to more open-ended discussion. The different phases show a progression from the goals of a local firm, "fabriquons et emballons chez nous des engins et vendons-les chez nous," to a global-scale operation that exploits the cheapest labor at each stage of the production, assembly and packaging processes. Finally, the company plans to diversify, to transform itself into a huge investment firm, "[une] gigantesque société de placement." Eventually the company would replace local governments and religions in its ultimate project of world domination, "faire du monde une seule et immense entreprise." This project certainly provides much material for discussion, both on a theoretical and practical level, as students discuss the roles businesses should play, and currently do play, in the world. Additionally, discussion can center around the narrator's position in the firm and his function as chronicler of the company's demise, as well as around the symbolic nature of the firm's collapse. The religious allusions should be noted, many of them quite subtle (the director's name is Saint-Ramé, the firm's headquarters are in Des Moines, "the monks") and examined. The use of time in the opening pages is also quite significant, since the novel opens with a future promise, "Je vais raconter l'histoire...," but the events refer to a distant past, since we learn that the company has since been long forgotten, "elle a perdu sa place dans la mémoire des citoyens et elle n'a creusé aucun sillon dans l'Histoire."

Since the narrator and General Director are the only two characters introduced in the passage, and they do not interact, it is somewhat difficult to create role-play situations. Nonetheless, at one point the narrator states that he was soon going to be promoted from Associate Director to Director of Human Relations; students can recreate the scene in which Saint-Ramé informs him of the fact. They can also imagine a phone conversation between the narrator or a secretary in the company and somebody who wants to know details about the firm's operations. In addition, some good writing exercises can be devised. Students can write a want ad for a position in the company, such as for the Associate Director of Human Relations once the narrator is promoted. Also they can write a letter to the headquarters in Iowa, describing their fears over cracks found in the building. Even though the passage is not rich in character development, it does provide many details about the company that can be used in role-playing and writing exercises.

Repetition of words and phrases are apparent in the introductory passage to *L'Imprécateur*. The very first words, "Je vais raconter l'histoire de l'effondrement et de la destruction," are repeated at the beginning of the sixth paragraph, less for comic effect than to reinforce the narrator's intent and the terrible fate that befell his company. The greatest use of repetition occurs in the description of the company's operations, where the verbs *fabriquer, emballer,* and sometimes *vendre* are used in nine different places within two pages. The use of these verbs takes on the tedium and monotony of assembly-line production while, from another perspective, their use becomes a kind of incantatory mantra recited in response to questions about the company's business. Issues involving circulation may not be readily apparent upon first reading, but just like the engines the firm manufactures, the company itself is a pump, circulating money and influence into the economies it touches, and its plans for foreign production and export maintain a flow of goods and money among many countries. One area in which the firm seeks to halt circulation, however, deals with power, since it wants to take political control away from governments for its own benefit, "le pouvoir temporel appartiendrait aux entreprises et aux banques." In this megalomaniac vision, the company sees itself as having a controlling role in society and the social life of the global work force, since business policies have enormous effects on people. Indeed, the company takes on the role of the world's salvation, hoping one day to end hunger, thirst, and sickness. But the story of this fantastical vision, which turns apocalyptic, is told by a marginal character who holds a middle management position, and who was not involved in decision making, "ma fonction m'avait tenu à l'écart des principales décisions financières, commerciales et techniques."

The position of the narrator in contrast with the aspirations of the company provides one of many ironic situations in the passage. Certainly the fact that the company sought world dominion, while the building in Paris decayed and collapsed, is a highly ironic and symbolic detail. Other aspects of the passage are more satirical and sinister. The various titles and attributes after Saint-Ramé's name when he is first mentioned indicate a general practice in business, while humorously critical of an exaggerated, inflated ego. The importance of management (*gestion*) itself takes on a religious fervor. People are no longer separated by sect and creed, but by whether or not they are good managers. Washington has become the new Jerusalem, in the new faith of global business domination.

The world of Sembène Ousmane's *Xala* is far removed from that of Pilhes' *L'Imprécateur*, although they are linked by two crucial elements. While the Parisian *filière* of Rosserys and Mitchell sought world domination, a kind of entrepreneurial colonization, the business leaders in Senegal are in the process of decolonization, of emancipating themselves from European political and economic power. And, in both novels written in the 1970s, characters must deal with a curse. The entire company was placed under an imprecation in Pilhes' novel, whereas it is only the protagonist in Ousmane's work who is cursed with *xala*, a Wolof word meaning impotency. El Hadji Abdou Kader Bèye is a corrupt businessman who has risen to prominence. A symbol of the newly rich African bourgeoisie, he occupies the position of a former European colonialist, and serves as a middleman for their continued economic presence. On the night of his marriage to his third wife, he suffers sexual impotency, brought about by a man whom he had robbed and who has gotten revenge through a spell.

The opening five pages of the novel describe the protagonist and the general social and economic climate of the country at a time when a double celebration occurs. The first African President of the Chamber of Commerce has been named, and El Hadji is about to be wed to his third wife, thus elevating him to the social status of a *capitaine*. General vocabulary relating to the festivities of this wedding needs to be covered and used in exercises, since words such as *festoyer*, *libation*, *conviés*, and *mosquée* appear in the text. In addition, a vocabulary of power and intention expresses the rise of the native African businessmen, as found in such terms as *prendre en main*, *velléité*, *visaient*, and *revenaient de droit*. Cultural items referring to local customs, such as marking an important date with a white stone, as well as the numerous allusions to Islamic tradition (mosque, pilgrimage) mixed with tribal practice (polygamy) require explanation. The use of honorific titles is important in the passage, since the "hommes d'affaires" (a designation placed in quotes in the first sentence of the novel) are assembled to honor the first African President of the Chamber (a man whose name does not yet appear in the text) and also Abdou Kader Bèye, who acquired the title "El Hadji" upon returning from a pilgrimage to Mecca. This use of titles can be compared with those of the businessman and little prince in Saint-Exupéry's text, and with the Associate Director of Human Relations and the *imprécateur* in Pilhes' novel, since people are often described by a role or function rather than a name. In Ousmane's *Xala*, we learn later in the novel that the titles are hollow and meaningless.

The vocabulary of business is fairly extensive in the opening passage, and we find terms like *Chambre de Commerce et d'Industrie, commerce de détail, demi-gros, avoir bancaire, action syndicale, revente, intermédiaire, concurrence, redevances, fin d'exercice,* and *rentrée.* Both the future aspirations of the African businessmen in general, and the specific business dealings in El Hadji's past are described in useful and current business terminology, found in standard Business French phrases. The businessmen who demand African *indépendance économique* wear English suits, drive Mercedes, and speak the language of the European French.

Basic content material to be covered in true-false and fill-in-the-blank exercises concerns the setting of the novel in Senegal, the naming of an African as President of the Chamber of Commerce, the ten-year fight by the local community for this honor, the impending third marriage for El Hadji, and issues related to the identity of the protagonist and how he acquired his title. A long list of failed business ventures which eventually brought him to a position of prominence, if not wealth, and his current corrupt practices provide many items for objective, factual exercises as well as for discussion, once the general facts are all clearly understood by students. A former instructor who was fired for his union activity, El Hadji began his business career with the resale of food products, then became an intermediary in real estate transactions. At one point he held a monopoly in the sale of rice. Upon the country's independence, he became an importer of dried fish, but financial problems ended various importing ventures, and he ended up acting as a front for foreign investors. Local law chose to ignore his illegal activities.

Other issues to be discussed involve the mood of the businessmen in the opening paragraph, including what their hopes are and why they are so keenly felt. The mixture of European and African practices also elicits good discussion comments, which can be placed in the context of the two major events of business and marriage. Role playing can be used to reshape the material in the passage from a different perspective. Students can take the role of the African businessmen, describe their own backgrounds and aspirations for the future, and describe the President of the Chamber and El Hadji. One student can claim to be his friend, another a critic, and they can argue his good points and weaknesses. Finally, students can recreate a scene involving El Hadji's first two wives, and their reaction to the addition of a third spouse.

With regard to the comparative thematic issues, repetition occurs in the use of titles, and in the fact that El Hadji is about to celebrate his third marriage. Terms such as *Chambre, chers collègues, responsabilité, and notre gouvernement* emphasize the importance of the meeting of the businessmen, and their political dreams and drive for independence, ideas which are invoked to hide personal, selfish greed, *a rêve d'embourgeoisement*. Money and power are intended to flow from Europeans to Africans at the time of decolonization, yet we see how the circulation is slowed and channeled through certain individuals, such as El Hadji. Unlike the characters in the texts we have examined before, El Hadji is a central figure in his society, but we learn later in the novel that he, along with all Africans, is being marginalized and kept from real social and economic power. Yet his central role is also a problem since, due to his corrupt practices, he should be pushed out through criticism, reprimand, or even a jail sentence. His leadership role is at the very least ironic. Indeed, the entire novel is a satire on the decolonization of Africa, symbolized by a corrupt businessman who is cursed by *xala*, an impotency that extends from the sexual to include his social and economic identity as well.

The methodological procedures we have discussed can be applied to a wide range of literary texts, not just the four texts we have analyzed. While space in this article does not allow an exhaustive list of appropriate literary works, a few titles can be helpful in orienting the Business French teacher to possible texts. One of the earliest texts is *La Farce de Maître Pathelin*, especially scene 2, in which Pathelin and the drapier negotiate. Portions of Rabelais (Pantagruel, 17; Tiers Livre 3), Molière (*Le Bourgeois gentilhomme, Le Malade imaginaire*, I, i), La Fontaine (*Fables*, 4, 20 "L'Avare qui a perdu son trésor;" 7, 10 "La Laitière et le pot au lait;" 8, 2 "Le Savetier et le Financier;"), La Bruyère (*Caractères*, 6, 83 "Giton et Phédon"), and Voltaire (*Candide*, 17) furnish humorous insights into pre-Revolutionary dealings, although language and cultural references may hinder some students. The 19th and 20th centuries are quite abundant in sources for texts which are more readily comprehensible, including Balzac's *Père Goriot and Eugenie Grandet*, Stendhal's *Le Rouge et le Noir*, Hugo's *Les Misérables*, Flaubert's *Madame Bovary*, numerous short stories by Maupassant ("Les Bijoux," "Le Collier"), Zola's *L'Argent* [about *la Bourse*] and *Au Bonheur des Dames* [about a department store], Becque's *Les Corbeaux*, and Gide's *Les Faux Monnayeurs*. A number of literary critics have recently begun to analyze economics and exchange in literature. Jacques Derrida discusses Baudelaire, Goux examines Gide, and other studies pertain to Montaigne, Molière, and Becque. Teachers of Business French may wish to consult these critical works for insights and approaches to adapt to their classes, and also for bibliographical source material.

Many contemporary novels contain at least a passage that involves money, business or finance. Teachers can be guided in their selection by their interests, those of their students, and the level of the course. We encourage the use of Francophone texts in order to provide a richly varied perspective. Our bibliography indicates some useful articles that discuss numerous Francophone literary works, such as Jacques Godbout's *Salut, Galarneau!*, André Langevin's *Poussière sur la ville* (Canada), Mongo Beti's *Ville cruelle*, and Charles Cheikh Sow's *Cycle de Sécheresse* (Africa). A number of significant works by women authors are definitely worth including in the Business French syllabus. From French Canada, texts include Gabrielle Roy's *Alexandre Chenevert* and *Bonheur d'occasion*, and Anne Hébert's *Kamouraska* and *Les Fous de Bassan*. From Africa and the Caribbean, texts to examine for business content include Myriam Warner-Vieyra's *Juletane*, Mariama Bâ's *Une si longue lettre*, Aminata Sow Fall's *L'Appel des arènes*, Philomène Basseck's *La Tache de sang* and Maryse Condé's *Traversée de la Mangrove* or *Pension les Alizés*. Given these possible choices, it is indeed difficult to select a few passages to include in the curriculum of a Business French course. Students may wish to read some passages outside the course assignments, and they could report back to the class, present a scene, or lead a discussion of issues raised in the text they chose to read.

A curriculum is a path, traveled and negotiated by instructor and students, as they cover a great deal of ground, gaining greater experience and knowledge. Among the growing list of materials and approaches available for the study of Business French, short literary passages dealing with economic and financial issues can provide useful reinforcement and a fresh perspective to factual documentation. As Rusterholz concludes, "We can never prepare all our students adequately for the variety of working situations in which they may eventually find themselves, but by teaching them to be skillful readers, we can give them the tools to continue to teach themselves" (433). We can guide them by demonstrating in our courses that business and literature are not only compatible, but equally necessary and mutually supportive for achieving cultural competence.

WORKS CITED

Literary Texts

Molière. *L'Avare*, ed. Louis Forestier. Paris: Hachette, 1965.

Ousmane, Sembène. *Xala*. Paris: Présence Africaine, 1973.

Pilhes, René-Victor. *L'Imprécateur*. Paris, Seuil, 1974.

Saint-Exupéry, Antoine de. *Le Petit Prince*.. Paris: Gallimard, 1984.

Economic Themes in Literature

Araujo, Norman. "The Language of Business and the Business of Language in Becque's *Les Corbeaux*," *French Review* 63, 1 (October, 1989): 66-77.

Derrida, Jacques. *Donner le temps: la Fausse monnaie* [Baudelaire]. Paris: Galilée, 1991.

Desan, Philippe. *Les Commerces de Montaigne: le Discours économique des Essais*. Paris: Nizet, 1992.

DiGaetani, John Louis, ed. *Money: Lure, Lore and Literature*. Westport, CT: Greenwood Press, 1994.

Force, Pierre. *Molière ou le prix des choses*. Paris: Nathan, 1994.

Goux, Jean-Joseph. *Les Monnayeurs du langage* [Gide]. Paris: Galilée, 1984.

Rogers, Nathalie Buchet. "Nouveau Réalisme, nouvelle monnaie: l'Economie des signes dans *L'Imprécateur* de René-Victor Pilhes. *Romance Languages Annual* 6 (1994): 151-59.

Francophone Literature

Abrate, Jayne. "Teaching the Literature of Quebec: Culture et langue de base." *French Review* 67, 6 (May 1994): 954-965.

Chevrier, Jacques. *Littérature africaine: Histoire et grands thèmes*. Paris: Hatier, 1990.

Harrow, Kenneth. "Sembene Ousmane's *Xala*: The Use of Film and Novel as Revolutionary Weapon." *Studies in Twentieth Century Literature* 4, 2 (Spring 1980): 177-88.

Kingué, Angèle et Odile Cazenave. "Pour une approche comparée des œuvres africaines d'expression française: quelques exemples appliqués." *French Review* 70, 1 (October 1996): 65-80.

Willen, Margaret Moore. "The New (Mé)Tissage: Weaving Black Francophone Literature into the Curriculum." *French Review* 69, 5 (April 1996): 762-74.

Teaching and the Teaching of Literature

Barnett, Marva A. *More Than Meets the Eye: Foreign Language Reading Theory and Practice.* Englewood Cliffs, NJ: Prentice-Hall, 1990.

Bernhardt, Elizabeth B. *Reading Development in a Second Language: Theoretical, Empirical and Classroom Perspectives.* Norwood, NJ: Ablex, 1991.

Blackbourn, Barbara L. "Transition from Language to Literature." *French Review* 60, 2 (December 1986): 196-202.

Carney, William J. "Integrating Commercial French into the Traditional Foreign Language Curriculum: A Marriage of Convenience That Works." *ADFL Bulletin* 17, ii (1986): 43-49.

Davis, James N. and Linda Bistodean. "How do L1 and L2 Reading Differ ? Evidence from Think-Aloud Protocols." *Modern Language Journal* 77, 4 (Winter, 1993): 459-472.

_____, Lynn Carbón Gorell, Rebecca R. Kline and Gloria Hsieh. "Readers and Foreign Languages: A Survey of Undergraduate Attitudes toward the Study of Literature." *Modern Language Journal* 76, 3 (Autumn, 1992): 320-332.

Dowling, Carol and Anita Mitchell. "Reading in a Specific Purpose Foreign Course: A Case of Technical Japanese." *Modern Language Journal* 77, 4 (Winter, 1993): 433-444.

Dugan, J. Sanford. "A Rationale for Broadening the Perspectives of Business French Programs." *French Review* 57 (1984): 356-65.

Harper, Sandra N. "Strategies for Teaching Literature at the Undergraduate Level." *Modern Language Journal* 72 (1988): 402-08.

Kramsch, Claire. "Literary Texts in the Classroom: A Discourse." *Modern Language Journal* 69 (1985): 356-66.

Labarca, Angela, ed. *Issues in L2: Theory as Practice/Practice as Theory.* Norwood, NJ: Ablex, 1986.

Prince, Peter. "Second Language Vocabulary Learning: The Role of Context versus Translations as a Function of Proficiency." *Modern Language Journal* 80, 4 (Winter, 1996): 478-493.

Purcell, John M. "Cultural Appreciation Through Literature." *Foreign Language Annals* 21 (1988): 19-24.

Raymond, Patricia Mary. "The Effects of Structure Strategy Training on the Recall of Expository Prose for University Students Reading French as a Second Language." *Modern Language Journal* 77, 4 (Winter, 1993): 445-458.

Rusterholz, Barbara L. "Reading Strategies for the Business Foreign Language Class." *Foreign Language Annals* 20, 5 (October 1987): 427-33.

Swaffer, Janet K. "Readers, Texts and Second Languages: The Interactive Processes." *Modern Language Journal* 72, 2 (Summer 1988): 123-49.

Wolf, Darlene F. "A Comparison of Assessment Tasks Used to Measure Foreign Language Reading Comprehension." *Modern Language Journal* 77, 4 (Winter, 1993): 473-489.

BRINGING IT BACK HOME: FRENCH FOR BUSINESS EXPLORES THE USA

Annette Sampon-Nicolas

In the past few years, higher education has been encouraged to improve the learning experience of students, and to build stronger ties between the classroom experience and the global community.[1] French for Business must be responsive to the needs not only of our students but also of the international community in which our students will soon be working. As French teachers, we have both the responsibility and the resources available to enhance student learning. For a course to successfully prepare students for a global marketplace where business, language, and culture skills are essential, it is necessary to modify course materials. Through extended research projects on the Web, students learn about employment opportunities, study economic developments both in France and in the United States, while using their newly acquired French business terms in authentic settings. By bringing our French for Business courses back to the United States, where the majority our students will be looking for employment, we are building stronger ties between what goes on in the classroom and what is happening in the world.

The primary object of most Business French courses is to master a new vocabulary, and to hone the four skills while learning about the French business world. In his article "French in the Workplace," Joseph Morello explains that the course has frequently been used to prepare for an exam, the Certificat Pratique de Français Commercial et Economique, offered by the Chambre de Commerce et d'Industrie de Paris (CCIP) (845). "Yet the question of whether or not the content of that exam and of my course has anything to do with the real life needs of an employee using French in the work world remained unanswered in my own mind" (845). We have probably all asked ourselves the same question over the past ten years. While I have relied on feedback about the usefulness of my Business French course from alumni, Morello surveyed French-owned companies in the United States regarding the use of French in the workplace (846). The results suggest that in order to be more responsive to the needs of the international marketplace, we need to prepare our students better by emphasizing oral communication, and the reading and writing of authentic documents[2] (848). The surveys also indicated that students need better knowledge of French culture as it relates to the business world (849).

I continue to use Claude LeGoff's fine text *French for Business*, and to prepare students for the *Certificat pratique*. However, the exam is not my focus.[3] I teach the important core material presented in LeGoff's book, continue to bring in articles on French economy and business, while emphasizing the interconnections of everything we study to the global marketplace. I want students to have a body of knowledge, as well as skills, to go beyond French business culture, to see both the divergences and the similarities between our cultures. This paper introduces the changes I have incorporated which improve oral and written skills as well as promote better understanding of the international marketplace. Thanks to the wealth of information on the Web, we focus our research on the business and economic aspects of both France and the United States.

Over the semester, students are assigned the following research projects: 1) the employment market, 2) a specific French Trade Commission, 3) a metropolitan area, state, or region of the United States, and 4) French exports and investments in the United States. Research projects incorporate technology while reinforcing French business vocabulary and concepts. The vocabulary from the fields of banking, corporations, chambers of commerce, transportation, stock market, sales, taxes, communications, advertising, import-export, economics, is effortlessly and constantly reintroduced in oral and written assignments relating to the research projects. While exploring the business connections between France and the United States, students also start focusing on their career goals.

The Job Market

Students are interested in taking Business French in order to enhance their resumes and their careers. They are also interested in finding employment upon graduation. Most institutions offer career counseling centers to help students define their goals, evaluate their qualifications, and direct their job searches. Although it might not be our responsibility as French teachers to help students find jobs, helpful suggestions are encouraged by the administration and appreciated by students.

During the first class meetings, we discuss internships, employment experiences, goals, and jobs our alumni have found with their French majors. In order to help our students, we publish a handout entitled "Careers for French Majors" in which our alumni describe their jobs.[4] Since approximately 80% of our students will be looking for employment directly after graduation, we encourage them to start exploring the job market early through internships. During our winter term, students have interned in Franco-American and Canadian-American Chambers of Commerce, Alliances Françaises, in French Trade Commission offices, and in French offices and companies both in France and in the United States. While internships might not procure jobs for them in the future, they are a good introduction to how French is used in the workplace.

However, even after internships, many seniors do not have a clear idea of how to go about searching for employment. Our first research assignment, therefore, focuses on the job market. While studying the first chapter on "Le secrétariat," where assignments include job application letters and résumés, we begin our study of the complex world of employment. The Web site "Pages France," under the heading "Emplois," lists many organizations for searching the job market in

France and in the world.[5] As students learn how to read job descriptions, they discover the range of employment possibilities.

I assign readings on the Web in the section "Guide de la recherche d'emploi," provided by the ANPE (Agence Nationale Pour l'Emploi). Students answer questions on topics that range from goals, the job market, CVs, application letters, to interviewing. The first section on "S'orienter dans les métiers," helps students who are unsure of their career goals. In order to know their options, they must first define their interests, and determine their professional goals through documentary research. Once students have decided which type of job they would like to have, they need to check its feasibility according to their skills and the current state of the job market. This is also the perfect opportunity for discussing the state of the economy and job markets in both countries.

"Le Marché de l'emploi," gives information on how to proceed after choosing an employment area. The first step is to research a particular professional sector, the companies which comprise that sector, their sizes, geographic locations, and recruiting practices. Research can be carried out on the Web, in national and international newspapers, and in specialized professional publications. The Web site "Career Mosaic," for example, has an amusing analysis of the state of the employment world where jobs are divided according to the following categories: "Ils vont bien et ils embauchent, Ils vont mal mais ils embauchent, Ils vont bien mais ils n'embauchent pas, Ils vont mal et ils n'embauchent pas." Another way to obtain information is to interview professionals in a field of interest, to ask questions regarding job descriptions, how they found their jobs, and the necessary requirements for the job. The more information a student has, the more productive the job search will be.

After narrowing down a sector, job descriptions and possibly potential companies, students examine whether their skills qualify them for the job they desire. With double majors in Economics or International Studies, French majors are able to find employment more easily. However, not everyone has a double major nor the intention of continuing their studies immediately after graduation, and those with French majors need to market themselves according to their experiences and interests.

The section on "Les écrits du candidat," has extensive suggestions and examples on how to write a job application letter and a résumé. Students learn the subtle cultural differences between a curriculum vitae and a résumé, requests regarding personnel information, and typed letters versus handwritten letters commonly used in France for handwriting analysis.

Once students have defined their professional goals, they are ready to research the job market through the reading of classified ads on the Web. Under the heading "Emplois," there are over a dozen sites where students can research employment opportunities. Under "Cadremploi," for example, students fill out a "Recherche multicritère." They define the job listings that interest them according to four topics: 1) job description, 2) sector, 3) salary, and 4) geographic location. I ask them to select two job offerings and report back giving the following information: the job title, sector, company name and address, job description, and necessary qualifications. I encourage them to search the Web sites of several organizations that list job openings and to choose those for which they are qualified. While they will probably not find their first jobs through these research projects, they are learning the research tools to help them down the road.

The French Trade Commissions and the United States

The next project has two parts: 1) the study of the role and function of the French Trade Commissions (Postes d'Expansion Economique), and 2) the study of a particular area in the United States. The Postes d'Expansion Economique (PEE) located under the Trade and Technology heading at the Embassy of France Web site, are an excellent source of information. The PEE, under the Ministère de l'Economie et des Finances, promote and defend the interests of French exporting businesses in foreign markets. They are located in Washington, Los Angeles, San Francisco, Chicago, New York, Miami, Atlanta, Houston, and Detroit. Although there are only nine PEE, there is sufficient information available for students to team up if the class is large. After choosing a PEE, students answer basic questions regarding the area covered, duties, responsibilities, services offered, general and recent activities, trade show schedules, sector notes, letters and publications.

From the starting point of a PEE, students examine the economic and business profile of a metropolitan area, state or region where they might want to work one day. Sample questions elicit information about natural resources, demography, economic conditions, communication infrastructures, tourism, exports, French presence and investments in the United States. Although some research can be conducted in the library, students are required to use the Web's resources. In her article, "Teaching with Technology: What is at Stake," Gilberte Furstenberg calls on us to create tasks that will "exploit the associative nature" of available technology, and turn our students into "photographers, guides, videographers, investigators, or reporters" (24). These research projects take advantage of the tree-like structure of the Web, since most projects start out at the Embassy of France site, and proceed from there to multiple sites. Given that each PEE offers various degrees of information from "Fiches économiques" to detailed "Profils économiques" about metropolitan areas and states, students must explore the Web for the most recent and complete information.

Since the PEE also specialize in specific sectors, students start narrowing down their research to a particular industry for the final project. For example, New York dominates consumer goods, food and wine sectors, while Washington is responsible for agricultural products, trade, and telecommunications. Los Angeles covers multimedia, audiovisual, air, space and ground transportation sectors. Although there are many different sectors, most students choose from the ever popular "Secteur Biens de Consommation," which includes clothing, shoes, health products, perfumes and the "Secteur Agro-Alimentaire," which covers wine, champagne, mineral waters, cheese, cookies, and chocolate.

However, once the more intimidating sectors have been explained and their significance for the United States presented, students become more adventuresome. Sectors such as environmental, audio-visual, tourism, sporting goods, telecommunications, entertainment, and transportation offer fascinating research possibilities. And while industrial equipment might not seem the most exciting area to study, bringing class discussions closer to home is another way to obtain diversity in research projects. I have found that studying a region to which they have close ties is often enough incentive for students to explore an unknown sector.

In Houston, for example, which is responsible for energy, chemical and environmental sectors, one can find French multinational groups such as Elf, Thomson, Saint-Gobain, Aérospatiale, and Rhône-Poulenc. Discovering that the Houston PEE is responsible for the environmental sector inspired a student from Texas to study Rhône-Poulenc USA and the developing environmental market. A student from California, surprised to find out that the subway BART in San Francisco was built by the French GEC-Alsthom, proceeded to study this company and mass transportation problems in the US. A report about Wisconsin, which is covered by the Chicago PEE, informed us that French cheese producers have bought dairy factories and are producing their products in the United States. Students come to realize that all sectors are equally important and fascinating once they make the connections which bring their research closer to home.

While pursuing their research on a French product or company for their final project, students give short oral reports on recent economic developments in their region of study. They read weekly summaries of "Notes sectorielles," which analyze potential markets and recent developments in American culture that might open markets to the French. A sectorial note in the "agro-alimentaire" sector, for example, presents information regarding the presence of European groups on the American cookie and candy market. From this note we learn that the United States,

193

with major groups such as Nabisco and Hershey, is the number one market in the world for sweets. In spite of the dominance of the market by American groups, with consumer demand for sweets steadily increasing, there is room for foreign exports of high quality regional and ethnic food products. All the PEE discuss changes in the American market for products and industries of the many sectors and offer complete sectorial notes for more detailed information.

In addition to recent economic developments, we study the calendar of trade shows in each geographic area. Students present professional trade shows which relate to their sectors, the products, the exhibitors and the visitors. We learn for example, that the "Institute of Food Technologies Annual Meeting and Food Exposition," which is held in Orlando, Florida this year, is the most important trade show for the American food industry. The exhibitors are suppliers of raw materials, and producers of flavorings, of equipment, of laboratory measuring tools, of packaging and transformation materials. Visitors include distributors, large food industry groups (technicians, scientists, marketing/sales/management specialists). I also bring in video clips of French trade shows, such as "Salon de l'Agriculture," "Salon des Arts Ménagers," and "Salon du Bateau," which are available on video cassette from the *Hexagone* and *France TV Magazine* series. Students discuss their visits to trade shows and the benefits of attending and presenting at these shows. Since experiential learning is an important aspect of improving the learning experience, we also visit a trade show, such as the Home Show, in order to get a first hand view of exhibitors, brochures and the use of advertising. Through the materials we collect, we are able to distinguish "brochures" and "dépliants" from "circulaire" and "prospectus." Employment questions are also reintroduced in our discussions of international trade shows such as the World Dairy Expo, which employs many interpreters. The actual "hands-on" approach is most appealing, as students use their recently acquired French business terms in the context of the United States.

From their research projects on the PEE and on a geographic area of the United States, students learn not only about the economic conditions of their own states and country, but also about French presence, interests, and investments in the United States. They are now ready to start their final project on a specific French product or company.

Exploring French Products and Companies

In order to guarantee a maximum of information, students are encouraged to pick a French company or product with high visibility in the United States. Using both French and English search engines, students explore the history of a product or a company, its development, advertising campaigns, marketing strategies, problems encountered, and recent stock market developments.

Although some research projects studied French companies that were new to students, such as Rhône-Poulenc USA, and GEC-Alsthom, most students chose companies such as Evian, Perrier, Danone, Guerlain, and LVMH-Moët Hennessey Louis Vuitton. In addition to stimulating discussions about cultural differences, the studies of consumer food products and luxury items offer insights into the role of luxury products in the trade balance, as well as problems posed by counterfeit.

The "Danone Group," which includes Danone dairy products and Evian mineral water, provides extensive information on the history of their products, their research institute, and sponsorship of sports events. In addition, the Danone group gives information regarding employment opportunities, training programs in marketing, human resources, research, manufacturing, purchasing, sales and finance, as they search for the ideal "Danone person," to work for them.

Students found both the history of perfumes in France and the complex and competitive perfume industry of great interest. French perfumes are extremely popular in the United States and some of the major groups in the perfume sector are L'Oréal, and the Elf-Aquitaine Group, through its subsidiary Sanofi. However, students learned that the top American machine washing powder manufacturers such as Procter & Gamble and Johnson and Johnson, are now in this competitive market after acquiring famous perfume names.

A study of champagne starts out with a brief history, geographical data, production information and leads into an overview of the market, champagne advertising, and the complex network of distribution, imports and retail in the United States. It includes actions undertaken by the Bureau de Champagne in the United States, and finishes with the Bureau's orientation for the coming year. Thus a study of champagne includes not only a discussion of French products, but also of the American economy. Thanks to economic growth in the United States and an increase in champagne consumption, France is able to increase champagne exports. In addition to the study of the economic situations of both countries, students bring in cultural information to explain the increase in champagne consumption, namely, the increased recommendation of the health benefits of moderate wine consumption in the American press, as well as a more "hedonistic evolution" in consumption in general. American consumers are buying more delicate wines to accompany a more diversified cuisine.

Conclusion

By bringing our curriculum closer to home, thanks to creative Web sites, we have at our fingertips a unique means of enriching our courses. The study of the connections between the United States and France brings a new interest to the study of Business French. While mastering French economic and business terms and principles, in addition to studying recent economic developments in France, students study the American economic situation at the state and the national levels. Although these research projects might not lead to jobs, they do provide students with important research tools for seeking employment and offer new insight into the job market and the complex world of Franco-American business relations. More importantly, students make great strides toward the mastery of Business French, making themselves more marketable to both French and American companies.[6]

Appendix

DEVOIRS SUR L'INTERNET

Devoir sur l'emploi : Allez à http://www.pagefrance.com/

Cliquez sur «Emploi», allez à «Guide de la Recherche d'emploi». Lisez le texte et répondez aux questions suivantes :

S'orienter dans les métiers :

1. Que pouvez-vous faire pour vous aider à déterminer vos buts professionnels ?
2. Que devez-vous vérifier une fois que vous savez l'emploi que vous voulez exercer ?

Le marché de l'emploi :

1. Où pouvez-vous vous renseigner sur le marché de l'emploi?
2. Quelles ressources sont à votre disposition ?

Evaluer ses compétences :

1. Que pouvez-vous faire pour savoir si vos compétences correspondent bien au poste qui vous intéresse ?
2. Quelles possibilités existent si vous n'avez pas les qualifications nécessaires pour exercer l'emploi que vous voulez ?

Mettre en place une campagne de recherche d'emploi :

1. Une fois défini vos compétences en rapport avec vos buts professionnels, que devez-vous faire ?

2. Quelle est souvent la longueur de la durée de cette recherche ?

3. Que devez-vous faire en attendant de trouver l'emploi désiré ?

4. Qui peut vous aider dans votre recherche en France ? Aux Etats-Unis ?

Les écrits de candidature :

1. De quoi avez-vous besoin avant de contacter les entreprises ?

2. Que devez-vous faire avant de rédiger votre CV ?

3. Quel est le but du CV ?

4. Comment un CV est-il différent d'un «résumé» américain ?

5. En quoi consiste le contenu du CV ?

6. Quelles variations sont possibles dans un CV ?

7. Qu'est-ce qu'une «lettre de motivation» ?

8. Comment une lettre de réponse à une petite annonce est-elle différente d'une lettre de motivation de candidature spontanée ?

Chercher des postes vacants :

1. Comment pouvez-vous détecter les postes à pourvoir en entreprise ?

2. Que devez-vous faire pour préparer une campagne de candidature spontanée ?

3. Comment pouvez-vous utiliser vos relations ?

4. Y a-t-il d'autres pistes de recherche qui peuvent vous aider à trouver un poste ?

Entretien d'embauche :

1. Qu'est-ce qui est indispensable à l'entretien d'embauche ?
2. Comment pouvez-vous préparer un entretien ?

Recherche sur l'emploi : A «Pagefrance», par exemple, cliquez sur «Emplois». Vous trouverez ici une liste de sites où vous pouvez chercher : ex. Cardremploi, Bottin, Adecco, Initiatives Emplois, Cegos. A Cadremploi, par exemple, cherchez deux offres d'emploi. Dites ce que vous avez cherché, (recherche multicritère), décrivez les postes, donnez le nom de l'entreprise, l'adresse, le nom du poste, le profil, les qualifications. Préparez a) un exposé, b) un résumé écrit, c) votre CV et une lettre de motivation où vous posez votre candidature à une de ces offres d'emploi.

Devoir sur les Postes d'Expansion Economique et sur une région des Etats-Unis : Allez à http://www.info-france-usa.org/ Ambassade de France à Washington.

Cliquez sur «Trade and Technology», ensuite sur les Postes d'Expansion Economiques. Il y a dix PEE aux Etats-Unis : Washington, Los Angeles, San Francisco, Chicago, New York, Miami, Atlanta, Houston, Detroit. Regardez le réseau des postes, cliquez sur la carte, ensuite sur le nom de la ville qui vous intéresse. Vous aurez les informations sur le poste ainsi que son adresse pour obtenir d'autres renseignements. Lisez et prenez des notes. Vous devez a) répondre aux questions ci-dessous, b) préparer un exposé au sujet du poste de votre choix, c) faire un devoir écrit où vous décrivez le poste et ses activités, d) préparez un exposé sur une agglomération, un état ou une région des Etats-Unis, e) rendre un résumé de cet exposé.

Questionnaire au sujet d'un Poste d'Expansion Economique :

1. Quelle région ou quels états est-ce que ce PEE recouvre ?
2. Quelle est la description du poste ? Quelles sont ses responsabilités ? Ses services ?

3. De quels secteurs est-il responsable ?

4. Y a-t-il des salons professionnels au cours de l'année qui se rapportent à ses spécialités ? Lesquels ?

5. Est-ce que ce poste publie des revues, des études de marché ou des notes sectorielles ?

6. Quelles sont les activités générales du poste ?

7. Quelles sont les activités récentes du poste ?

8. Quelles sont les industries françaises principales qui se trouvent dans la région ?

9. Pourquoi ces industries françaises ont-elles choisi cette région ?

Questionnaire au sujet d'une région aux Etats-Unis :

1. Quelles sont les données fondamentales de votre région ? Quelles sont ses ressources naturelles ?

2. Décrivez la population. Quel est son pouvoir d'achat? Est-elle culturellement diversifiée ? La main d'œuvre est-elle qualifiée ? éduquée ?

3. Quel est l'état de l'emploi et du chômage ? Y a-t-il des congrès et des salons professionnels chaque année ? Lesquels ?

4. Quels sont les principaux secteurs d'activité de votre région? Quels sont les services principaux ?

5. Sur quoi est fondée l'économie locale ? Quels sont les industries principales qui s'y trouvent ? Où en est-elle du point de vue technologique ?

6. Y a-t-il des filiales d'entreprises françaises ?

7. Dans quels secteurs la France est-elle présente ?

8. Quelles multinationales y sont implantées ?

9. Y a-t-il des écoles françaises ? Lesquelles ?

10. Combien de Français y vivent ?

11. Quels sont les infrastructures de communication ?
    Comment sont les transports ? Y a-t-il des liaisons
    aériennes régulières à Paris ?

12. Décrivez le commerce de détail. Y trouve-t-on des centres
    commerciaux importants ?

13. Est-ce que le tourisme génère des recettes importantes ?
    Quel est le rôle du tourisme ?

14. L'économie est-elle ouverte sur l'extérieur ? Quelles sont
    les exportations ? Sont-elles importantes ?

15. Quelles sociétés américaines de votre région sont
    implantées en France ? Y a-t-il des villes jumelées avec la
    France ?

16. Quels problèmes est-ce que cette région pose aux Français
    qui veulent s'y implanter ?

17. Est-ce que votre région recherche des investissements
    étrangers ? Comment ?

18. Comment le gouvernement de votre région, aide-t-il les
    investisseurs ? Y a-t-il des exemptions d'impôts ou des
    dégrèvements fiscaux ?

19. Pourquoi est-ce un marché attrayant ?

Devoirs sur une entreprise ou un produit

Choisissez soit une entreprise française qui est implantée aux Etats-Unis, ou un produit français qui se vend aux Etats-Unis. Cherchez des renseignements au sujet de cette entreprise ou de ce produit à l'Internet, dans les revues et les journaux. Il s'agit de faire de la recherche sur l'histoire de l'entreprise ou du produit, d'étudier les marchés aux Etats-Unis où il se vend, son succès, la publicité utilisée, l'état de ses actions à la Bourse. Le devoir devra incorporer de la documentation, des statistiques et des publicités du produit.

WORKS CITED

Cantor, J. A. *Experiential Learning in Higher Education: Linking Classroom and Community.* ASHE-ERIC *Higher Education Report* 95-7.

Carbonnier, J.L. *Le Marché des Etats-Unis : Bilan de l'année 1996 et Perspectives pour 1997.* New York: KCSA Public Relations, 1997.

Furstenberg, G. "Teaching with Technology: What is at Stake?" *ADFL Bulletin* 28-3 (1997): 21-25.

Le Goff, C. *Le Nouveau French for Business.* Paris: Editions Didier, 1994.

Morello, J. "The Use of French in the Workplace." *The French Review* 70.6 (1997): 845-853.

WEB SITES CITED

- http://www.pagefrance.com
- http://www.info-france-usa.org
- http://www.danonegroup.com
- http://www.echange.fr/site&/emploi/ANPE/ANPEF1.html
- http://www.france.diplomatie.fr/label_france/ENGLISH/ECONOMIE/PARFUM/parfum.html
- http://www.frenchtradecgo.org/FRENCH/SECTEURS/agro/presta.htm
- http://home.dti.net/ftcny/miami/french/present.htm#presentation
- http://home.dti.net/ftcny/french/abstract/ny/biscuits.htm
- http://home.dti.net/ftcny/houston/french/present.htm#presentationPEE
- http://home.earthlink.net/~peela/french/secteurs/transpo/present.htm
- http://www.frenchtradecgo.org/FRENCH/illinois.htm
- http://www.dreeusa.org/ouest/la/french/secteurs/bienscons/

- http://www.dreeusa.org/info_us/agrisal.htm
- http://www.echange.fr/site&emploi/ANPE/ANPEF1.html
- http://www.careermosaic.tm.fe/web/career/

Notes

[1] Over the past few years, many studies, published by ASHE-ERIC *Higher Education Reports*, discuss the challenges to higher education. They emphasize the need to improve learning experiences, add experiential learning, and engage in curriculum reform to prepare students more effectively for the global community.

[2] The results showed that practice telephone interviews should be emphasized.

[3] Claude LeGoff, *Le Nouveau French for Business: Le français des affaires* (Paris: Editions Didier, 1994).

[4] Many of our alumni describe in great detail their careers, how they obtained their jobs, how their French major and their French for Business course have helped them in their careers. We list their jobs under the following categories: Arts and Communication, Social Service, Law and Government, and Business. Under the business heading alone, their job descriptions range from Travel Agent, International Trade Representative, Administrative Manager for Government Contracts, Commercial Market Representative, to Marketing Communications Manager and President of Investments. Anyone interested in our booklet can contact me at Email: asampon@Hollins.edu, or at P.O. Box 9545 Hollins College, Virginia 24020.

[5] I also encourage students to use search engines in English and to study the American job market in their specific area of interest.

203

[6] The results from Morello's survey suggests that French companies more than American companies recognize the need for employees highly skilled in French.

THE PRODUCT IS THE THING

Juanita W. Casagrande

One of the many challenges to those of us teaching a course in *Le Français des Affaires* is that of guiding students through material and topics with which they have little or no life experience. In addition to the unfamiliar technical vocabulary, there are concepts whose explanations require yet more technical vocabulary. The very necessary emphasis on vocabulary can lead students to focus excessively on the task of vocabulary acquisition. While no Business French instructor would deny how important vocabulary is in these courses, we are obliged to remind our students that vocabulary is necessary as a tool for access to a new area of knowledge but is not an end unto itself. A similar difficulty arises as regards culture. We may tell our students that understanding the culture is as important as speaking the language well, but they need to experience its importance for themselves.

Almost all of the textbooks that are commonly used in Business French courses treat one major topic per chapter. This is pedagogically sound as the students need to have the material presented in manageable units. I use Claude LeGoff's book, *Le français des affaires.* The students prepare the written exercises and oral exercises for each chapter with in-class discussions aimed at reinforcing important points and giving additional information to highlight cultural differences. All too often the students seemed to view each chapter or topic as a separate entity rather than as part of a whole. I came to believe that, in part, it was because they were concentrating on those daunting vocabulary lists and failing to see the avenues that this new area of language skill afforded them. My personal challenge was to create an activity to help the students synthesize many of the topics, while actively reinforcing vocabulary and concepts acquired in the course.

An obvious way of involving the students is to have them, as a class, create a fictitious business. This has often been suggested for this type of course. However, as most of the students are not business majors and have no thought of ever being entrepreneurs, the task does not excite them. In an average Business French class of twenty-five, the majority of students are French minors. Their major fields are journalism, business, and psychology. There are also a few French majors. But regardless of their major, they all have something of great importance in common: they are all consumers. Given the importance of peer acceptance, they even consider themselves quite informed consumers as to "what's hot" in the marketplace. It seemed to me, therefore, that the logical starting point for any synthesizing activity that would also motivate them should be the product. That is how the product project — or what students call "le grand projet"— came to be.

Each student is asked to select a product that he/she thinks would be successful in the French market. While this may seem a simple task at first glance, it is in fact the first big hurdle for the student. The choice of a product has to be approved by me before the work proceeds and, for me to approve it, the students must justify their choices on the basis of their knowledge of France and French culture. This step involves serious thought more than market research. It is indeed the quality of the student's reasoning that concerns me most at this stage. How much have they really learned about the culture? A proposal to sell American-processed cheese food because the French like cheese would indicate they haven't learned very much. On the other hand, one student's choice of a dog cushion-bed filled with western red cedar was very astute. He reasoned correctly that the large number of Parisian dog owners coupled with the space-saving advantage of this type of cushion-bed for small Parisian apartments gave his product possibilities. Every French course strives to teach cultural awareness. Yet, nowhere is it more important, nor is there a more practical application of cultural awareness, than in a course of this type.

The product chosen must be an existing product as opposed to a product that the student would invent. Inventing a product would allow the student to avoid dealing with problems that an already existing product might present. The student may choose to modify the product if those modifications can be justified on cultural grounds. An example of such a modification would be size or packaging. The student should realize the advisability of and suggest smaller sizes for refrigerated products to accommodate the typically smaller refrigerator in France.

It is preferred, although not required, that the product chosen be one that is not already on the French market. The student's first choice, then, is to find a product that is unique, or at least, out of the ordinary. In order to do that, students are encouraged to look to their own hobbies or special skills. A student who was an accomplished equestrian chose as her product a particular kind of saddle which was becoming popular in horse show circles but was made only in the southwestern United States. Having chosen a product with which she had familiarity in English, she was more interested in the outcome and better able to deal with the translation of a description of the product.

The product has to be American-made as the student will be playing the role of an employee of an American company that is hoping to expand its sales and enter the international market. The company has hired this person with expertise in French language and culture precisely because it recognizes the need for this expertise. Since many students do hope eventually to work in an international environment, this idea seems plausible and they see possibilities in their task. Also, by this point in the semester, students have done a fairly detailed study of marketing in *Commerce et Marketing* (Schmitt et Brillié Lutz). Some students get so enthused that they write or call the American company to get more precise information about the product.

Once this task is completed, the students are ready to start formalizing their work. Each step in the project requires the student to use technical vocabulary, business documents, and written French in a meaningful context. The vocabulary the student has struggled with now has a utilitarian purpose. The parts of the project are:

1. un rapport
2. une brochure
3. une fiche
4. une lettre
5. une présentation orale

The four written parts of the project have to be turned in together in a folder following the oral presentation, which takes place at the end of the semester.

Le rapport. This is an internal document that is longer than most and is submitted to a higher-up in the company. It is defined by Girault and Nony as "un texte dans lequel, après avoir analysé des faits, une situation, une documentation, on formule des propositions; ainsi le rapport donne des informations puis propose des solutions; il prépare les décisions des responsables" (p. 351, *Situations et Techniques Commerciales*). The student, as an imaginary employee, must prepare such a document concerning the product proposed for launching onto the French marketplace for his/her supervisor. The student's "rapport" must address product choice, the targeted market, transportation and distribution, and publicity.

Under product choice, the student must justify to his employer (as he has previously done to me) why French consumers will accept this particular product. Knowledge of the culture is paramount and the student may give reasons based on purchasing power of the French consumers, lifestyle, resources of the country, etc. A name for the product must be proposed. The students must confront the translation issue. Is the name suitable if left in English? Will direct translation work or must a new name be created for the product? One student's effort at translating "Handi-Vac" went first to "Aspirateur Commode." Realizing that this was not as descriptive as the English, he created "Aspirevite." This part of the exercise affords another opportunity to point out the importance of avoiding pitfalls of translation where "lavement" was incorrectly used in "lavage d'auto."

The student must also propose which consumer group to target. Will it be young adults nationwide, only city-dwelling young adults, or older consumers in the *Midi*? The student's knowledge of climate and demographics plays a role here. Most students need to refer to maps or review information on the economic regions.

The students have previously studied "les moyens de transport et les canaux de distribution." Their task in the "rapport" includes proposing what means of transportation will be the best and most economical based on the qualities and nature of their product. Heavy and bulky could call for maritime transportation as opposed to air transport for something fragile and lightweight. They must also recommend whether an intermediary such as a "grossiste" should be involved or, perhaps, suggest a type of retail outlet to which they could sell directly. The students are expected to be very specific in their proposed transportation, e.g., ship to Le Havre and truck to Paris.

Since culture plays an important role in advertising, the student must propose what tack to take regarding promotion of the product to the French consumer. At least one advertisement that is as French as possible must be proposed and recommendations for the "supports publicitaires" that would best reach the targeted consumers. Students are asked to be mindful of the fact that there is a budget for publicity, and television is not the only medium available. In order to get ideas as how to best reach their targeted consumer group, they may find it necessary to use the library to look through French newspapers and magazines. In this way, many students discover French publications with which they were unfamiliar before starting the project. "Une affiche publicitaire" is not a requirement, but some students enjoy the challenge of creating one to promote their product. A young lady who had spent a few months in France as an *au pair* was convinced that French children would be attracted to Pop-Tarts by her poster featuring "Pop, le pingouin et Tartie, la tortue."

All of the information which goes into the "rapport" must be written in French even though the student is playing the role of an employee of an American company. The students easily overlook this bit of lack of logic. Creating this business document is another opportunity for them to put into practice what they have learned about written business communication. As befits this type of document, the tone must remain impersonal and the style "soigné."

La brochure. The brochure gives the student the opportunity to be creative and imaginative while continuing to work on task. The brochure is usually a single- or double-folded page which contains a picture (or pictures) of the product and a detailed description of the product, which boasts of its quality and uses. It is consumer-oriented and requires the student to weigh cultural considerations. The quality of pictures or artwork varies depending on the artistic ability of each student but students are made to understand that this is of much less importance than the overall planning of the brochure. A student who enjoyed camping selected as his product a lightweight, folding chair suitable for camping and picnics. His "Conforchaise" was pictured beside a small Renault at a roadside picnic and in an obviously Alpine setting. His written message touted the ease of portability and storage.

La fiche. This document (p. 60, *Le Français du Secrétariat Commercial*) provides in a very concise manner some general sales conditions. Although it might not be particularly appropriate to the method of distribution suggested by the student in the "rapport," it is nonetheless a good exercise for making the student reflect on other important issues such as pricing and packaging. The fiche contains the following information:

1. What will be the product name and general description?
2. What will be the presentation for retail sale: in a box, a plastic bag, or hanging bag?
3. How will it be shipped — by a crate of ten, or a box of twenty-five? Who pays shipping charges?

4. What will be the minimum shipment?

5. What will be the delivery time — within one week, two weeks?

6. What will be the price? The establishment of a "tarif degressif" is encouraged.

La lettre. An excellent way to make a new product known is to exhibit it at a trade show. Each student must write a letter to a Paris address provided by me and ask to participate in the appropriate show, "Salon du Jouet," "Salon du Livre," etc. They must also specify the size of booth that they will need and request information on special services such as telephone and/or Internet accessibility. Finally, they must discuss the manner of payment of the rental fee.

In order for the students to feel confident about their work, it is important that they have early feedback. Each student is required to turn in his/her notes on the contents of the "rapport" about four weeks before the due date of the project. That allows the instructor to determine who, if anyone, is not on the right track. Notes returned with comments are very helpful to the students.

La présentation orale. Before the student turns in all the written parts of the project, an oral presentation is made to the class. The students in the class now assume the role of buyers and receive prepared forms to help them make their choices. The forms ask for their comments on what they think market potential for this product is and if the market segment targeted is appropriate; how well the proposed publicity has been adapted to the French market; and if they themselves would or would not buy the product and why. It is impressed upon all the students that classmate comments have no bearing on the grade received for the project. This exercise requires the students to use once again their acquired skills and allows them to satisfy their natural curiosity as to how other students have approached the task. In their roles as fictitious buyers, the students are allowed to ask questions of each presenter. This is another way of engaging the whole class in what would otherwise be an individual task.

While "le grand projet" is currently used in a two-semester sequence at the third-year level, it can and has been used in the more typical one-semester program. Our department added a second semester of Business French to our curriculum only recently. I used the project several times before the recent addition of the second semester.

The project can be limited or expanded to suit time constraints and the level of the students. The additional classroom time allowed me to add the oral presentation component. Students in past semesters had expressed a desire to see and learn from their classmates' work, but this activity had to be limited to one class period in which all the projects were displayed. Students would circulate in the classroom to look at them but there was not enough time to read each one or ask questions of the author.

As stated earlier, students are not allowed to invent a product for this project. However, we do use product creation as a class-wide exercise, as it prepares the students for the larger project and has been found especially valuable in a one-semester course. Students propose ideas for a new product and the class as a whole selects one. The class is divided into groups and each group is charged with tasks related to the larger project. The instructor reviews pertinent material already covered or supplies information not yet covered in the course. A subsequent class period devoted to discussion of each group's work orients the students to what they will be expected to do individually later in the course.

What I have variously described as an activity, or a project, assumes the mantle of methodology. The task is described in detail to the students early in the course. From that point on, the instructor can orient the course to suit the task. Students readily accept this and it becomes a very positive learning experience. Student evaluations bear this out as does improved performance on the cumulative final exam. Students feel that they have acquired practical knowledge that goes beyond the Business French course. A majority also feel that while a lot of work goes into the project, its completion gives them confidence in their ability to apply what has been learned in the course. Due to the multi-part make up of the project, each student also feels that there is at least one part that they can do particularly well. The journalism major with a concentration in advertising relishes preparing the publicity, the computer major loves doing computer graphics on the brochure and making attractive letterhead, the psychology major likes to emphasize the role that psychological needs play in marketing.

One last example will perhaps serve to illustrate what can be accomplished by using this activity. A student chose as his product an air filter. Readings on the concentration of industries in the Paris area and air pollution problems had piqued his interest. The air filter is made in table top and window models. In his "rapport," he proposed selling only the table top models initially because the window unit would not fit the typical French window. He pointed out the practicality of exporting only the dual-voltage models and providing an adapter for the plug. The theme he created for the advertisement was repeated on the brochure: "C'est un travail d'Hercule de protéger votre famille de la pollution!" And how better to symbolize this on the brochure than Hercules fighting off the Hydra of pollution with a HEPA filter as his sword?

WORKS CITED

Dany, M., Geliot, J., Parizet, M.L., Grand-Clément, F. *Le français du secrétariat commercial.* Paris: Librairie Hachette, 1977.

Girault, O. and Nony, D. *Situations et Techniques Commerciales.* Paris: Foucher/Hatier International, 1987.

LeGoff, C., *Le Nouveau French for Business: Le Français des Affaires.* Paris: Hatier/Didier, 1994.

Schmitt, Conrad J., Brillié, Lutz, K. *Commerce et marketing.* New York: McGraw-Hill, Inc., 1992.

Ricks, David. *Blunders in International Business.* Cambridge: Blackwell Business, 1993.

TEN TIPS FOR THE
FIRST-TIME BUSINESS FRENCH TEACHER

E. Nicole Meyer

While much has been written about teaching business foreign language courses, including specific rationales, techniques, exercises, and even textbook choice (Bousquet 1993, Elton 1990, LeGoff 1982)[1] as well as on teaching effectiveness in general (Eison 1990, Weimer 1990)[2], there has been no article specifically designed to help new instructors face the business foreign language class. The following ten suggestions should help you — the first-time or perhaps continuing business foreign language teacher — design and teach an effective and enjoyable class. I would encourage you to consider your goals for teaching a business foreign language course as well as those of the students enrolled in your course. Only then can you design a course that achieves these goals.

Tip #1: Examine why you want to teach this course.

The answers to the question of why you wish to teach this course may vary widely and may diverge sharply from those of an administrator. What is certain is that the number of Business French courses have increased. Many professors of these courses, however, come to them indirectly. For this reason, a Flaubert scholar such as myself might be responsible for a less than familiar area of the curriculum. I recommend doing as I did, that is, to welcome the challenge of teaching a new subject and to go about it in a practical way.

You may be nervous. Remember, however, that you are, I assume, already a good teacher. Carl E. Schorske perhaps states the "test of a good teacher" best:

> Do you regard 'learning' as a noun or a verb? If as a noun, as a thing to be possessed and passed along, then you present your truths neatly packaged to your students. But, if you see 'learning' as a verb, the process is different. The good teacher has knowledge, but tries to instill in students the desire to learn, and demonstrates the ways one goes about 'learning' (cited in McCleery, 106).

While a business foreign language course involves the learning of a great deal of technical vocabulary, the goal of the course should be to teach students to understand the "concepts that underlie the words," (LeGoff 1987, 143) and, more importantly, to *function* in the business context. Students need *cultural* knowledge to survive in the increasingly global business world.[3] This translates into both the specific ability to read high-level business documents such as faxes and financial reports and the general familiarity with general cultural practices of the target areas. Basic subject matter such as economics must be studied in relation to the particular target areas studied. Since French cultural practices differ according to the region in question (e.g., Sénégal vs. France), the teacher will need to reflect this diversity when discussing banking, export, import, sales, correspondence, transportation, etc.[4] Patricia Cholokian notes that our business foreign language courses should emphasize the development of communication skills (666-71). Christine Uber-Grosse and Geoffrey Voght concur, noting that the United States lacks "citizens in many specializations who can communicate effeitively in foreign languages and understand other cultures and value systems" (Uber-Grosse & Voght 1991, 184). The desire to incorporate global perspectives into higher education infuses many of our courses.

Once you have set your goals, be sure to clearly state some or all of them on your syllabus (see Browne 81-2). Tests and assignments should correspond to your goals. If they do not do so your students may become frustrated. This leads us to the second tip.

Tip #2: Examine why the student would want to take your course.

Cross and Angelo make the excellent suggestion of requesting that students make their goals explicit (91). I do this on the first day of any course and also make assignments that students can tailor to their needs (for instance the business research paper that I mention below). Such goal assessment should be a continuous process.

While student goals may very well coincide with our own, they are often articulated from a different perspective. Goretsky, LeGoff, Strand, Walker, Woloshin and many others have stated a primary motivation for students: to do well in their [first] job. To do this, students need to develop certain skills. They must be able to comprehend and communicate in an active and spontaneous manner[5] both with their employers and with their foreign contacts.[6] In order to facilitate this active communication the student and potential employee must acquire "the abilities to conceptualize, organize, and verbalize thoughts, resolve conflicts, and work in teams" as these skills are critical to a firm wishing to remain competitive, according to Carnevale, Gainer and Meltzer (7-8). In other words, students must learn how to *perform* their job, not merely be able to furnish a list of vocabulary or memorized phrases.

Opportunities must be created for students to practice using the language in a variety of appropriate contexts (see Omaggio, 51). Context must never be omitted as "it is not only *how* to say it, but also when and why and what to expect in reply" that counts (Jeffries 1). The teacher must target the students' goals in designing her course. She can do this according to the model developed by Van Ek and cited by Strand (670). The teacher recreates the situation in which the language would be used, develops activities in which the learners expect to engage, prioritizes the language functions which the learners are to fulfill, and aims at achieving a general skill level among the students. This can be done in many ways (see tip #4). I would like to stress here, nonetheless, that there is no point in reevaluating your and your students' goals if you do not follow through with appropriate activities. I designed the business research paper and corresponding exercises that I discuss elsewhere (Meyer 1995) in response to the goals that I established for my course. Similar class projects become learning experiences that help the student progress in their careers and can be described to business recruiters (Goretsky 34).

Tip #3: Enter each class with specific education goals and objectives.

This tip is self-explanatory. I would like to urge you, however, to be flexible and not too ambitious.

Tip # 4: Read to learn about the topic and also to find interesting exercises.

I recommend that you read the articles cited above. Many explain the rationales for course design, specific techniques and exercises. The previous volume in this series (Cummins 1995) also provides ample suggestions. Relevant cultural and Business French articles appear regularly in *French Review*, *Foreign Language Annals*, *French For Business and International Trade*, *The Modern Language Journal* and *The Journal of Language for International Business*. In reading about other approaches you may feel encouraged to innovate on your own. These journals can also help you learn of changes in the European economy (e.g., the state of the European Union).

While there is no perfect textbook available, there are many to consult. In so doing, you will begin designing your own course and revising your goals. I highly recommend that you consider the videos and CD-ROMs available (see Tip #8). There are many videos available that show general aspects of culture and provide an opportunity for the instructor to show how business infiltrates many aspects of our life. *French For Business and International Trade* and *French Review* provide reviews of these and many more. I enjoy looking at Commercial Spanish and Commercial German materials as well. *Exito Commercial* and *Deutsche Wirtschaftssprache für Amerikaner* are two popular texts.[7]

Current business journals in French such as *Nouvel Economiste, L'Expansion, Capital, L'Essentiel du Management* and *L'Entreprise* contain current articles on the economy, employment practices, marketing, technology, and specific case studies as well as interviews with business leaders. *Le Point* and *L'Express* can help you keep up with the latest developments. I will return to the use of such journals for teaching purposes under tip #8.

Your local newspaper can inform you of which local businesses operate globally.

And, last, but certainly not least, I recommend that all teachers continue to read about general teaching approaches that interest them. Articles that discuss active learning (e.g., those of Bonwell, Eison, McKeachie, Sheils and Friedrich), communicative language teaching, and proficiency-oriented approaches may help you make your Business French course more lively and effective.

Tip #5: Discover the outside sources that exist in your community.

Community experts bring real world concerns into the classroom (see Lance 1987 and Watts 1992). Visitors from a wide variety of industries and professions have lectured to my students. Farm machinery, paper machinery, paper-product producers, automated techonologies, translation, dairy industry, electrical products, printing, transportation and insurance, the fields most frequently represented in my classroom, reflect the community's international workforce. In addition to showing the wide variety of career opportunities available to students, these community experts can share a lot of information on how to attain similar jobs, what to do when actually working, and what problems they face daily. Most stress the difficulty and importance of communicating with others, whether face-to-face or through correspondence. They advise the students to travel to the target countries and learn as much about the culture (and language) as possible. The visitors also help students establish realistic expectations, for instance, of job availability and job mobility.

Site visits complement these classroom discussions. In addition, as they are conducted in the target language, students *see* their classroom learning in action. I select the particular site visits based on several criteria. In addition to the linguistic requirement of having a French native lead the visit, the companies must deal internationally and represent various aspects of business (e.g., marketing, production, sales, exports, pricing, financing and distribution). When I teach in Green Bay, the national sales director, a French native, gave us a thorough tour of an international award-winning cheese factory. In Milwaukee, another French native, the CEO of Froedert Malt, gave a marvelous tour explaining the agricultural process, specific business decisions and the international malt market. He also explained his career path and future plans. When I taught a course in Paris, the choice of businesses for site visits was large. I chose the leading cable TV station in Paris and the testing center of a major car producer because both businesses were international and very visual, which maintains the interest of the less linguistically able students. While I discovered these four companies through personal contacts, the Wisconsin World Trade Center, the Wisconsin Department of Commerce, the phone book, the Alliance Française or the closest consulate can offer suggestions. These resources can also help you to set up student internships by providing lists of French firms.[8]

The short student business research paper emphasizes resources that can be pursued easily by letter, phone call or e-mail. Topics vary greatly but include possible careers and job opportunities, further educational opportunities, presentations on international marketing and its cultural implications, interviews with successful business entrepreneurs and how to use the Internet to access further resources.[9] Each student chooses a topic and focuses his or her paper on providing actual contacts and resources. He or she receives copies of the entire class's papers in booklet form. In this way, they produce a secondary course text that should serve them in the future.

Students learn how to find resources, organize, and then present them in useful fashion to their peers. They learn problem-solving skills, how to get things done quickly, establish actual contacts, obtain results and feedback and get the satisfaction of completing a project. Teacher and student roles are expanded. The teacher functions as resource, facilitator, stimulator, and adviser, while the student enjoys greater independence from the teacher and becomes responsible for his or her own intellectual development.

Tip #6: Select a text that fits your purpose and personality.

Choose your textbook to fit your own goals. My personal strategy is to promote the active learning of the integrated skills of the business world. The active learning of integrated skills that I propose combines "active learning" (Bonwell and Eison 1991) and "communicative" language teaching (Jeffries 1986) with proficiency-oriented goals (Magnan 1986, 429). Thus, my ideal textbook promotes student responsibility and autonomy, in part by urging the students to create the "knowledge" that is learned (Johnson et al. 1991). I design student activities that engage students in meaningful and realistic activities that develop creative thinking skills. My course is interactive in nature and prioritizes a skill-based rather than knowledge-based approach.

Unfortunately, current textbooks neglect both my integrated skills-based methods and the multicultural realities of the Francophone business world. I choose to supplement heavily (over 300 pages of additional handouts). For a beginning teacher, however, this is unrealistic. I suggest that you consider the popular textbook of Claude LeGoff (*French for Business*) or those of Michel Danilo.

Tip #7: Become more knowledgeable through workshops, seminars and conference attendance.

The Eastern Michigan University Conference on Languages for Business and the Professions has always been very useful for foreign business language teachers to meet and share ideas. If it resumes, I highly recommend attending at least once. The American Association of Teachers of French annual conference and the American Council of Teachers of Foreign Languages annual meeting frequently feature Business Foreign Language sessions. Your regional CIBER or Bureau de Coopération Linguistique et Educative (of the Consulat Général de France) often arrange "Stages Pédagogiques Régionaux." Various Chambres de Commerce (e.g., those of Paris, Strasbourg or Grenoble) offer scholarships to attend a variety of seminars.

Tip #8: Supplement your text with realia and visual aids.

I find Claude Le Ninan's video "Le Français des affaires" and support materials to be quite useful in providing vivid case studies that help explain marketing and other concepts. The case studies feature a large variety of authentic companies dealing with realistic situations, and the workbook has some excellent exercises. "Attention à la démarche!" is a series of three videos produced in France and available through PICS.

Students can see actual job interviews and discussions by personnel directors of what they desire in a résumé or candidate. Hinshaw's "Radishes & Butter," available through Schoenhof's Books, deals with similar topics. CD-ROMs, such as "A la Recherche d'un emploi" and "L'Acte de vente," provide authentic materials as well.

There are multiple ways of using realia and visual aids to create interactive exercises. Some examples of active-learning exercises that I enjoy include the following:

A sorting exercise (a fun and active way to learn about marketing and its various methods) involves distributing various examples of catalogues, brochures, *dépliants*, *prospectus* and *circulaires* to the students who then group with students with like materials. They must justify their choice of term for what they are holding in their hands.

Given quite a few examples of *formules d'attaques*, the students categorize them according to the purpose of the letter, e.g., a thank you letter, an order letter, etc. This exercise can provide the occasion to discuss the different situations and letters that require such opening phrases, in other words, to introduce students to broader cultural information.

Students use my actual correspondence to reply to the sender or simply analyze the letter(s).

Several business magazines contain useful material to supplement such activities. For instance, *L'Essentiel du management* of September 1997 includes a section on recruiting candidates with sample curriculum vitae, employee questionnaires, and another with thirty-five models of letters related to dealing with the Administration ("Comment vous défendre face à l'administration").

Students learn to write business letters by doing small-group role-playing exercises, e.g., a client writes to a bank to report a change of address or a student requests information on internships. I keep a variety of French correspondence to provide models for these activities.

My French checkbook, banking receipts, etc., provide ideas and props for role-play activities as well. Students change traveler's checks, open an account and reenact other realistic situations.

Many different lists of international businesses exist as resources for information. Students can use them to request information or investigate job possibilities or invite speakers to class. Similarly the *Sources d'information et de documentation,* available from the Chambre de Commerce et d'Industrie de Paris, lists a large number of resources. I distribute the list and ask the students to pick a company listed and write or fax them for information that they may share with their peers. The *Pages du soleil* (Paris Yellow Pages) can be used to role-play, to order items, write complaints or inquire about products. Many pair activities can be devised.

Catalogues from a variety of Francophone countries can also provide ample material for active exercises. For instance, a catalogue of resources available from the business school of Chicoutimi lists a number of books that contain a plethora of resources, such as the *Bottin international du Québec.* Students can either order these bulletins or go one step further and order directly from the company. The catalogue itself contains a great deal vocabulary (*sociétés, multinationales, informatisées, format, logiciel, frais de port,* etc.) that can be learned in a more *active* manner by using authentic material. Receipts, which I save from my travels, reveal both general cultural distinctions (e.g., between Bénin and France) and specific business differences (individual restaurant receipt vs. wholesale order).

The June or July issues of French business magazines contain announcements of *rapports annuels.* I do a circulation activity in which students search for their "partner" who has the same company's *rapport annuel* announcement. They ask each other questions, without naming the company, in order to determine who has the same announcement. They then answer questions, either furnished by me or by another group, and compare and contrast reports to see if they have similar information or ways of expressing information. Such exercises are much more effective for learning vocabulary such as *l'effectif, CA, activité d'une entreprise.*

The subscription forms from magazines can be used to learn about marketing. The students each get one and then we compare and contrast them (some have different vocabulary, or offer different *cadeaux* when you subscribe). Canadian forms should be used as well as they differ somewhat. Students practice filling in a variety of such forms (e.g., order forms, credit card applications).

Using want ads from journals and newspapers, small groups form companies chosen from the ads, and then "interview" candidates. I build up to this by completing exercises from LeGoff and especially from Danilo's *Français de l'entreprise.* Advertisements promote lively discussions on marketing.

When I get a postal package from a French-speaking country, I bring it into class and we open it up while I ask questions about how can we tell where it comes from or about the contents, etc.

Guest speakers foster discussion and provide female business role models (see Tip # 5).

Cassette tapes or videos of news broadcasts, interviews, etc., can improve listening skills.

There are bountiful possibilities for interactive learning in an appropriate cultural context on the following Webpages:

Our home page:
http://www.uwgb.edu/~modlang/french/FRLINKS.htm

Janice Paulsen:

http://www.urich.edu/~jpaulsen/ecolecom.html

Gilles Bousquet:
http://polyglot.lss.wisc.edu/frit/affaires/Affaires2.html

Tennessee Bob:
http://www.utm.edu/departments/french/french.html

Africa Online:
http://www.africaonline.co.ci/AfricaOnline/coverbusiness.html

Students are particularly good at suggesting useful Internet addresses and resources as well.

All of these activities share the same assumption: people learn best when they are actively involved in the learning process. The activities encourage small-group work that also enables students to participate fully while developing high-level thinking skills. The use of realia motivates the students while teaching real-life business activities and vocabulary.

Tip #9: Share your knowledge with someone else. Maybe they'll have some creative ideas to share with you.

When you share your knowledge with others, you often learn from them. Their feedback can help you improve your teaching (Eison 1990) and their interest helps motivate you to increase your knowledge.

Tip #10: Be relaxed about admitting when you don't know something.

You'll learn each time you teach the course and you can incorporate changes.

Conclusion

My ten suggestions are designed to help a teacher inaugurate or improve the business foreign language course. They share at their core the careful consideration of teacher and student goals, thorough teacher preparation (both of methods and materials), and the instruction of students on how to *function* in a realistic business context through the active-learning of integrated skills (e.g., using community experts, site visits, internships, class projects and recreating realistic situations with authentic documents). The Business French course is a cultural course which should reflect the diversity of the Francophone business world. Sharing knowledge with others and admitting your own weaknesses will help you learn more. Any teacher who gives systematic thought to his or her courses can only become a better teacher.

WORKS CITED

Allwright, R. L. "The Importance of Interaction in Classroom Language Learning." *Applied Linguistics* 5.2 (1984): 156-171.

Bonwell, Charles C. and James A. Eison. *Active Learning: Creating Excitement in the Classroom*. ASHE-ERIC Higher Education Report, No. 1. Washington, DC: The George Washington University, School of Education and Human Development, 1991.

Bousquet, G. "Integrating Business, Technology and Area Studies for a New Era of Euro-American Business Relations: a Case-Study in Interdisciplinary Curriculum." pp. 5-11 in Nzegwu, L. I., ed. *Implementing Cultural and Language Awareness into International Business Curriculum*. Platteville, WI: University of Wisconsin — Platteville, 1997.

_____. "Vers une culture des affaires? Mentalités, comportements, représentations dans la classe de français commercial." *French Review* 66.6 (May 1993): 908-918.

Brod, Richard I. "Careers and the Foreign Language Department." *ADFL Bulletin* 6.2 (1975): 16-22.

Browne, M. Neil and Stuart M. Keely. "Achieving Excellence: Advice to New Teachers." *College Teaching* 33.2 (1985): 78-83.

Byrnes, Heidi. "Second Language Acquisition: Insights from a Proficiency Orientation," pp. 107-31 in Byrnes, Heidi and Michael Canale, eds., *Defining and Developing Proficiency: Guidelines, Implementations, and Concepts.* The ACTFL Foreign Language Education Series. Lincolnwood, IL: National Textbook Co., 1987.

Cannon, Emilie Teresa. "Commercial, Legal and Medical Spanish." *Foreign Language Annals* 16.3 (1983): 213-215.

Caré, Jean-Marc and Christian Richard. "Jouer, improviser." *Le Français dans le monde.* 204 (1986): 52-57.

Carnevale, A. P., Gainer, L. J. and Meltzer, A. S. *Workplace Basics. The Skills Employers Want.* Alexandria, VA: American Society for Training and Development and US Department of Labor Employment and Training Administration, 1988.

Carney, William J. "Integrating Commercial French into the Traditional Foreign Language Curriculum: A Marriage of Convenience that Works." *ADFL Bulletin* 17.2 (January 1986): 43-49.

Cholakian, Patricia F. "Commercial French: An Opportunity for Innovative Classroom Techniques." *French Review* 54 (1981): 666-71.

Conlin, C. *Unternehmen Deutsch.* St. Paul, MN: EMC Paradigm, 1995.

Crane, Robert and Kitzie McKinney. "Langues, culture, et le cursus des études de commerce: Europe — Amérique du nord." *French Review* 60.1 (Oct 1986): 71-78.

Cross, K. Patricia and Thomas A. Angelo. *Classroom Assessment Techniques: A Handbook for Faculty.* 2nd ed. Ann Arbor, MI:

National Center for Research to Improve Postsecondary Teaching and Learning, 1988.

Cummins, P. W., ed. *Issues and Methods in French for Business and Economic Purposes*. Dubuque, Iowa: Kendall/Hunt Publishing, 1995.

Danilo, Michel and Béatrice Tauzin. *Le Français de l'entreprise*. Paris: Clé International, 1990.

Doyle, M., B. Fryer and R. Cere. *Exito Commercial*. Holt, Rhinehart and Winston, 1997.

Dugan, J. S. "Rationale for Broadening the Perspectives of Business French Programs." *French Review* 57.3 (February 1984): 356-65.

Eison, James. "From the Reference Desk: Texts on College Teaching." *Journal of Staff, Program, and Organization Development* 5.3 (1987): 131-133.

_____. "Designing Effective Peer Observation Programs." *Journal of Staff, Program and Organization Development* 6.3 (1988): 51-59.

_____. "Confidence in the Classroom: Ten Maxims for New Teachers." *College Teaching* 38.1 (1990): 21-25.

_____ and G. Hoover. *Using Student Feedback to Improve Classroom Instruction*. Cape Girardeau, Missouri: Southeast Missouri State University, Center for Teaching and Learning, 1989.

Elton, Maurice G. A. "French For Business Bibliography." *French Review* 64.1 (October 1990): 119-122.

Finel-Honigman, Irène. "Rationale, Structure and Methodology of a French Language Program for American Bankers and Traders." *Foreign Language Annals* 19.1 (1986): 27-31.

Forti-Lewis, Angelica. "Facing the Challenge: Teaching a Business Course in Italian." *Italica* 666.1 (Spring 1989): 1-2.

Fuller, Carol S. "Language-Oriented Careers in the Federal Government." *ADFL Bulletin* 6 (September 1974): 45-51.

Gerulaitis, R. "Essential Cultural Information in German Business Courses, and Suggestions for Teaching it." *Die Unterrichtspraxis* 19 (1986): 41-48.

Gill, June M. "Québec — Resources for French for Business." *French for Business and International Trade* 8.1/2 (Winter/Spring 1993): 1-2.

Gleason, Maryellen. "Ten Best on Teaching: A Bibliography of Essential Sources for Instructors." *Improving College and University Teaching* 32.1 (Winter 1984): 11-13.

_____. "Ten Best on Learning: A Bibliography of Essential Sources for Instructors." *College Teaching* 33.1 (Winter 1985): 8-10.

Goretsky, M. Edward "Class Projects as a Form of Instruction." *Journal of Marketing Education* 6 (Fall 1984): 33-37.

Herman, Gerald "Teaching the Skills of French Business Correspondence to American Undergraduates: Problems and Techniques." *French Review* 61.1 (October 1987): 12-20.

Higgs, Theodore V. "Foreword" and "Language Teaching and the Quest for the Holy Grail," p. v and pp. 1-9 in Theodore V. Higgs, ed., *Teaching for Proficiency, the Organizing Principle.* ACTFL Foreign Language Education Series. Lincolnwood, IL: National Textbook Co., 1984.

Hoegl, Juergen K. "Education for the World System: The Demand for Language and International Proficiencies in Economic Development and National Security." *Foreign Language Annals* 19 (1986): 281-287.

Honig, L. J. and Brod, R. I. *Foreign Languages and Careers.* New York: MLA, 1979.

Inman, Marianne. "Foreign Languages and the US Multinational Corporation." *Modern Language Journal* 64.1 (Spring 1980): 64-74.

_____. "Language and Cross-Cultural Training in American Multinational Corporations." *Modern Language Journal* 69.3 (1985): 247-255.

Jeffries, Sophie. "The Teacher in the Communicative Curriculum." New York State Association of Foreign Language Teachers *Language Association Bulletin* 38.1 (September 1986): 1, 3-5.

Johnson, D. W., Johnson, R. T., and Smith, K. A. *Active Learning. Cooperation in the College Classroom.* Edina, MN: Interaction Book Company, 1991.

Lance, L. M. "Variety in Teaching Human Sexuality: Involvement of Community Experts and Guests." *Teaching Sociology* 15.3 (1987): 312-315.

LeGoff, Claude "Pour une pédagogie de la correspondance d'affaires." *French Review* 56.2 (December 1982): 241-49.

_____. "Teaching French for Business." pp. 143-151 in Spencer, S. I. *Foreign Languages and International Trade: A Global Perspective.* Athens, GA: The University of Georgia Press, 1987.

Magnan, Sally S. "Assessing Speaking Proficiency in the Undergraduate Curriculum: Data from French." *Foreign Language Annals* 19.5 (1986): 429-438.

McCleery, William. *Conversations on the Character of Princeton.* Princeton, NJ: Princeton University Press, 1986.

McKeachie, Wilbert J., Paul R. Pintrich, Yi-Guang Lin, and David A. F. Smith. *Teaching and Learning in the College Classroom: A Review of the Research Literature.* 2nd ed. Ann Arbor: Regents of the University of Michigan, 1990.

Merrifield, Doris F. *Deutsche Wirtschaftssprache für Americkaner.* 3rd ed. New York: John Wiley & Sons, 1994.

Meyer, E. Nicole "Active-Learning Approaches to the Business French Course. The Business French Research Paper." *Foreign Language Annals* 28.1 (Spring 1995): 135-146.

_____. "Integrating Business Foreign Language into the International Business Program" pp. 47-55 in Nzegwu, L. I., ed. *Implementing Cultural and Language Awareness into International Business Curriculum.* Platteville, WI: University of Wisconsin — Platteville, 1997.

Michael, Colette Verger. "L'Enseignement du français commercial et ses problèmes." *French Review* 55.1 (October 1981): 17-26.

Omaggio, A. C. "The Proficiency-Oriented Classroom." pp. 43-84 in Higgs, T. V. (Ed.). *Teaching for Proficiency, the Organizing Principle.* Lincolnwood, IL: National Textbook Co., 1984.

Paulsell, P. R. "The Importance and Implementation of a Business Foreign Language Overseas Internship Program." *Foreign Language Annals* 16.4 (1983): 277-286.

Rusterholz, B. L. "Reading Strategies for the Business Foreign Language Class." *Foreign Language Annals* 20.5 (1987): 427-433.

_____. "Developing Oral Proficiency in the Business French Class." *French Review* 64.2 (December 1990): 253-260.

Saito, Y. "Assessing Perceived Needs for Japanese Language Training in US Business Education: Perspectives from Students, Business Faculty and Business Professionals." *Foreign Language Annals* 28.1 (Spring 1995): 103-115.

Scaglione, J. "Cooperative Learning Strategies in the Business Education Curriculum." *Business Education Forum* 46 (April 1992): 15-17.

Sheils, J. *Communication in the Modern Languages Classroom.* Strasbourg: Council of Europe, Council for Cultural Cooperation, 1988.

Simon, P. (1987) "Teaching Foreign Languages. Policy and the Federal Role." pp. 23-28 in Birckbichler, D.W. (Ed.). *Proficiency, Policy, and Professionalism in Foreign Language Education.* Lincolnwood, IL: National Textbook Co.

Spinelli, E. "Principles, Content and Activities for the Foreign Language Business Curriculum." *The Journal of Language for International Business* 2 (1985): 1-11.

Strand, D. "French for Field Work: A Specific Purpose Language Course." *French Review* 57.5 (April 1984): 669-74.

Strasheim, Lorraine A. "Proficiency in the 'Real World' of the Professional Classroom Teacher," pp. 29-42 in Birckbichler, Diane W. (ed.) *Proficiency, Policy, and Professionalism in Foreign Language Education.* Lincolnwood, IL: National Textbook Co., 1987.

Uber-Grosse, Christine. "Attitudes toward Languages for Business at Two South Florida Universities." *Foreign Language Annals* 16.6 (1983): 449-453.

_____. "A Survey of Foreign Languages for Business and the Professions at US Colleges and Universities." *The Modern Language Journal* 69.3 (1985): 221-226.

_____. and Geoffrey M. Voght. "Foreign Languages for Business and the Professions at US Colleges and Universities." *Modern Language Journal* 74.1 (1990): 36-47.

_____. and Geoffrey M. Voght. "The Evolution of Languages for Specific Purposes in the United States." *The Modern Language Journal* 75.2 (1991): 181-195.

Voght, Geoffrey M. "Commercial Spanish at Eastern Michigan University" pp. 71-81 in Garfinkel, A. (Ed.). *ESL and the Foreign Language Teacher*. Report of the Central States Conference on the Teaching of Foreign Languages. Lincolnwood, IL: National Textbook Co., 1982.

Walker, L. "Commercial Language Course: Supply and Demand." *The Journal of Language for International Business* 2 (1985): 17-21.

Watts, Françoise. "The Art of French Business Letter Writing: Our Modern Form of *'Préciosité'*." *Foreign Language Annals* 26.2 (Summer 1993): 180-187.

_____. "The Cultural Implications of International Business: Three French Experiments in the United States and Their Classroom Dimension." pp. 237-242 in Voght, G. M. and Schaub, R. (Eds.). *Languages and Cultures for Business and the Professions*. Ypsilanti, MI: Eastern Michigan University, 1992.

Weimer, Maryellen G. "Study Your Way to Better Teaching." 117-130 in Marilla D. Svinicki, ed. *The Changing Face of Teaching*. New Directions for Teaching and Learning No. 42. San Francisco: Jossey-Bass, 1990.

Woloshin, David J. "The Undergraduate Curriculum: The Best and the Worst." *Modern Language Journal* 67 (1983): 356-64.

Notes

[1] Other relevant articles include: Caré and Richard 1986, Carney 1986, Crane and McKinney 1986, Dugan 1984, Finel-Honigman 1986, Forti-Lewis 1989, Fuller 1974, Grosse 1983, 1985, Grosse and Voght 1990, 1991, Herman 1987, Hoegl 1986, Inman 1980, 1985, LeGoff 1987, Michael 1981, Paulsell 1983, Rusterholz 1987, 1990, Scaglione 1992, Spinelli 1985, Voght 1982, Watts 1992, 1993.

[2] See also Allwright 1984, Browne and Keely 1985, Eison 1987, 1988, 1989, Gleason 1984, 1985, Weimer 1987, 1988, 1989.

[3] See Meyer 1997 and Bousquet 1997 on the increased globalization of business practices. Kramsch, Tsongas, Carney and others stress the necessity that our course curriculum respond to economic pressures facing the United States. This response includes the creation of Language for Specific Purposes courses.

[4] Dugan discusses the need to expand our discussions to include all French-speaking countries (1984). See Gill (1993) and Cummins (1995) for some suggested resources.

[5] For this reason Business French courses must stress proficiency-oriented principles as well as those of the communicative method.

[6] See Strasheim, Cholokian, Jeffries, Omaggio, Higgs, Grosse and Voght 1990, 42-43. Remember that these skills are not always present in English for native students.

[7] See Conlin for a more lively and somewhat easier text.

[8] See Paulsell 1983 for more on overseas internship programs.

[9] See Meyer 1995 for more on this project.

FRENCH AND BUSINESS
AT THE UNIVERSITY OF MARYLAND:
«UN MARIAGE REUSSI»

Jo Ann Hinshaw

I n the late 1980s, a group of sixty-five prominent leaders in the public and private sectors issued a report calling for the internationalization of business education: "Business schools must internationalize the entire course of study including comparative business practices and foreign languages and the analysis of other countries and cultures" (Starr, 309). Later, in 1989-1990, the US Department of Education surveyed eight major US companies employing more than 400,000 people worldwide to determine their personnel needs. The final report, well known to many business language instructors, made clear that "US corporations are beginning to value second language proficiency more highly." In addition, it was stated that "[c]ultural sensitivity and an ability to act differently in different countries are qualities that employers are recognizing as extremely valuable in their international and domestic operations" (Adelman, 13).

These reports simply confirm what business language instructors have known all along: a foreign language is a necessary ingredient for success in business. It is refreshing to note that experienced international businesspeople and employers are finally recognizing that language skills increase the value and contribution of employees working across borders. Consequently, it is no wonder that our students desire more "real-world" skills; this desire may in part be fueled by the needs of their future employers in the business world.

Yet, despite highly vocal demands — from students and employers — for greater internationalization of the business curriculum, with more emphasis on marketable skills, many universities in the US have not yet structured undergraduate programs that encourage cross-fertilization and cooperation between language departments and business schools. The University of Maryland (UMD) is one of the rare campuses offering a program — Business, Culture & Languages — that bridges the two disciplines, and although the structure is relatively new (1991), recent graduates appreciate the value of combining business and languages.

> "The IBFL program offered me a much needed rounding to the standard business curriculum. It provided me with the tools necessary to understand and appreciate the importance of the differences in business cultures around the world."
>
> — Kristine Mahoney, recent graduate of the International Business and Foreign Language double major program.

Program Overview

The Business, Culture & Languages program of studies distinguishes itself by offering a flexible structure of study options, an interdisciplinary curriculum, and a menu of "non-traditional" course choices using interactive methodologies and technology. The basic program is a double major in International Business and Foreign Languages (IBFL). Students work toward a BS in International Business and complete the Business Language Option (Business French, Business Spanish, etc.) in the foreign language of their choice. For students who prefer to carry a single major but still want emphasis in either business or languages, the College of Arts & Humanities is proposing a citation (similar to a minor) in either business language or business and management.

Students choose between the two basic major/minor combinations listed below:

1. Double major in International Business and Foreign Languages (IBFL); within the foreign language major, the business language option is selected.

2. Single major in Business & Management or Foreign Languages with Citation:

   a. Students major in Foreign Languages (Business Language) with a Citation in Business & Management, or

   b. Students major in Business & Management with a Citation in Business Language.

The choice of an IBFL double major or a citation allows undergraduates flexibility in their major (with the possibility of finishing their Bachelor's degree in the standard four years), while emphasizing skills in both business and a foreign language. The business language option differs from other avenues of language study, such as literature, in that it concentrates on language for commercial purposes. In the business language curriculum, students benefit from an experiential methodology integrating technology and a participatory approach to learning.

History

In 1990 the University of Maryland leadership, encouraged by President William E. Kirwan, adopted a campus-wide approach to develop a foreign language training capability sensitive to student and research needs for the next decade and beyond. As a result of this initiative, the University submitted a proposal to the US Department of Education to establish an International Business major, and Business Spanish and Business French options, creating a double major in International Business and Foreign Language (IBFL) for undergraduates that would be used as a prototype for other languages: German, Russian, Japanese and Chinese.

Under the grant, monies were set aside to develop new courses in both majors, support faculty advisors, coordinate the internship program and set up a lecture series involving business, government and industry. Funds were allocated also for the purchase of educational materials and for outreach efforts not only campus-wide, but also to area high schools. The brainchild of a UMD business professor who served as Director of CIBER-Maryland, the IBFL program was originally managed out of the CIBER office. In 1993, the program lost its CIBER funding and was subsequently directed part-time by a faculty member in the French & Italian Department. Finally, in Fall 1997, the College of Arts & Humanities (ARHU) took the initiative of enhancing the program by the creation of a Director's position. The College of Business & Management (BMGT) agreed to co-finance the project mainly by supplying the operating budget. Subsequently, the name was changed from International Business & Foreign Languages (IBFL) to "Business, Culture & Languages," although the double major still retains the name IBFL. Both Colleges see the value in the joint program, but ARHU may well have more to gain in the long run, given its desire and need to recruit new students in languages. BMGT will benefit from a greater degree of internationalization of its curriculum, and from the opportunities the program provides for students to study languages and other cultures.

The Business, Culture & Languages Program of Study

The program provides undergraduates a comprehensive education designed to make them more competitive in international business. The joint venture of the Colleges of Business & Management and Arts & Humanities offers qualified students a double major in International Business and Foreign Languages. In addition, ARHU is currently reviewing a "Business Citation" with 15 credits in selected courses for language majors, while Business majors can earn a "Business Language Citation" with 15 credits of upper level course work.

The main objectives of the program are...

- to provide the fundamental principles of business from an international perspective,
- to equip future business leaders with knowledge of language and culture, and
- to expose students to real-life experiences through internships and study abroad.

Students double major in International Business and one of six languages, all of which are widely used in international business (Chinese, French, German[1], Japanese, Russian or Spanish). Within the double major, International Business is the primary major, affording students a basic foundation in traditional business courses complemented with a series of international business classes. In addition, students take on average 36 credits of a foreign language (requirements vary according to language), including a sequence of courses in Business Language, which emphasizes culture, translation, and specialized business vocabulary. Students complete all course work within the 120 credits required for a baccalaureate. The International Business and Foreign Language (D3FL) double major leads to a B.S. in Business & Management with the student's transcript reflecting the two majors in business and language. Spanish is the most popular language, with French and Chinese in second and third places, respectively.

The Business Language Option

"Popular opinion seems to be that the knowledge being taught in [US] colleges and universities is not the kind of knowledge that would be of much practical help in real-life situations; that is, foreign language instruction seems to be more focused on the teaching of literature than on practical communication skills" (CIBER).

The controversy surrounding the teaching of literature versus language for specific purposes, albeit a topic worthy of debate, does not seem to be as crucial as the more urgent issue of declining numbers in our classes. In light of decreasing enrollments in French, we are compelled to respond to our students' needs and desires, if we want not only to maintain our language programs, but also to see them grow and expand.

However, students are not the only ones clamoring for curriculum innovations. In a 1984 report, firms in the southeastern US were queried about the qualifications of future employees. "Respondents gave the highest preference to the traditional business major with an international business orientation and a proficiency in a foreign language emphasizing business terminology" (Ball and McCulloch, 385).

To respond to this demand from students and the private sector for more practical language skills, the six language departments at UMD offer the Business Language option, a requirement for students in the IBFL double major and an elective open to all other students. This option emphasizes specialized business vocabulary as well as crosscultural understanding. Each language requires two or three upper-level commercial language courses (six credits) in addition to additional courses at the 200-300 levels. Below is the entire course of study for the Business Language Option available to French majors:

FREN 204   Review Grammar and Composition
FREN 250   Readings in French
FREN 301   Composition and Style
FREN 302   Introduction to Translation
FREN 303   Practicum in Translation
FREN 306   Commercial French I
or
ARHU 439   Doing Business in French or European Business Cultures
FREN 311   Advanced Comprehension and Expression in French
FREN 312   Introduction to French Civilization: The French Press
FREN 401

or
FREN 402	Stylistics or Advanced Grammar and Phonetics
FREN 406	Commercial French II
FREN 473	Cross-Cultural Approaches to the Study of Contemporary French Society
FREN 474	Contemporary France: Sociocritical Approach

Native speakers would be able to complete the Business Option by taking three upper-level courses in place of FREN 204, 301 and 311.

The enrollment numbers for business language majors, although not exceptionally high, are growing; all six languages totaled 106 majors in 1996-1997, representing a 100% increase over a two-year period. Currently about one-third of the French majors have opted for this program. Although Business Language Option students are not required to take business courses, the College of Business & Management has opened several courses for the Business Language students who are encouraged to increase their understanding of business language and culture. Language majors must meet the necessary prerequisites for the business courses (for example, ECON 203 Principles of Economics I, is a prerequisite for most BMGT courses). Up to three courses may be selected from the sequence listed below:

BMGT 110	Introduction to Business & Management
BMGT 350	Marketing Principles & Organization
BMGT 360	Human Resource Management
BMGT 364	Management & Organization Theory
BMGT 372	Introduction to Logistics Management
BMGT 380	Business Law
BMGT 392	International Business

The Citation Program

Students wishing to pursue only one major may choose the citation program, similar to a "minor." Language majors receive recognition for their course work in Business & Management, selecting five courses (15 hours) from the above list. Business & Management majors may pursue a citation in Business Language, also 15 credit hours, with each language requiring two upper-level commercial language courses in addition to three courses at the 200-300 levels.

Special Program Curriculum

"The IBFL program provided me with the necessary skills to compete at a time in which business is being conducted in a global market where multi-language proficiency and cultural understanding are becoming a necessity."

— Bonnie Elgarnil, 1996 graduate of the International Business and Foreign Language double major program.

One of the key tenets of the program is its emphasis on culture. Several courses in the French and Spanish Departments, for example, teach students valuable intercultural communication skills. In one course, FREN 306 entitled "Doing Business in French," UMD undergraduates are thrust into the world of high-powered international negotiation through a computer-assisted simulation. Assuming the role of corporate decision-makers, students negotiate a joint venture agreement via e-mail with their French counterparts at CERAM, the business *grande école* located in Nice.

During the first few weeks of the course, students explore joint venture theory, negotiation, and crosscultural issues, with guest speakers intervening to demystify balance sheets and negotiation theory for both instructor and students alike. As the class is divided into small groups, a scenario is presented and each team is required to set forth its negotiation goals and strategies. The simulation scenario in the form of a case study, is based on a real joint venture between General Electric and the French aerospace giant, Snecma. Students seem to enjoy the high-tech flavor of the case and its accurate reflection of what happens in the real world.

About mid-semester, the drama escalates as the "negotiators" spend three weeks on-line in real-time negotiations with the French teams, who have also been preparing strategies for negotiating a joint venture. In order to allow each team to work in authentic language, the negotiations are held in English and French on alternate days. In between classes, the two teams exchange e-mail messages to keep the negotiation pace at a relatively high level, and to reflect what would happen in the corporate world. Some of the issues that the teams have to resolve are quite complex and sophisticated: the name of the joint venture, the organizational structure, the ownership and participation of each parent company, etc. Students are not penalized if a joint-venture agreement is not concluded; rather, their performance is evaluated on the quality of the negotiations. The final weeks of the class are devoted to processing what has transpired, writing up a report for "management," and preparing an oral presentation for the class, all in the target language.

One quickly realizes that this pedagogical scheme is an instructor's dream: students actually use the target language to perform real-world tasks, such as negotiations, contracts, correspondence e-mail messages. The challenge for instructors is to maintain a "hands-off" attitude and allow students to communicate with their French-speaking counterparts, unfettered by grammar rules and spelling; instructors must constantly remind themselves that in the real world there are no language instructors intervening in business negotiations.

Given the complexity of the simulation, the process is not devoid of pitfalls. One semester the special software for conferencing failed and students had to resort to e-mail messages, which was certainly a less authentic and exciting experience than real-time electronic communication. The time difference can also be problematic, although

French schools are fortunately more flexible than US colleges in their class scheduling. Other cultural issues are bound to complicate the drama: French students might be on strike; student expectations and level of business knowledge can differ greatly between the two negotiating teams, and finally, different concepts of time can be an issue. One year the US students, expecting the French negotiators to be late, took their time in responding to messages until the French threatened to cut off the negotiations and take their proposal to a competitor of the fictitious US company. These cultural issues, however intrusive they appear to be to the process, are in reality stimulus for enriching, memorable learning experience. They also mirror reflections of what happens in business on a daily basis.

The simulation does not necessarily require partnership with another school. Recently, the instructor, lacking faith in the Internet, opted to run the simulation within the borders of the classroom, dividing students into French and American teams. The effect was less dramatic, but the logistics were certainly easier, making for a more controlled learning environment. Regardless of the parameters of the simulation, students appreciate the dynamic quality of this experiential, interdisciplinary and open-ended approach to language acquisition, which represents quite a deviation from the traditional language course. The Spanish Department offers a similar scenario with a Mexican business school.[2]

The second French course in the Commercial French sequence is FREN 406, Commercial French II. In this more traditional course, the emphasis is on written skill development. Students prepare their CV, as well as several types of commercial correspondence and translation exercises. As technology evolves, the curriculum attempts to keep pace. Research assignments now involve the Internet and on-line services, and sometimes Web-page development, an exercise that students grasp and appreciate more easily than faculty! The course prepares qualified and interested students to take the Paris Chamber of Commerce exam for the *Certificat*, administered every Spring at UMD. It is recommended that students maintain a B average in the course in order to sign up for this test.

Another popular course offered in the IBFL sequence is "European Business Cultures," emphasizing European integration, crosscultural communications and working in Europe. Students spend the first weeks exploring the events and actors contributing to the development of the European Union. The second part of the course emphasizes interactive crosscultural activities. The final weeks are devoted to a student simulation in which teams go through the motions of setting up a company in a European country, justifying their selection of product, site, marketing strategies and personnel recruitment based on cultural considerations. Recently, a French-language section of this course was offered. Students meet faculty once per week for a French discussion class; tests, papers and oral presentations are also prepared in French. Thanks to the proliferation of articles and brochures accessible from the European Union and the press, many of the class readings are available in French. Students respond well to the interdisciplinary and participatory nature of this course which allows them opportunities to build valuable skills in research and teamwork.

Internships

A very special feature of the Business, Culture & Languages agenda is the internship program that allows students to take full advantage of UMD's proximity to the rich resources of the Washington, DC, and Baltimore area. In their junior and senior years, students are placed in an internship in an industry, business, or organization that has a strong component of international commerce. As a means of assessing performance and achievement in an internship, a learning contract is developed and agreed upon by both the sponsoring organization and the student prior to the initiation of the assignment. These contracts enumerate what is required of the undergraduate, the type of "hands-on" experience he or she will obtain, as well as the amount of credit being offered by the internship. One of the office's goals in the coming academic year is to develop language internships in Washington's many international non-profits, businesses or associations. The director is currently working with locally based companies and organizations to assure that students placed in language internships use their foreign language skills at least once a week.

Study Abroad

Students in Business, Culture & Languages are encouraged to participate in a study abroad program. In addition to UMD's study abroad programs around the world, Business, Culture & Languages currently has established programs in France (Nice), Spain (Madrid), and Germany (Kassel), in which students can earn credit for both language and business courses. The University of Nice's business school, l'Institut d'Administration des Entreprises, provides students with the essential knowledge of France's economic, fiscal, legal, and cultural activities with the European Union and the global economy. Participants have the option of residing in local apartments, in campus residence halls, or with families. The Business French faculty at UMD work closely with the on-site internship coordinator in Nice to assure that UMD students in France follow courses equivalent or complementary to those offered at UMD.

Career Advising

One of the advantages students enjoy in the double major program is access to several career and placement offices. The College of Business & Management as well as the College of Arts & Humanities assist students of Business, Culture & Languages in career advising and placement. Both colleges support participants in the program by identifying potential employers, conducting résumé and interview workshops, and coordinating campus visits of companies, government, and nonprofit organization recruiters. In addition, students have access to sophisticated software in the BMGT Career Center that permits instantaneous matching of their résumés (which are online) with potential employers' needs. The Director of Business, Culture & Languages also assists students in orienting them to the appropriate college career center and informing them of relevant career and professional workshops across campus that will enhance their placement possibilities.

Business, Culture & Languages Workshops

A series of distinguished speakers are brought to campus to discuss relevant topics in international business practices. The proximity of the University of Maryland to Washington, DC, affords access to internationally recognized experts in every area of world commerce and to distinguished leaders in industry and trade from other countries. In an effort to keep students informed of what Business, Culture & Languages offers, a career and information workshop was held in Winter 1997. The event, which was extremely successful and very well attended, involved the participation of academic advisors from Business & Management and Arts & Humanities as well as the Study Abroad and Career Center directors. Guest speaker Dr. Irène Finel-Honigman, Senior Advisor at the US Department of Commerce, discussed current trends and issues in international business, including expectations of potential employers. Students had the opportunity to ask questions about career prospects and courses of study here and abroad. Given the interest generated by this event, another workshop is being planned for Spring 1998 focusing on women in international business.

The first of a series of faculty development seminars was offered in 1992: "Teaching Foreign Language in an International Business Environment." The aim of the workshop was to stress the importance of teaching the fundamental principles of business from an international perspective in addition to the language and culture of international clients.

A series of round tables and guest lecturers emphasized the importance of uniting business and language in interdisciplinary instruction. This, however, was just the first step in recognizing the needs of foreign language faculty called upon to teach business language without having the opportunity to develop relevant skills.

Subsequently, the business and foreign language faculty teamed up and conceived the highly successful "Getting Started," a faculty development workshop designed to assist language instructors seeking to design and/or teach courses in business language. The workshop attracted instructors from various universities across the country. As a result, one participant at Salisbury State University is involved in the development of a project similar to Business, Culture & Languages. Faculty members have also been invited to take this training seminar "on the road" to campuses elsewhere interested in the concept of internationalizing their curricula not only in foreign languages, but also in a variety of disciplines ranging from history to mathematics.

Pedagogical Materials

The Business, Culture & Languages office also supports students and faculty through the development of tailored pedagogical materials. For example, faculty in the French and Spanish Departments have scripted and produced a video on international joint ventures and negotiation. "US-Euroventure" is a video-based case study modeled after a Busch Gardens theme park, Port Aventura, that actually exists in Barcelona. Additionally, with a grant from the French Cultural Services, faculty have scripted and produced "Radishes and Butter: Doing Business with the French," a French-language video course. The intercultural nature of the story line makes it appropriate for Business French, civilization or language courses.

Currently, faculty in the French Department are preparing a script for a video course, modeled after the "Getting Started" workshop, targeted at French instructors desiring to teach or develop courses in Business French. The video, with possibility of conversion to CD-ROM, will assist instructors in decoding the complexities of business vocabulary and concepts, while offering crosscultural examples of business practices in the US and France. Detailed explanations of the intricacies of banking, logistics, and insurance, among others, will complement demonstrations of proven techniques used in teaching business language. Funding for research of this pedagogical tool has been provided by the French Embassy.

Additional Programs

In addition to courses offered in the Business, Culture & Languages curriculum, faculty in the French & Italian Department also teach in the Business School's IBM-TQ Program. This unique honors curriculum teams up Business and Engineering students in four core courses emphasizing total quality. One of the courses, "Cross-Cultural Perspectives of Customer Service," popularly known as "Theme Parks 101," focuses on French, Spanish and Japanese amusement parks. Students explore the challenges and issues involved in satisfying customers around the world. Although the course is taught in English, students are required to meet with French-speaking focus groups who provide insights into different products and notions of quality in France. The entire course is held in UMD's state-of-the-art teaching theater designed and built by IBM. The facilities allow for teleconferencing with industry and academic specialists and the cutting-edge computer software permits electronic brainstorming, opinion polls and Internet access. The challenge for faculty is to stay one technological step ahead of the business and engineering students, who seem to master computer technology with enviable ease.

Other avenues for marrying business and French have developed with help from the French Embassy's *Services Culturels*, which furnish grants for pedagogical workshops organized and hosted by the

Department of French and Italian. In previous years, a spirited, animated lawyer-turned professor of the University of Paris, Laurence Garnier, has been the main attraction at workshops focusing on legal French ("Business French Expanded: from Business to Legal French"). Garnier's talent lies in making a seemingly dry and complex subject entertaining, lively and relatively easy to grasp. Vivian Curran of the University of Pittsburgh introduced a cross-cultural approach to understanding basic legal principles and representatives of the French and US governments and the European Commission provided overviews of current events and trends in business.

In 1997, a new workshop, "La pédagogie de l'interculturel," was initiated, focusing on content and methodology in teaching culture. The 40 French instructors who attended the workshop especially praised the practical approaches to the sometimes challenging, but increasingly frequent, requirement to incorporate culture into the French language and literature curriculum. In fact, the workshop was deemed so successful and helpful, faculty in the Department are considering delivering it on-site to interested campuses nationwide.

Conclusion

The proliferation of free-trade agreements, instant communication, and greater international marketing efforts confirm that we are all increasingly in contact with what is popularly called the "global marketplace." It is abundantly clear that people working in this marketplace must be familiar with, and fluent in, languages and cultures other than their own. A newly defined set of skills is needed for our graduates if they are to succeed in business, development, health care, or nearly any discipline within or outside the border of the US. Those of us in languages are well placed to help students, school administrators and future employers of our students define those skills and incorporate them into the curriculum. By so doing, we better serve our students, while advancing our own interests and enhancing our recruitment efforts.

Although Maryland's Department of French & Italian offers an established course of study based on literature and language acquisition, it has recognized the necessity of recruiting students interested in following less traditional disciplines, such as Business French. In this era of declining enrollments in French, applying entrepreneurial principles to course offerings may be a wise strategy. That is, French departments will have to give their "clients" what they want: language for specific purposes, as well as practical business and intercultural skills that equip them to become the new leaders of the 21st century. At Maryland, the French faculty is pleased that the less traditional courses are helping to attract more students, and the prospects for continued growth appear promising. However, the French & Italian Department is not alone in this enterprise. The College of Business & Management has proven to be an indispensable partner in this *mariage réussi*. After all, the driving principle behind the alliance comes from business theory: "customer satisfaction results in increased sales," or in this case, student satisfaction results in increased enrollments.

WORKS CITED

Adelman, C. "Putting International Skills to Work." *NAFSA Newsletter*, August/September, 1994.

Ball, D. & W. McCulloch. "The Views of American Multinational CEOs on Internationalized Business Education for Prospective Employees." *Journal of International Business Studies*, second quarter, 1993.

Center for International Business Education and Research (CIBER). "Report on Survey of Foreign Language Faculty." Durham, NC: Duke University. 1994.

"Radishes and Butter: Doing Business with the French." (video) Cultural Services of the French Embassy. Cambridge, MA: Schoenhof's Foreign Books, 1996.

Starr, M. *Global Competitiveness*. New York: W.W. Norton & Co., 1988.

"US-Euroventure." (video) College Park, MD: University of Maryland, in progress.

Notes

[1] The Department of Germanic Studies encourages the double degree, rather than the double major. Students in Business & Management and German seek a baccalaureate in both disciplines and receive two degrees (BS and BA). They must complete 150 credits and all the requirements of both degrees programs.

[2] For copies of the French or Spanish scenarios, contact the author of this article.

ABOUT THE AUTHORS

Jayne Abrate

Jayne Abrate (Southern Illinois University) is the newly appointed Executive Director of the American Association of Teachers of French (AATF) and co-editor of volume 2 *Making Business French Work*. She has taught Business French for nearly 15 years and is the author of many publications on the use of Internet technology in the teaching of Business French and French and Francophone cultures.

Eileen Angelini

Eileen Angelini (Philadephia College of Textiles and Science) is Director of the Foreign Language Program and Assistant Professor of French. She received the AATF's Award for Young Teachers of French and a grant from the San Diego State University CIBER to study Business French in Strasbourg. Angelini also serves on the AATF National Commission on French for Business and Economic Purposes.

Juanita W. Casagrande

Juanita W. Casagrande (University of Florida) has created a second course in Business French to offer a two-semester sequence to students. Co-author of a forthcoming book on French pronunciation, she has served as coordinator of the Intermediate French program.

Raymond Eichmann

Raymond Eichmann (University of Arkansas, Fayetteville) is Professor of French, Chairman of the Department of Foreign Languages, and Director of the European Studies Program. His research and teaching interests include French Medieval Literature, Twentieth Century Drama, and French Culture and Civilization. He is the author and co-author of four books, and numerous articles and grants to develop Business French courses and area studies programs, and to internationalize courses in Business Administration.

Salvatore Federico

Salvatore Federico (Thunderbird-The American Graduate School of International Management) directs the French program at Thunderbird and is co-editor of the *Journal of Language for International Business*. He is the co-author of *Cas Pratique pour le Français des Affaires* (McGraw Hill, 2nd ed. 1997) and *Business French Case Studies* (Transparent language, forthcoming 1998).

Irène Finel-Honigman

Irène Finel-Honigman (US Department of Commerce) was appointed in the first Clinton administration as Senior Advisor in Finance Policy and is Adjunct Professor in Johns Hopkins University's Master's of International Business Program. Finel-Honigman has published over 40 articles on European financial issues, international relations, French intellectual and cultural history, and management training strategies. She is editor of a forthcoming volume on European Union banking issues.

Hervé de Fontenay

Hervé de Fontenay (McGill University) is Director of the French as a Second Language Program in the McGill Center for Continuing Education. He is the author of *Français, Inc.,* which will soon appear in second edition. He is a member of the AATF National Commission on French for Business and Economic Purposes and has been instrumental in forging a strategic alliance between the Quebec and Paris Chambers of Commerce and Industry.

Michael P. Fronmueller

Michael P. Fronmueller (Boise State University) is Associate Professor of Management and Chair of the Department of Management. A native German, Fronmueller teaches courses in International Management and has taught Business German for the Department of Modern Languages at Boise State University.

Michel Gueldry

Michel Gueldry (Monterey Institute of International Studies) is Associate Professor of French. He teaches a wide variety of courses that includes Business French, French Politics and Society, and French Cinema. He is currently writing a book on France and the European Union and is co-editing a book on the teaching of civilization via film.

Jo Ann Hinshaw

Jo Ann Hinshaw (University of Maryland-College Park) is Director of the Business, Culture & Language Program and author of the video course "Radishes & Butter: Doing Business with the French." She teaches a variety of Business French courses including "European Business Cultures" and "Quality in France."

Steven J. Loughrin-Sacco

Steven J. Loughrin-Sacco (San Diego State University) is a co-editor of this volume, along with Jayne Abrate. He is the Co-Director of the Center for International Business Education and Research (CIBER), Chair of the National Commission on French for Business and Economic Purposes, and the new editor of the French for Business and International Trade (FFBAIT) newsletter. He has been teaching Business French since 1979 at both the secondary and postsecondary level.

E. Nicole Meyer

E. Nicole Meyer (University of Wisconsin-Green Bay) is Associate Professor of French, Humanistic Studies and Women's Studies. She is the author of numerous publications on Business French, Flaubert, and Nineteenth and Twentieth Century French and Francophone women authors. She has been teaching Business French since 1989.

Catherine Moore

Catherine Moore (Western Illinois University) is Associate Professor of French and co-author of *Cas Pratique pour le Français des Affaires* (McGraw Hill, 2nd ed. 1997) and *Business French Case Studies* (Transparent language, forthcoming 1998).

Annette Sampon-Nicolas

Annette Sampon-Nicolas (Hollins College) is a department chairperson who has been teaching Business French for the past ten years. She has successfully prepared many students for the *Certificat pratique* offered by the Paris Chamber of Commerce and Industry. She is presently working on an interdisciplinary project with the Departments of Economics and International Studies to create an international business track in French and Spanish. She is a published translator, and the author of publications on contemporary French literature.

Fernande Wagman

Fernande Wagman (Academy of the Holy Angels, Demarest, NJ) is a secondary school French teacher who has pioneered the teaching of Business French at the secondary level. She is the author of *Faisons des affaires,* which has recently appeared in second edition. She is a member of the AATF Executive Council, and serves on the AATF National Commission on French for Business and Economic Purposes.

Allen Wood

Allen Wood (Purdue University) is Associate Professor of French and Associate Editor of *Global Business Languages*, which is published by the CIBER at Purdue. He teaches Seventeenth Century French Literature and Business French.

259